Shirlee Taylor Haizlip

THE
S WEETER
THE
JUICE

SIMON & SCHUSTER
New York   London   Toronto   Sydney   Tokyo   Singapore

SIMON & SCHUSTER
Rockefeller Center
1230 Avenue of the Americas
New York, New York 10020

SIMON & SCHUSTER and colophon are registered trademarks
of Simon & Schuster Inc.

Designed by Carla Weise/Levavi & Levavi
Manufactured in the United States of America

1   3   5   7   9   10   8   6   4   2

Library of Congress Cataloging-in-Publication Data
Haizlip, Shirlee Taylor.
The sweeter the juice / Shirlee Taylor Haizlip.
p.   cm.
Includes bibliographical references.
1. Taylor family.   2. Haizlip, Shirlee Taylor—Family.
3. Racially mixed people—United States—Biography.   4. Racially
mixed people—Washington (D.C.)—Biography.   5. Washington (D.C.)—
Race relations.   6. United States—Race relations.   7. Washington
(D.C.)—Biography.   I. Title.
E185.96.H175   1994
929'.2—dc20   93-33532
                                        CIP

ISBN: 0-671-79235-0

All photographs appear courtesy of the author's personal collection except where noted.

"Cross," from Selected Poems of Langston Hughes. Copyright © 1926 by Alfred
A. Knopf, Inc. Reprinted by permission of the publisher.

"The Mulatto to His Critics," from Joseph Seamon Cotter, Jr.: Complete Poems.
Edited by James Robert Payne, Copyright © 1990 by The University of Georgia Press.
Used by permission.

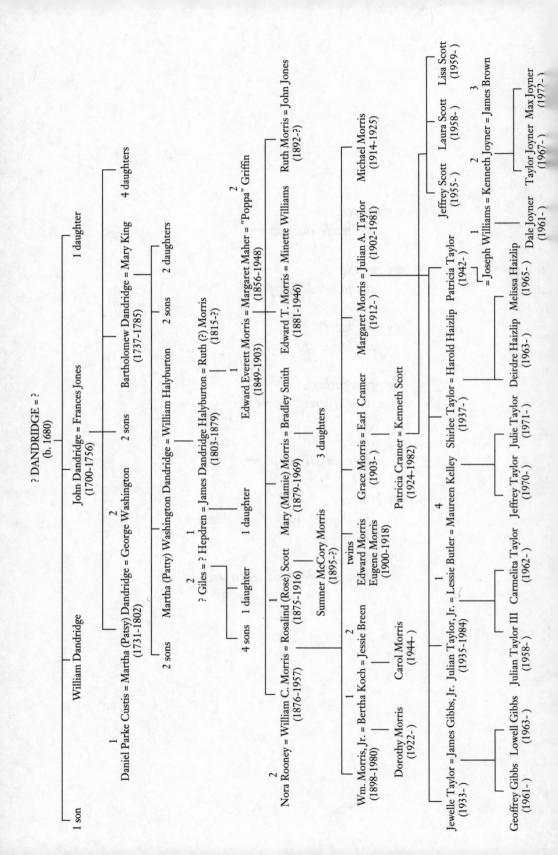

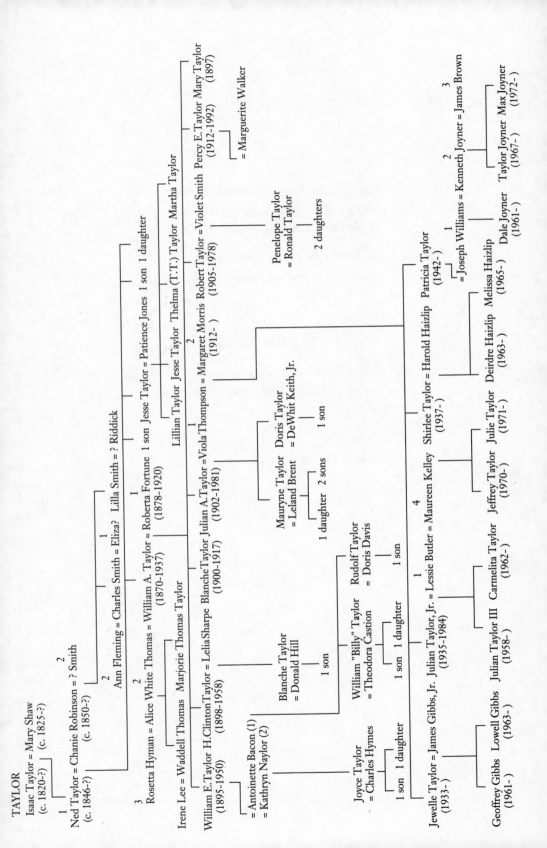

TAYLOR

Isaac Taylor = Mary Shaw
(c. 1820-?)   (c. 1825-?)

1
Ned Taylor = Chanie Robinson = ? Smith
(c. 1846-?)   (c. 1850-?)   **2**

                    2
Ann Fleming = Charles Smith = Eliza?   Lilla Smith = ? Riddick
                        1

3
Rosetta Hyman = Alice White Thomas = William A. Taylor = Roberta Fortune 1 son Jesse Taylor = Patience Jones 1 son 1 daughter
                          (1870-1937)   (1878-1920)

Irene Lee = Waddell Thomas   Marjorie Thomas Taylor   Lillian Taylor Jesse Taylor Thelma (T.T.) Taylor Martha Taylor

                                                    1
William E. Taylor H. Clinton Taylor = Lelia Sharpe Blanche Taylor Julian A. Taylor = Viola Thompson = Margaret Morris Robert Taylor = Violet Smith Percy E. Taylor Mary Taylor
(1895-1950)   (1898-1958)   (1900-1917)   (1902-1981)   **2** (1912-)   (1905-1978)   (1912-1992)   (1897)

= Antoinette Bacon (1)   Mauryne Taylor Doris Taylor   = Marguerite Walker
= Kathryn Naylor (2)   Blanche Taylor   = Leland Brent = DeWhit Keith, Jr.   Penelope Taylor
                             = Donald Hill   = Ronald Taylor

                                   1 son   1 daughter 2 sons   1 son   2 daughters

                         William "Billy" Taylor Rudolf Taylor
                         = Theodora Castion   = Doris Davis

Joyce Taylor   Shirlee Taylor = Harold Haizlip Patricia Taylor
= Charles Hymes   1 son 1 daughter   1 son   (1937-)   (1942-)
                                                                                                                          = Joseph Williams = Kenneth Joyner = James Brown
                                      1   **1**   **2**   **3**
         1 son 1 daughter Jewelle Taylor = James Gibbs, Jr. Julian Taylor, Jr. = Lessie Butler = Maureen Kelley
                            (1933-)   (1935-1984) **4**

Geoffrey Gibbs Lowell Gibbs Julian Taylor III Carmelita Taylor Jeffrey Taylor Julie Taylor   Dale Joyner Deirdre Haizlip Melissa Haizlip Taylor Joyner Max Joyner
(1961-)   (1963-)   (1958-)   (1962-)   (1970-)   (1971-)   (1961-)   (1963-)   (1965-)   (1967-)   (1972-)

My family was here and loved the land
    before the Vikings, before the Spanish,
    before the Italians, before the English.

My family came here as aristocrats,
    loved the land and claimed most of it
    as their own.

My family came here unwillingly and in chains,
    loved the land and built the country.

My family came here as immigrants,
    loved the land and lived some of their
    dreams.

This then is my claim: I am in all America.
    All America is in me.

                        —S.T.H.

Preface

This book is based on a variety of materials, including oral histories, interviews with family members, correspondence, diaries, photographs, newspaper clippings and archival material such as census tracts, city directories, school records, birth, death and marriage certificates, alumni records, historical tracts and so on. To reconstruct my family's story, I traveled from California to Richmond, Virginia, North Carolina, Washington, D.C., New York City, Connecticut, Buffalo, Cleveland, Maryland and back to Anaheim, California.

I am indebted to the staffs and resources of the Buffalo Erie County Library, the Cleveland Public Library, the Library of Congress, the Pusey Library and Archives at Harvard University, the Los Angeles Public Library, the New Haven Public Library, the New York City Public Library, the Museum of the Confederacy, the Moorland-Spingarn Research Center at the Howard University Library, the National Archives of the United States of America, the Schomburg Center for Research in Black Culture, the Southwest Film/Video Archives at Southern Methodist University, the State Library and Archives of Virginia, the Sterling Library at Yale University, the Valentine Museum, the Virginia Historical Society and the Yale University Law School Library.

Elicia Pegues gave me access to information that would otherwise have been barred to me. Charles Proctor helped me meet a deadline by copying my manuscript at the eleventh hour. Doris Haizlip Sanders and her colleague Mollie Smith, of the School Attendance and Records Branch of the District of Columbia Public School System, searched through musty records on my behalf. ADR Investigation Corporation in Cleveland, Ohio, provided technical assistance. Elgin Charles, Blake Little and Natalie MacGowan Spenser made sure I put my best face forward. My dear friends Trudy Barnes and Mariah Richardson read my manuscripts and assisted the creative process in a dozen other ways. My surrogate sisters, Sandra Michael and Phyllis Miriam, also waded through my evolving pages and provided me with a loving haven, as well as a place to rest my mind and body. From England came encouraging words and incisive suggestions from my lifelong friend Lucy Wynne. Libby Clark, my West Coast mother, cheered and supported me through each step. And through it all, I could sense the guiding spirits of my father and my cousin Ellis Haizlip, who over many years urged me to "tell the story and tell it true."

My father always told me that Faith would bring me through, and he was right. My agent, Faith Childs, was key to my getting over, thanks to her belief in my project and her tenacity in its development. Debbie Goodison fueled the book's progress. On the other side, there was Becky Saletan, my editor, who took reams of pages and mounds of words and helped shape them into the story I was determined to tell. Fred Chase made certain I was as correct as I could be. Frank and Julie Metz gave the book a jacket that invited the reader to open the book in the first place, and Eve Metz brought the pictures to life. Denise Roy put the finishing editorial touches on the manuscript and guided it through its final production phases. And Carolyn Reidy sent my spirit soaring with her personal encouragement.

Finally, it is with deep and abiding gratitude that I thank all the members of my family, on both sides, who gave me their time and their memories. First and foremost among that group is my mother, Margaret Taylor Hancock, who, despite old pain and new discomfort, kept peeling back layer after layer of memories until we had reached her core. I owe much to my aunt Grace Cramer, who was the most important link with the unknown past. I am especially grateful to my sister Jewelle Taylor Gibbs, who was my highly unpaid research assistant, family tour guide, fellow conjecturer, and probably "right" most of the time. I give great credit to my sister Patricia Taylor Brown, who nourished and housed me, physically and emotionally, on my treks east.

I am indebted to my daughters, Deirdre and Melissa Haizlip, who read the manuscript in its earliest stages and who sweetly but firmly told me what worked and what didn't. Deirdre found some of the basic keys to my story, while Melissa helped me step back and look at some of my deepest feelings about past events. I could not have done any of the work without the support and love of my husband, Harold, who assisted me in archival research, Xeroxed manuscripts, returned library books and kept our household going while I lived at the computer, on the road, and in the archives.

❧

(Note: I have varied the terms I use for African-Americans in keeping with the customs of the eras that my family story spans, from the eighteenth century to the present. "Black" is therefore used as appropriate, along with "Negro," "colored" and "African-American"; "mulatto" is also used from time to time. In the case of Native Americans, "Indian" is used in the same manner.)

Prologue

This color seems to operate as a most disagreeable mirror, and a great deal of one's energy is expended in reassuring white Americans that they do not see what they see.

—JAMES BALDWIN
"White Man's Guilt"

Sometimes I look at people and wonder if they are related to me. I do this in public places and private spaces. There I am, in airport terminals, and train stations, on ballroom floors and sandy beaches, studying people who might be my relatives. At parties and dances I have become momentarily distracted by familiar yet unknown faces. I scrutinize the shape of the nose, the cast of the eyes, the curve of the lips and the jut of the chin. Whenever I see a tall white man with the slightly kinky golden brown hair, subtly flared nostrils and large ears of my brother, I say, "There's a Morris."

I often wonder what those I observe would think if they knew what I was doing. Would they be amused, insulted, nervous? I have indulged in this curious pastime since I was eight years old, when I first understood that all but one of my mother's family had become white.

I am a black woman, but many of you would never know it. On the other hand, I do subscribe to the racial mythology that black people know their own. My skin is as light as that of an average white person. The skin of my sisters and brother is as light as, if not lighter than, mine. But we have lived as, worked as and mostly married black people. Our psyches, souls and sensibilities are black. Sociologists would say we have been "socialized" as black people. Yet our lives have been deeply colored by our absence of deep color.

The mirror would say that my mother's skin is the fairest of them all. She has always been a beautiful woman with dark hair, large and expressively sad, dark eyes, a heart-shaped face and a gracefully defined mouth. Her nose is prominent and long. All of her life, like many other people whose light color does not immediately define their race, she has been called "exotic-looking." I too have inherited that label and unwillingly passed it along to my daughters.

Most of us are curious as to who we are and why we look the way we do. Many of us know the answers to those questions. Some of us have no idea. This primeval need to know informs my search for my relatives. I liken my curiosity to that of adopted children looking for their kin. I am not entirely sure, if and when the time comes, that I will be comforted to know the sculpture of their cheeks or the architecture of their noses.

Mysteries of color have encased my family for five generations. Putting together the bits and pieces of my past creates a quilt of melanin patches shading from dark to light, red to brown, tan to pink. There are ragged edges and missing segments. I dream I will find some of myself in those holes and gaps. I need to finish the quilt, wearing it smooth until its edges feel soft to my touch, blending its clashing colors to my own notion of harmony. Only then can I store it away in a safe place, taking it out every once in a while to look at.

Make no mistake. I do not lust after my whiteness. More often than not, I feel ambivalent about the white part of me and those circumstances, both known and imagined, that resulted in the mix. I am not really sure what the white portion of me means, if anything. Is it a separate self? Does it think differently from my black self? Does it have a subconscious racial memory? How can I love it when it may not love me?

Finding the missing souls of my family has supplied some of the answers. I will keep looking for those who can provide the vanished biographies; those who can restore the limbs amputated from the family tree. In searching for my family, I yearn to close the circle of my existence.

What is it I will get from confronting these living ghosts? A knowledge of life on the other side? The opportunity to feel superior? The revenge of exposure and embarrassment? Recognition,

contrition, forgiveness of what might have been their sin of abandonment? A gathering unto their bosoms? Sometimes I believe I
want all of these things. Often I think I want none of them. More
than anything, it is the attempt to understand and consolidate identity that drives my exploration.

In a broader sense, my family's story reflects white and black
America's historical attitude toward skin color. Our experience suggests that America is not what it presents itself to be. Some ge-
neticists have said that 95 percent of "white" Americans have widely
varying degrees of black heritage. According to *The Source: A Guide-
book to American Genealogy*, 75 percent of all African-Americans have
at least one white ancestor and 15 percent have predominantly white
blood lines. All statistics, of course, are subject to interpretation
and reinterpretation, but the fact that anthropologists and biologists
continue to glean these truths from their study of genetic data gives
weight to the claim that there are no "real white Americans." As
Adrian Piper wrote, "The longer a person's family has lived in this
country, the higher the probable percentage of African ancestry—
bad news for the DAR, I'm afraid."

In other words, many Americans are not who they think they
are; hundreds of thousands of white people in America are not
"white." Some know it; others don't. Ten thousand people each
year cross the visible and invisible color line and become "white."
If a new sociological method of determining race were devised,
equal numbers of black people might no longer be black. What
happened in my family and many others like it calls into question
the concept of color as a means of self-definition.

Genes and chromosomes from Africa, Europe and a pristine
America commingled and created me. I have been called Egyptian,
Italian, Jewish, French, Iranian, Armenian, Syrian, Spanish, Portuguese and Greek. I have also been called black and Peola and
nigger and high yellow and bright. I am an American anomaly. I
am an American ideal. I am the American nightmare. I am the
Martin Luther King dream. I am the new America.

❦

In the first part of the twentieth century, my parents grew up
in a then legally segregated Washington, D.C. It was a city as rigidly

stratified in its way as Victorian England. What follows is the story of my parents' lives and the options the color wheel spun for them. The brushes and tongues of oral history, family records, historical documents and written testimony have painted the pictures and given me the words to tell how my multihued family of diverse racial and ethnic strains journeyed through two color-conscious societies in America: black and white.

This is the story of a family that is black, white and Indian.

This is the story of how color separated that family.

This is the story of a family that accepted its color but rejected its race.

This is the story of a family that accepted its race but rejected its color.

This is the story of how the black family prospered and became visible.

This is the story of how the white family fled and became invisible.

This is the story of the black family's search for the white family from one generation to the next.

This is the story of the white family's denial of the black family.

This is the story of how the family lived with the choices it made.

This is the story of choices still to come.

This is all one story.

This is the story of my family.

Chapter One

It is his life and no mere abstraction in someone's head. He must live it and try consciously to grasp its complexity until he can change it; must live it as he changes it.

—RALPH ELLISON
Shadow and Act

On a January day so achingly cold the streets of Manhattan were almost empty, Julian Taylor, a man the color of fresh-baked ginger cake, married Margaret Morris, a woman the color of eggnog. Emerging from the judge's chambers at City Hall, the bride nearly slipped on a sidewalk covered with black ice. Crystalline slivers were beginning to fall.

As they made their way carefully to the car, the groom checked his inside coat pocket several times to make certain the future he had planned was still there. Carefully folded in a small white envelope was the handwritten letter he had received days before.

Rev. Julian Taylor
In our regular church meeting, we the First Baptist Church of Stratford do hereby extend to you a call to serve beginning the first Sunday and lasting as long as satisfaction is given. We are yours in Christ. Done by order of the Church.

In payment for his leadership, Rev. Taylor's weekly salary was set at twenty-five dollars. And so it came to pass that Julian took his mostly white bride, Margaret, to the poor white town of Stratford in the rich white state of Connecticut.

❧

In 1933, Stratford was a sleepy coastal village that had once been known for its shipyards and oyster beds. It was not a place of rolling hills, large estates or English gardens like its sister towns, Southport and Greens Farms. Although there were a number of large, well-preserved homes, for the most part the houses were small and painted white or gray. A few adventurous souls chose yellow or barn red. Overall it was a nondescript town with a few colored residents. For them, there was one church, First Baptist, a tiny wooden house of worship with a little more than one hundred members.

The church's congregation lived mainly in the neighboring city of Bridgeport. As in many New England towns and cities during that era, it consisted of two groups. There were families whose relatives had been in the town since either colonial times or shortly after the Emancipation. Many had the cultured mannerisms of those who work around the very rich—which, in fact, they did, in places like Westport, Fairfield, New Canaan and Darien. The other group was the majority, uneducated through no fault of their own, hard-working and respectable; they were the first trickle of the streams of Negroes who migrated from the South to find new jobs and new dreams.

❧

The installation of a new minister is a time of celebration, renewal and optimism. Old quarrels are put aside and new ambitions are revealed. Julian's first order of business was a proper introduction to the church. His father, his four brothers and his stepmother journeyed from Washington in a shiny LaSalle. With their elegant attire and big city airs they dazzled the congregation. A few hours after the service, however, Julian's stepmother, Miss Alice, had a heart attack and was put to bed. The next day they managed to get her into the car for the return journey. Miss Alice would die a few weeks later.

For the new pastor and his wife, that first year in Connecticut included the expected weddings, funerals and christenings. Julian's diary also recorded "lawn fetes," garden parties, a baby contest, "smokers," chicken suppers, theater, chitterling dinners, bingo parties, a bus ride to Coney Island and "intertainments," as Julian called them, at various members' homes. In his spiritual ledger, the titles of his sermons that year suggested high drama or deep intrigue: "Influence," "Fatal Decision," "The Blood Taken," "Palace of Happiness," "The Rich Fool," "Contrary Winds," "Bitter Water Sweetened," "The Sublimest Theme."

It had been a full year and at its end, on an unusually warm November day, Margaret felt the first contractions of labor. She claims she was not unduly upset that her doctor would not give up the Yale-Princeton football game at Yale Bowl to be at her bedside. Margaret's "sister," Thelma Lazenberry, and a neighbor, Matiel Robinson, served as midwives. Once the real work was done, Julian took charge and named the infant Jewelle.

Two more Taylor children were born in the Stratford bungalow. First came Julian, Jr., in 1935. After his birth, homesick and frequently ill, Margaret was often depressed and showed little interest in the business of running a household. It was clear that she needed someone else in the house full-time to bolster her spirits and help with the two young babies. Through a minister's wife who was a social worker, Julian heard of a nine-year-old girl in an orphanage who needed a home. Memories of her own childhood gave Margaret a deep cushion of empathy for children who had no relatives to take them in. She was eager to meet the little girl. Her name was Margaret Jackson, the first in a long line of additional "daughters" in the family. "Little Margaret," as she would thereafter be known, quickly became a conscientious older sister to Jewelle, Julian and, later, me. On occasions when they were out with the family, the young minister and his wife introduced Little Margaret as their daughter. Because she was dark like Julian, people said she looked like him, a comparison she cherished.

My own birth was duly recorded by my father on September 3, 1937. Like many other mothers that year, my mother named me after the reigning child star, Shirley Temple. Margaret found no dissonance in giving to her infant Negro daughter the name of an apple-cheeked Hollywood princess. But when I reached high school I would drop the "y" and add an "e" to my name to distinguish it from all those other Shirley Temples. I took more solace that one of my middle names, Anne, was from my paternal great-grand-mother, an Indian. Her Native American name was White Cloud, and in my own fanciful process of deduction, I figured I could claim it too.

The year I was born, five young men were freed from the Alabama prison where they had been incarcerated since 1931. They were part of the group that became known as the Scottsboro boys, the name given to nine young Negro men who had been falsely accused of raping two white girls while traveling in boxcars on a train in Alabama. In a series of trials starting in Scottsboro, Alabama, the boys were convicted, and some of them sentenced to death. Subsequently an Alabama judge set aside the verdict. Three more were freed in the 1940s, and in 1948 the fourth escaped from jail to Michigan, which refused to return him to Alabama. But I would not read that tale until 1950, when it would deepen my adolescent awareness of what it means to be black in America.

To help care for me, my father hired Mrs. Arrington, a widow from his church who needed a place to live. The expanded family remained for more than four years in the cozy house on Stratford Avenue. It had a lawn many times its size, with trees and a brook at one end that was inhabited by frogs and minnows. It was also said to be haunted by a child who at the turn of the century had drowned in the swollen stream after a week of steady rain. At night the moonlight's phosphorescence revealed an insubstantial childlike form running and jumping through the trees and along the water's edge. For my parents, the image held no fear. They were accustomed to ghosts.

In the new house a new tradition established itself. Julian's young teenage daughters by his first marriage, Mauryne and Doris, came from Washington to stay for the summers. Mauryne was only nine years younger than my mother, and the presence of two adolescents befuddled by divorce added to the strains on the growing household.

It was during those years that Mauryne and my father began to sing duets in concert. Mauryne had a well-developed singing voice and a mature stage presence. The handsome dark father and his beautiful egg shell–colored daughter performed the light classics and the popular love songs of the day, in churches and at the gingerbread bandshell in Seaside Park in Bridgeport. In addition to expanding his reputation, extra money from these concerts was a much needed supplement to Julian's meager income.

In those Depression years, collecting his full salary was a challenge. Each Sunday, beside the title of his sermon in his diary, he recorded what the church owed him. One such entry was typical: "Balance owed, $287.63. Received, $8.45." There was no way he could support his family on his church earnings alone and he constantly sought other sources of income.

When Franklin Roosevelt was elected president in 1932, politics began to capture Julian's attention. From his father he had learned that having political power could help him change the laws of the country and the lives of his people and, equally important, would give him access and clout that he could translate into financial gain. Most of the members of the Stratford church were Republicans, but admiring Roosevelt and his New Deal, Stratford's new minister decided to throw his lot in with the Democrats. It was a break not only with the church's congregation, but with his father's Abe Lincoln Republicanism.

Julian also began to look for other flocks. His father, then a vice president of the New England Baptist Convention, wrote to Julian about a church in Providence that needed a minister and offered his support. But the light-complected congregation privately agreed he was too dark and, besides, he was divorced. The elder Taylor wrote to his son, cushioning the blow. "Funny about Providence," he mused. "Maybe they are not anxious about having a pastor." He offered to scout for another position.

Julian would not have his father's help for long. I was born the year my grandfather died. That same year my father got the "call" to lead Macedonia Baptist Church, the largest and by far the most influential of the three black churches in the small town of Ansonia, Connecticut.

Macedonia had been founded in 1888 by freedmen and former slaves. The church stood on the west side of town, at the head of the major bridge that joined the two sides of the city. The church did not, however, own a parsonage. The church's trustees and deacons made it known that they wanted their new minister to find a residence suitable to his position and encouraged him to look wherever such housing might be available. But housing discrimination was formidable, and Julian had almost given up looking when he found and rented a three-story furnished home in rural Shelton, a factory town two miles from Ansonia.

The town had two or three black families, who could trace their ancestors to the Civil War. Otherwise the population was white and poor, except for the Andersons, a family who claimed both Negro and white heritage. Not by chance, it was the Andersons who owned the house my father rented, an unpretentious, comfortable New England gray frame structure not far from the main street. It especially pleased my mother, who found it more like the homes she had known in Washington, with space for retreat and privacy. But unbeknownst to my parents, everyone in town considered the house to be inhabited by the spirit of the previous owner.

At first my mother was the only one who nightly heard footsteps on the stairs and felt strong, intimidating, nonhuman presences. They were everywhere and nowhere, the air of the rooms growing thick with restless inhabitants. Then my father and Mrs. Arrington and Little Margaret felt them too. They never saw a physical manifestation, but each night at two o'clock, everyone in the house, adults and finally the children, would be awakened simultaneously, jolted into an uneasy consciousness. The menace increased, and after only a year's tenancy, my parents decided to leave the house and to look again in Ansonia.

∽

My mother's state of body and mind echoed the condition she'd been in after the birth of my brother. She suffered from a then indefinable malady for which there seemed to be no balm. "I weighed ninety-five pounds for months after you were born," she recalls. I believe it is likely that after the birth of each of her children, my mother experienced that special sadness known medically as post-partum disorder.

The sight of Ansonia did little to cheer her up. A town of few graces, Ansonia was—and is—a blue-collar valley community in southeastern Connecticut. Compared to the grandiose beauty of the District of Columbia and the Victorian primness of Stratford, it seemed dreary, bleak and unattractive. There were no tree-lined boulevards, no leafy parks, no elegant neighborhoods, no zoos, no department stores. There was little to please the eye, occupy the mind or nourish the soul.

In the days when entrepreneurs saw rivers and people first as sources of power, Anson Phelps had erected factories beside the railroad tracks that followed the curving Naugatuck River as it drifted down from the Berkshires. In Ansonia, at least, it was a dead river, which glittered with rainbow ribbons of oil and gave off a slightly metallic smell. As children we knew that if no creatures lived in the water, we couldn't either. No one was tempted to swim in the shallow stream.

As in Stratford and Shelton, a handful of black families had been in Ansonia as freedmen or runaway slaves, or arrived there shortly after the Emancipation, bearing names like Boone, Green, Tinney, Austin, Rogers and Mayo. Their small number had made them unthreatening, and good fortune and industry had allowed them to purchase homes away from the middle of the town. Most of them had a high school education.

Later, the mills attracted the bulk of Ansonia's Negroes, who came in family groups during the great migrations from the South to the North in the late 1930s and early 1940s. Most of them came from North and South Carolina hamlets with names like Society Hill, Bennettsville, Hartsville and Darlington. Fewer than half a dozen family names covered the entire population. You were either an Antrum, a Gatison, a Thomas, or a Douglas or a cousin thereof. For lack of opportunity, few of Ansonia's newest residents had more than a third-grade education—the age when, in the South, they were required to leave school and play and take on adult-size jobs in the cotton or tobacco fields. They were clustered in small, poorly maintained, poorly heated wooden tenements in easy walking distance of the mills.

My father canvassed the town and located another large, run-down Victorian house on Locke Street on the east side of town, in a neighborhood of Irish, Italians and Polish. It was owned by a white family who were willing to rent to Julian and Margaret for one year. Next door lived an Irish family named Maher. For at least six months, the Mahers acted as if the Negroes who lived next to them did not exist.

The rambling Locke Street Victorian with its spacious sunny rooms and generous yard became my mother's enchanted castle. My parents repainted the outside, which brought a thaw in their relationship with their neighbors but left them little money to furnish the inside. But the sparseness enabled Margaret to dream of rooms filled with mahogany tables, velvet loveseats and silk-upholstered chairs. Twelve months after they had moved in, however, the owner sold the house. Margaret was heartbroken. She was also pregnant again, and still with no place that she and her husband could call their own. Julian was unsuccessful in finding another Ansonia residence and they moved to Waterbury, eighteen miles away.

❧

One of Connecticut's largest, oldest cities, Waterbury is a town of steep streets and mean houses, most of them dating back to the turn of the century. As in Ansonia, the Naugatuck River runs through the center of town, shaping its history and defining its future. In 1940, it was a bustling industrial center. The schools were filled and the parks were empty. Hailed as the "brass capital of the world," its factories would soon be geared to supporting the efforts of World War II. Like Ansonia, Waterbury had attracted large numbers of European immigrants and Southern black emigrants, who worked side by side in the brass, steel and rubber mills.

My mother was beginning to feel like a nomad. There were days when she felt like packing up all the children and going back to Washington. For a short time, we stayed with Mack and Sarah Keyes, well-to-do Negro undertakers who had a taste for European furniture and expensive, conservative clothing. They had befriended my parents after meeting them at church functions. It was no small thing for the undertaker to be looked upon with favor by the minister, since the man of God was the first to know of a death. Hide-and-seek with my brother in the mortuary's basement showroom became a favorite game, and once the proprietors' nephew closed Jewelle in a coffin when she refused to play "doctor" with him.

It was in Waterbury that Little Margaret took me to see my first feature film, at the Palace, as a reward for surviving my first vaccination. I thought that the twenty-year-old edifice that seated over three thousand people really was a royal residence. We sat in the dark red-velvet balcony, equally mesmerized by our regal surroundings and the images on the screen. But when would the king make his appearance?

Several months later, on a bitter winter's night, I would return to the Palace, this time with my father. Fussing and grumbling, saying it was too cold, too late for the children and too expensive, he took my mother, my brother, my sister and me to see the Ink Spots. To me they were tall, dark, handsome men dressed in white who sang songs that made my mother act and smile in a strange way.

From the funeral home we moved to a snug, light-filled apartment on the second floor of a two-family house on Long Hill Road at the edge of the city, in an area just beginning to undergo development. The house was bordered by scrubby woodlands in a hilly neighborhood of Irish and Italians, with one other Negro family. The neighbors seemed to get along but it was in that community that I had my earliest sense of being the Other.

Our landlords were an elderly Italian immigrant couple named the Amatas. They called my father "Reventay" and treated him with the respect that the uneducated often have for the well educated. Of greater interest to them was my mother, whom they thought at first was Italian. They called her "Missatay" and said she looked like their eldest daughter, Connie. They invited Connie and her husband, Pat, a dark-haired sailor in a white uniform, to meet the look-alike.

Margaret did resemble their black-haired, pleasant daughter, although Margaret was far prettier. The two light-skinned young women with dark curly hair and prominent noses were drawn to each other and quickly became friends, trading recipes and visiting each other's homes. My mother, who began to cook only after she was married, learned Italian recipes and how to bake bread from the women downstairs.

From the Amatas I often heard the phrase "old country." Where was this place with only old people, old buildings, old cars, old dirt and old trees? It was a place, they told me, where every day they baked Italian breads and pastries, tended flourishing grape arbors in side yards, and made their own wine, which they told Missatay was good for her babies.

Most afternoons, my mother took us downstairs to visit. Little did my father know that his wife and children giddily sipped wine on the long, cold winter days. I can still taste the tablespoons of the strong, red liquid the landlady gave me. I can still smell the bread she baked and remember the way she held it under her arm against the side of her large bosom as she broke it up, piece by piece. Then, she was the only adult who fit my picture of a grandmother.

∾

My younger sister, Patricia, first known as Patty, then Pattee, was born in Waterbury in 1942, when I was five. Much of my mother's time in Waterbury was consumed in caring for Pattee, a whiny, demanding baby with skin fairer than mine and curly, sandy brown hair. Mrs. Amata loved the chubby little baby with rosy cheeks, and liked to look after her when my mother had an errand to run. Each time my mother returned, Mrs. Amata would say, "Baby no looka like Reventay," rubbing her own cheek and pointing to her skin.

Family life in Waterbury revolved around my parents and sisters and brother, since we had no aunts or uncles or cousins or grandparents nearby. My father often talked about his many family members who were in Washington, a place that at first seemed far away. Some of their pictures were on the console radio, others sat casually on shelves or end tables. Most were in a large, old tattered scrapbook that we liked to riffle through at least once a week.

Less frequently, my mother spoke of two Washington relatives, a "sister," Thelma, and an aunt named Mamie Smith. There was no photo gallery for her family. She had only a picture of Thelma, whom I knew she regarded as a sister, but I also knew Thelma was not her sister by blood. In my mind I equated Thelma's relationship to my mother with Little Margaret's relationship to me. Once in a while my mother talked about some cousins. I knew her own mother had been dead a long time, and that her father had "gone someplace." I put him and Amelia Earhart, who disappeared the year I was born, in the same category.

❧

My mother doted and waited on my father. Around his needs and whims, she planned her schedule and the routine of the entire household. Dinner was served precisely at four, except on Sundays, when it was at one. Julian's tea water had to be boiling hot, and his eggs had to be scrambled to the exact soft consistency. Holding his cup with his small finger elegantly arched, at least twice a week he would say, "Margaret, this water is not hot." We could count each "t" in that sentence. My mother accepted or ignored his dictates with good humor and grace.

Later we sat in the living room and listened to *The Lone Ranger*, *The Inner Sanctum* and *The Shadow* on the radio, beneath which there was a large dark red leather hassock I always claimed. From my perch I could see the kitchen, and on the wall beside the slew-footed sink hung my father's chart of enemy airplanes and a large pair of black binoculars. In the vigilant spring of 1942, from four to six in the afternoon, he entered the world of military reconnaissance. He had been asked to be a chaplain, but he did not want to leave his family or his church and instead volunteered to be a plane spotter. I never knew exactly where he went to spot his planes but figured it was probably the top of Long Hill Road. Since he did not offer the information, I happily supposed it was a military secret.

Plane spotting was not his only military duty. His calm demeanor and authoritative manner made him an exemplary air raid warden, his delicate face dwarfed by the huge helmet he was required to wear during the alarms. We loved the blackouts; there couldn't be enough of them. We rushed to pull down all the green shades in the kitchen and the living room and then be very quiet. In our cinema world of fighter planes that lit up the night skies and carried heroes who would end the war, we had no real idea of the danger.

Often my father met with something he called a ration board. He explained it was not a piece of wood, but a group of men who because of the war decided how much of certain scarce items people could have. One of my earliest awarenesses of privilege was knowing that my father had extra ration sheets, freeing us from the worry of running out of the things we liked.

In the evenings, if he was not listening to a radio program, my father read or did crossword puzzles, a pastime he had taken up during the puzzle fad of the 1920s. My mother went back and forth among the children, mediating spats or helping with homework. Unless my father had an evening meeting or he and my mother were at the movies, we were always together.

It was in Waterbury where we all sat listening to the fights of Joe Louis and cheering his victories, even my father, who abhorred violence. It was in Waterbury that I remember seeing for the first time the *Crisis* (the national publication of the NAACP), the *Negro Digest* and *Our World*, a forerunner to *Ebony*. And it was in Waterbury that I began to trail my brother like a shadow, wanting to do everything he did.

"Brother," as Julian, Jr., was called, inherited my mother's temperament and my father's charm. He had round cheeks, slanty eyes and soft, light brown hair that in summer became the red some people called "rhiney." His elegant nose, his ready grin and a cleft in his chin were predictors of future handsomeness. Brother's best friend was a thirteen-year-old white boy whose stunted growth made him look six and resulted in his nickname, Little Man. He had a big head, wispy, pale blond hair, and round blue eyes that looked as if they never blinked. The three of us played with toy trucks and cars in the back of the house at the edge of the woods.

One day, Brother, who was six at the time, and Little Man invited me into the woods to see something special. It was Little Man's swollen penis. The pale, fat flesh held little interest for me. Disappointed, I returned to the yard. Little Man zipped up and we all went back to playing with the trucks and cars in our backyard dirt. I never told my parents about the incident, but I stayed away from Little Man after that.

My sister Jewelle was four years older than I, her skin tone slightly more olive. Heavy eyebrows gave her face immediate authority, while large, round dark eyes, a long nose that resembled our father's, full, sensually curved lips and deep dimples gave her an arresting, mature expression. She was chatty and inquisitive, and related easily to grown-ups. She carried the confidence and assurance of the firstborn lightly on her shoulders. In Waterbury her life revolved around school and violin lessons. Directing my behavior and activity became second nature to her, though generally I ignored her baton.

She was much the little lady, while I was a tomboy, preferring overalls and uncombed hair. Having combed hair was a major mark of respectability for colored people then. Unkempt hair represented slattern ways and deserved poverty. I was forbidden to go outside unless my hair was presentable. My way around that edict was to wear hats rather than face the comb's teeth, a solution I employ to this day.

My hair was soft and came to my shoulders. It was not quite "nappy," but it tangled, knotted easily, and required a light pressing with a hot comb. During my first summer away at camp I put on a hat and did not comb my hair for two weeks. When I came home, it was so matted that my mother had to cut it.

Because my mother did not have to press her own hair, she had little experience with hair that napped. And because I was tender-headed, and my mother let my hair dry completely before she pressed it, each hair-doing session was torture for both of us. There were no such things as conditioners or softeners then. The only hair dressing we had was a pomade called Dixie Peach, a scented step up from Vaseline.

When the appointed time came, I would sit in the kitchen beside the stove with a towel around my shoulders. Each time my mother tried to get the comb through my hair, I pulled away. The more I pulled, the more it hurt. I screamed. I yelled. I prayed. I pounded on my thighs. I stomped my feet. I bit my hand. I arched and humped my back. I held on to the edges of the chair. I slid out of the chair onto the floor. I told my mother she was killing me.

After what seemed like several hours, she was finished. Exhausted, she did not try to curl my hair, but braided it instead. My scalp felt as if it had been fastened to a clothesline by every strand. It was a milestone for us both when I was old enough to go to a beauty parlor.

❦

By the age of two, children begin to notice differences between themselves and others. I learned the vocabulary of those variations shortly after I began to talk. I could see the heterogeneous skin colors around me, and their descriptions were part of my everyday life. In my immediate family, every color was good and had value. My mother was light, my father was dark. I am light but I always thought I was medium brown. I did not understand until I went away to college that I could be mistaken for anything other than colored. At seventeen, my perception of my color was skewed by the layers of brownness that had swaddled both my mother and me from birth.

In spite of the trauma and cost of being born with colored skin, we black people have always had a delicious way of describing ourselves. To a white person, a black person is simply black. Black people see an infinite range of hues. We call ourselves honey, caramel, ivory, peaches-and-cream, mahogany, coal blue, red, bronze, amber, tar, rhiney, snow, chocolate, coffee, ebony, clear, bright, light, dark, alabaster, tan, rosy, molasses, toffee, taffy, café-au-lait, nutmeg, leafy, high yellow, paper-bag-tan, and purple.

Color for blacks is intensely subjective. How we see it is affected both by our feelings toward the skin tone as an abstraction and by the reality of the person cased in that skin. If you ask a group of black people if a person they know is lighter or darker than another person they also know, you will get wildly divergent answers.

Long ago, someone told black people that their hair was "good," "nice" or "bad." The labels, which used "white" hair as their standard, stuck. In the "good" and "nice" categories were straight, wavy, curly, "Indian," heavy, coarse or soft. Nappy, kinky and short fell into the "bad" group. Long hair was favored over short, and long hair that had to be pressed with a hot comb fell somewhere in between. In the 1990s, despite the fashionability of dreadlocks, braids, corkscrew curls and a never-ending variety of geometric haircuts for men, hair dressers, black and white alike, make good money on chemically straightened, woven and otherwise ingeniously lengthened black hair. "Good" hair can be had, for a price.

In my family, we knew my mother and Pattee had "good" hair. My mother said the rest of us, even my father, had "soft hair"— that is, it did not require a hot and heavy press. Privately, although he kept it short and manageable by wearing a nylon stocking cap each night, I would have called my father's hair "nappy," but not "bad." When he was in his seventies, he experienced a regrowth of his hair, and it came in straight, like an Indian's. It was as if some recessed Native American hair gene had escaped and overpowered its African-American brothers and sisters.

✑

There are dozens of pictures of me in my mother's scrapbooks. From black-and-white snapshots to faded Polaroid portraits, I can chart my physical progress from infancy to the present. Through those images I can see the fashions, the seasons and my interests change. Although we change imperceptibly every day and the reflection in the mirror can sometimes be a surprise, I am familiar with *what* I look like, but the *who* is another matter. There is no such tracking for my mother.

I have a need to see the aspects of my mother's face when she was a teenager. I remember the surprised joy of my own daughter when, in her twenties, she found a picture of me as a teenager. Although she is a rich, red, chocolaty brown, and I am shades lighter, she was fascinated with her close resemblance to my high school picture. "Cool," she said. So far, I have been denied the opportunity to compare myself to the girl who would become my mother. The few pictures of my mother as a girl that did exist burned in a fire the year she left her last home.

As far as I know, the one exception is a picture taken in 1916 when she was four. In the small candid, she is standing in the summer sun behind her younger brother, who has a small hump on his back. Someone dressed her in a white, angel-sleeved frock. Her hair sports an oversized bow, and the flyaway auburn strands look golden in the high sunlight. Her expression is one of delight and pleasure. The picture was taken around the time her family vanished.

✑

They say that as early as infancy a child can read the expressions on its mother's face. Was I that young when I began to absorb her sadness? As a little girl, and later as an adolescent, I was convinced that big chunks of my life were missing. There were no gray-haired grandparents waiting to welcome and spoil me on holidays or vacations. There were no letters or presents or cards from the parents of my parents. There were no stories about my mother when she was a little girl.

Three of my grandparents died before I was born. The remaining one, my mother's father, William Morris, whom my mother called Willmorris (I heard it as one word), was inaccessible to me. As a "white" man who could not admit colored people into his world, he lived a distant life in a distant place. I knew he was alive, because whenever the subject of her father came up, my mother, with uncharacteristic venom, referred to him as "Willmorris that-bastard-in-Maryland." I never met him, but his absence was a presence in my life. His looks were an intriguing mystery; in those days, I never got to see a picture of him because my mother, in a fit of anger, destroyed the only one she had. I knew he did not want to see my mother, or me, or any of the rest of our family. But I could not understand why.

I was even more confused when my mother told me that she was not with her father, or her brothers and sister, because she was "too brown." My mother was not brown; she was light. I knew that this missing grandfather did not care that I liked to read and was a straight-A student. I knew that he did not know that my mother alternately loved and hated him, and wished she could visit with him. I knew that he did not know how she cried for and cursed him with equal passion.

No matter how beautiful the autumn, its onset signaled the beginning of a seasonal sadness for my mother. Her melancholy would deepen as Christmas approached. Poignantly she spoke of her feelings. I remember feeling helplessly protective of her as she talked of childhood holiday wishes unfulfilled.

For us there were luxurious, indulgent Christmases always at home. We received hundreds of Christmas cards from church members and scores of pies and cakes. Each year, my father would buy a tall Douglas fir tree that he hung with ornaments and lights. Our job was to hand him the icicles, strand by strand. When he finished, he would step back, ask one of us to turn on the lights, and admire his handiwork. Then, invariably, he would begin to hum the "Hallelujah Chorus."

During the succeeding nights, either he or Jewelle would play the piano and we'd all sing Christmas carols in the living room. Brother could not carry a tune, so his job was to pull my hair or breathe on Jewelle's neck. At the edge of the group, my mother sang shyly, holding Pattee on her hip or clinging to her hand. Sometimes my Uncle Percy came from New York. He and my father would sing "O Holy Night" and "Ave Maria" together as they had when they were boys. Then we all sang together, Percy directing with a thumping foot or a waving hand.

On Christmas morning, there was always a roomful of toys, clothes and books. After we opened the presents, my father would go out to visit the members of the church, to bring them his personal greetings and to accept their gifts. Every year we would ask my mother why he could not stay at home and enjoy the day like other fathers. We knew the answer, of course. When he came home, he was usually several hundred dollars richer.

Most of us have yearnings and longings for the holidays of times past. My mother never had anything for which to yearn.

❧

My search for the missing part of my family has been with me consciously and unconsciously all my life. I inherited it, I absorbed it by osmosis. This need, this pain, of my mother's became mine. Her loss and rejection gave shape to my development. It touched me in ways I am yet unable to fathom. As my mother approached her eightieth birthday, I made a conscious decision to use whatever means possible to find her family. I knew that I would find them. Lawyers and census takers and city directories and utility companies and alumni offices prepare lists of names that I could scan.

Whenever I traveled, to Cleveland, Buffalo, Philadelphia and the Eastern Shore of Maryland, my preoccupation with the vanished family came to the surface. I knew that somewhere out there the living ghosts went about their daily lives. I was ambivalent about my quest. I didn't know what I would do or say when I found my missing kin. Some were undoubtedly dead. Others had no knowledge of their black ancestry. Should I visit their parents' sins upon them? This was not a theoretical question for me, the daughter of a minister, with inherited bonds to the church.

Sometimes, in moments of reflection or frustration, my sisters and I talked about what was ethical and what type of responsibility we had to these relatives we didn't even know. Would my revelations of familial connections bring pain, shame, anger, horror, revulsion, suicide? It has meant all of those things to be black in America. There is strong evidence that light-skinned blacks still receive preferential treatment in white and black America. I wondered how many of my cousins who had been free, white and twenty-one would claim their colored relative and heritage.

If the division in my family has caused so much pain, why did I seek them out? Because my children and I need to know the rest of what has shaped us. Simply put, part of their genetic codes belong to us as well. But also, my mother's story mirrors the lives of tens of thousands of Americans who have racial schisms in their own families. Wherever I share the story, someone invariably tells a similar one.

My mother's history suggests that race and color in America are not interchangeable. From bitter experience, black people have always understood that color and race are exquisitely arbitrary. White people in America take their whiteness for granted. But if we adhere to traditional notions of race, many of them are not white. Nor are all black people black. The heritage of this country and all of its people is mixed. A subtext of this story is, What is white? What is black? What is race?

Those who can claim to be Americans of pure African descent are few and far between. No matter what we call ourselves, the ethnic range of America lives within us. Currently, one of the country's major black political figures is married to a woman whose sisters pass for white in Tennessee. In Buffalo, there is a man who lives as white, but frequently returns to his black high school reunions in Washington, D.C. In New Haven, a friend of my family who used to be black moved to neighboring Hamden and is now white. The D.C. police force was integrated by a black man taken for white in the 1920s. A woman I knew as black when I was young is now white and no longer speaks to me. Multiply these instances many times over and the footprints of those who have crossed the color line become infinite and untrackable.

Chapter Two

My old man's a white old man
And my old mother's black.
If ever I cursed my white old man
I take my curses back.

If ever I cursed my black old mother
And wished she were in hell,
I'm sorry for that evil wish
And now I wish her well.

My old man died in a fine big house
My ma died in a shack.
I wonder where I'm gonna die,
Being neither white nor black?

—LANGSTON HUGHES
"Cross"

My mother's family story begins as many American stories begin, with a transatlantic journey. The year was 1860, and the family travelers were Irish, from County Tipperary: William Maher, my mother's great-grandfather, his wife, Mary Katherine, and his daughter, Margaret. It was the desperate era after the great potato famines and fever in Ireland, when more than 750,000 died of starvation. Corpses had been found with grass stuffed in their mouths. Dogs and donkeys had become staples of the diet. Scores of bodies lined the roads.

This was Maher's seventh journey between Ireland and America. According to Margaret, change was as much a part of her father's life as travel. Like other country boys in search of city dreams, when he was eighteen he had left the ancient town of Thurles, nestled beside the quiet Suir River in the rich agricultural region called the Golden Vale. Leaving Thurles, the Suir meanders south, passing Kilkenny and Cashel, and before it turns east and flows into the Irish Sea the river has, as the Irish would say, the good sense to touch the shores of Tipperary. Taking his lead from the river, and from those who had gone before, the young Maher called Tipperary his first home away from home. It was not long before the local boys were calling him "The rolling Tip from Thurles," a name his daughter would keep locked in her memory.

Maher was not alone long. He married, had seven children, and became a widower. His second bride, Mary Katherine, would become my great-great-grandmother. He also took advantage of every business opportunity that presented itself. Before long, Maher began making entrepreneurial trips to Washington, D.C. In time he opened a store that sold groceries and sundries on M Street in Georgetown, where Irishmen had taken over the grocery business while groups of Jewish merchants from Germany and France favored the clothing and shoe trade.

Maher's store was one of many small businesses that welcomed the flood of Irishmen and other immigrants who had come to Washington looking for jobs. They found work in the foundries and flour mills of then industrial Georgetown and helped build the Chesapeake and Ohio Canal. For those who built her and those who sailed her, the C&O Canal was a failed dream of passage to western wealth. But Maher's benefits from the waterway were lasting and substantial. He prospered.

⟨∞⟩

Three of Maher's children from his first marriage had joined him in the capital city, but three daughters stayed behind in a convent school and became nuns. Alcoholism prevented a brother and a son from making the journey. Maher's seventh voyage was to be a journey of restoration. He would re-create the family he had lost to death, to religion and to the bottle. His young second wife and their daughter would make a new start in a new place.

Transatlantic voyages in the 1860s were not for the fragile. The weather could be severe and conditions aboard ship were appalling. Fresh foods were in short supply. The stench of excrement filled the hold. Fever would break out and no medicines would be available. With little time for funeral rites, bodies were thrown overboard. An estimated twenty thousand people perished on the ships carrying the Irish immigrants. As Gerald Keegan tells us in his *Famine Diary*, those who survived staggered out of the hatches and "looked for all the world like specters coming out of tombs with their ghastly complexions and gaunt, emaciated bodies."

One of those who did not survive was my great-great-grandmother. As the ship rolled and groaned in the water, Mary Katherine tossed and moaned in a narrow berth. Her last sight was that of her husband holding her hand, and her four-year-old daughter resting her head beside her on the pillow drenched with a fever's sweat. She was dead before they reached their first stop, New York City. What family history does not tell is why, upon subsequently arriving in Washington, William Maher left his daughter at St. Vincent's Orphanage and Convent. Some in the family suggest that his grief as well as his constant traveling prevented him from caring for a young child. Others speculate that the much older half brothers and sisters had no interest in this child of a woman who was not their mother. Whatever the reasons, we do know that William Maher set a pattern of abandonment for his family.

∞

Margaret Maher remained in the orphanage until she was sixteen. She was petite, with pale skin and electric blue eyes that gazed imperturbably from an oval face framed in light brown hair. Some in the family called her pretty, but I think she had an unattractive mouth that gave her face an unpleasant cast. I saw her once, when I was a girl of eleven and she was an invalid in her nineties. All I can remember is someone very old, very white and very small. She looked at me and did not smile and I recall that I was afraid of her, whether because of her age or her whiteness I am not sure.

St. Vincent's Orphanage and Convent provided a strict classical education for its white charges. The institution was located at the bustling corner of 11th and G streets, now the site of Woodard & Lothrop, Washington's oldest department store. St. Vincent's goal was to develop well-read young women of culture, eligible for marriage, teaching or the sisterhood. Margaret Maher told her grandchildren that during her convent years she had been a conscientious student who loved to read and study nature. From time to time, her father would visit with news of her relatives on both sides of the Atlantic and to check on her progress. Otherwise she was left in the care of the women in black.

Sometimes the sisters found positions for the girls as companions for wealthy women. The patrons' wealth often exceeded their learning, and they relied on others to broaden their intellectual lives. When it was Margaret Maher's turn to make the choice between the convent and life outside, she chose life. A position was found for her in the rambling house of an elderly, wealthy white spinster.

Margaret's new home sat in an elite district up in the hills overlooking the city from the northwest. She acquired her own comfortably appointed room, with a four-poster mahogany bed instead of a cot. Clusters of miniature lilacs on a pale yellow background replaced the chalky walls of her orphanage cell. She could see a garden and beautiful grounds from her window seat, upholstered in lavender velvet. The furnishings included a marble fireplace, a deep, dark green chintz armchair where she could daydream or nap, and delicately etched, frosted sconces over the gas lights that enabled her to read her beloved books.

In exchange for room, board, clothing and a modest allowance, Margaret read, embroidered and chatted with her companion during the day. She cradled the old woman's arm and kept her steady when they took their daily walks. She could not talk much about Ireland because she did not remember it. Nor could she talk about Washington, because she did not kow it. Instead Margaret spoke to her companion of books, poetry, nature and art.

One day each week, Margaret had her freedom. She headed for the colorful open-air markets that were numerous in Washington at the time, shopping and studying the variety of people who crowded the noisy, wide streets. There were light people and dark people and people in uniforms. There were horses and carriages and pushcarts and stalls. One of the people who caught her eye was a handsome young man named Edward Everett Morris. He would become my mother's grandfather, my great-grandfather. And he had been a slave.

꒰꒱

One hundred years before Margaret Maher came to America, there was proportionately more sex and marriage between whites and blacks than at any other time in the country's history. In *Mixed Blood*, Paul Spickard writes that many of those mixed couples were indentured servants or a free black and an indentured white. Spickard notes that Jews in New Orleans frequently married black women in the nineteenth century.

Counts from the 1860 census tallied mulattoes at more than 12 percent of the nonwhite Southern rural population. Those, of course, were the ones who were known. Mary Chesnut, a friend of Jefferson Davis, wrote, "Our men live all in one house with their wives and their concubines, and the mulattoes one sees in every family exactly resemble the white children—and every lady tells you who is the father of all the mulatto children in everybody's household, but those in her own she seems to think drop from the clouds, or pretends so to think."

The English word *mulatto* is derived from the Latin *mulus*, for "mule," traveling down through Portuguese and Spanish. Its original meaning was much the same: a mixed breed. But mules are sterile, while mulattoes were not. And historically, "mulatto" was a pejorative term that blacks used with ambivalence. Those who bore it had no choice in how they came to be born into what one observer called "a society long quietly familiar with illicit sex based on ownership." Their straight, wavy, curly, kinky or nappy hair was blond, brown, auburn, red and black. Their eyes were hazel, green, blue, gray, brown, black and even lavender. My family has all of these colors and textures.

The desire to label racial differences took exquisite turns. Besides "mulatto," there was "quadroon," the offspring of a white person and a mulatto, and "octoroon," the offspring of a quadroon and a white. Some Southern states adopted the West Indian terminology, by which the child of a quadroon and a white was a "mustee," and the child of a mustee and a white person a "mustefino." In Jamaica, to be born a mustefino was to be born free, because that was as close to white as one could get. At the other end of the spectrum were the children of mulattoes and blacks, called sambos.

When I reread all those definitions recently, they triggered both profound sadness and high hilarity in me. What would my mother, the daughter of a mustee and a mulatto, be—a "mustatta"? Surely my sisters and I would qualify for the sambo category—or would that be "sambelina"?

As American society polarized into black and white, most of the nineteenth-century labels fell out of use. It was just too difficult to measure and track how much black or white "blood" was flowing, and in what direction. Some form of the "one-drop rule" was adopted in most states.

Edward Everett Morris was the son of James D. Halyburton, who served as a federal judge of the Eastern District of Virginia from 1844 to 1861, and a mulatto house servant whose name has come down through the family as Ruth Morris. Oral history, photographs, census records, physical features and a genetic flaw give substance to Morris's lineage. In those days, to those for whom such things mattered, he was a quadroon. His name, however, had a story all its own.

On the banks of the Charles River in Cambridge, Massachusetts, a boy from the South met a teacher from the North whose influence would remain with the boy forever. The year was 1819: the boy, my ancestor, James Halyburton. The teacher, a classical scholar, Edward Everett. The setting, Harvard University.

Edward Everett was born in Dorchester, Massachusetts, in 1794, one of eight children of a Congregational minister of modest means. One of the top scholars in a class of forty-nine that included Samuel Gilman, author of the school's song, "Fair Harvard," Everett graduated from Harvard and became a Unitarian minister in Boston. He gave up his active ministry to teach Greek literature at his alma mater, then left academia to become first a representative, then governor of Massachusetts, and later a senator from the state. A principled abolitionist, he resigned from the Senate in his second year because of the Whig Party's compromise on slavery. He went on to higher and higher posts, becoming a minister to England, president of Harvard and secretary of state in the last four months of President Millard Fillmore's administration.

When Everett was president of Harvard in the late 1840s, a Negro student, Beverly Williams, applied for admission. Williams, a Hopkins School student who ranked as one of the best Latin scholars in his high school class, also tutored one of Everett's sons. When word got out about Williams's application, some within the college let it be known that although he might pass the examinations, he would never be admitted.

Everett's written response to the rumor was, "The admission to Harvard College depends upon examinations: and if this boy passes the examinations, he will be admitted; and if the white students choose to withdraw, all the income of the College will be devoted to his education." Everett's resolve was not put to the test. Consumption claimed the life of Beverly Williams in 1847, before he could take the admissions test.

During the Civil War, Everett traveled throughout the North speaking for the Union cause and drawing immense audiences. His best-known speech, now almost forgotten, was the principal oration given at Gettysburg on the same occasion when Abraham Lincoln delivered his famous address. More popular in its time was Everett's speech, entitled "The Character of George Washington." So great was its reception that he donated $70,000 of the proceeds from that speech alone for the restoration of Mount Vernon in 1859.

Everett's student, Judge Halyburton, was born in New Kent County, Virginia. At the peak of his career he presided over a federal court and a large household in Richmond, Virginia. He lived on one of Richmond's most important thoroughfares, Marshall Street, within blocks of the home of his friend and colleague Jefferson Davis, whom the judge swore in as president of the Confederacy. The neighborhood was known as Court End because it was populated mostly by lawyers and judges. After Davis, its most famous resident was John Marshall, who became chief justice of the Supreme Court. After the war, Halyburton opened a law firm on Main Street with his brother-in-law, Thomas Giles.

History suggests that Halyburton was not a confident man. George Christian, another Richmond judge, wrote of him, "He was so much afraid of doing wrong, that he frequently hesitated to decide at all, and thus, to some extent at least, impaired his efficiency as a judge." Of the Halyburton-Giles firm, Christian commented, "They were too distrustful of themselves, and too slow for the times, and therefore, did but little in the way of practice. It was a common saying at the time that Judge Halyburton doubted, and Mr. Giles doubted about Judge Halyburton's doubts, and so on almost ad infinitum, so that they rarely reached a conclusion satisfactory to either themselves or their clients." Halyburton was one of the first professors of the law school of Richmond College. Christian observed it was "a position for which he was eminently suited by his learning, but I suspect unfitted for by reason of the fact that he was hardly dogmatic enough in his style to be a successful teacher."

Halyburton was a tall man with a large frame, deep-set, soulful dark eyes, a prominent nose with a hump and flaring nostrils, and uncommonly large ears. The judge had a health problem described as a "paralysis" that recurred from time to time. Along with his other genetic traits, it seems he passed on a neuromuscular defect to at least one member of each succeeding generation. In my generation and the one after, it affected my cousins. In the generation after that, it affected my brother's grandchild.

∽

In the census of 1860 Halyburton reported four slaves: three mulattoes and one black. Three were women, two sixty years of age and one forty-five. The sole male listed was a sixty-year-old mulatto. Halyburton's forty-five-year-old mulatto slave was my great-great-grandmother. I know her only from the handwritten roster of the census. Each entry is scrolled in an elegant script that looks as if it has catalogued precious and cherished possessions. But they were neither precious enough nor cherished enough to be listed by their names, any names. My great-great-grandmother is simply listed as a forty-five-year-old "F," for female. Beside her surname, in the appropriate box, is the designation "M," for mulatto.

I touched that page when I first saw it, as if my fingers on the paper would help to conjure up visions of the woman, the forced mistress, the concubine, the wife's competitor, the sexual receptacle of the esteemed judge. My fingers just felt sorrow. I look in the mirror and have no idea where I would find that forty-five-year-old F/M in any of my features.

The judge's Henrico County property abutted that of several white Morris families, headed by R.F. and Adolphus. The designation for the thirty-eight slaves on the R. F. Morris property was B for black. The designation for each of the eight slaves on the Adolphus Morris properties was M for mulatto. I wonder how many of their descendants eventually became white. Since the slave usually took the name of its original owner, I believe that my great-great-grandmother had come to the judge's home from the Adolphus Morris place, where mulatto slaves were clearly preferred. For one of my middle names, my mother added Morris, and I have passed it on to one of my daughters. For years I simply accepted it as my mother's family name, and as an early feminist, I was pleased that my mother had given her last name to me. Some fifty years after my birth, the unvarnished reality of seeing the name on an old census form, in the space reserved for the slaveholder, makes me more ambivalent about owning it.

Twice married, the judge had two daughters and four other sons. But the family story passed down from those Virginia days is that the judge favored the slave son he'd named for his beloved teacher and took a special interest in him. Edward lived in the house with his parents, his white half siblings and their mother, the official mistress of the Marshall Street home. He was almost as light as his siblings, and his golden brown hair had a slight curl. His ears were large like his father's, and he had also inherited the distinctive long nose with the prominent hump and flaring nostrils.

Once I began to track my family's history it became an obsession. Each step revealed still more mysteries, secrets and riddles. From the time I was a little girl, I had been told by my mother's Washington relatives that we were "descendants of the first families of Virginia." My sister and I laughingly edited that to "descendants of slaves of the first families of Virginia." But the relatives had been especially proud of their lofty connections. I decided to find out more about my allegedly aristocratic progenitors.

A request for information from the Virginia State Archives brought a thick yellow envelope in the mail. It contained newspaper clippings and abstracts from legal and historical journals. From an obituary in *The Richmond Daily Dispatch* I learned that James Dandridge Halyburton was indeed a member of the aristocratic Dandridge clan of New Kent County, Virginia. I knew of only one other Dandridge—Dorothy, who was black and a movie star. The white Dandridges were wealthy tobacco planters whose graceful plantations were built along the Pamunkey, one of the rivers that flow into Chesapeake Bay. They had been there since colonial times, having claimed vast expanses of free land. They were among the richest 1 percent of pre-Revolutionary Americans.

Among the papers was a genealogy of the Dandridges of Virginia. At first I wondered why it had been included, since I had not requested it. I studied it carefully and made my own lineage chart. Directly above Judge Halyburton's name was the maiden name of his mother, Martha Washington Dandridge. The name jumped out at me. Clearly this Martha who married a Halyburton was not the Mother of Our Country, but why that name? Following the line up the chart just one generation above I found the answer: Martha Dandridge Custis Washington, wife of General George Washington, was her namesake's aunt. The general's wife had a favorite brother named Bartholomew Dandridge, who was little Martha's father. There are several references to Martha Washington Dandridge Halyburton in Anne Wharton's biography of Martha Washington. She was said to be the first lady's favorite niece and was called Patty, as were all the Marthas in the Dandridge family.

Could I, would I, want to claim Martha Washington as an ancestor? Instead of six degrees of separation there were seven generations between us. My first thought was that I could be eligible for membership in the DAR. I called my mother.

"Mother," I said, "Guess what? You are a great-niece, six generations removed, of Martha Washington."

I called my sister Pattee and told her of the two illustrious forebears with the same nickname. I called my daughters and Jewelle, who was in England for a month studying the problems of England's black young men. She had just come in from dinner with the crème de la crème of England's black aristocracy, the first black peer and peeress in the House of Lords. I told her it was too bad she did not have this evidence of her own aristocratic pedigree beforehand.

I found it difficult to sleep that night. I had never given Martha

Washington much thought. For me she had been frozen in time as the quintessential colonial dame, embroidering a lawn handkerchief while her husband defended and then created America. It never occurred to me that she had been someone's restless teenager, someone's daughter to be married off. In the next few weeks, I read as much about her as I could find, and studied her portraits in books and in museums. She was a short woman with thin lips, a wide pursed mouth and lidded eyes. I kept coming back to her hooked nose, which looked like mine, and her thin mouth, which reminded me of my mother's aunt Mamie Morris Smith.

Martha Washington's father, John Dandridge, had immigrated to Virginia from Worcestershire, England. He owned hundreds of slaves who worked his tobacco fields along the Pamunkey. Martha's life revolved around balls, horseback riding, private tutors, presents from England and slaves for every need or whim. It was no secret that she was one of the richest women in Virginia when she married George Washington. She has been depicted as a devoted mother and a feisty defender of her husband, qualities that bring to mind my own mother.

But it was not Martha Washington who fascinated me. It was her personal maid, Oney, to whom there are numerous references in the biographies and in the few letters Martha did not destroy. Oney, a slave described as a handsome mulatto, was presented to Martha when both were young girls. Oney was said to be devoted to her mistress and then to the general. Wherever Martha went she took Oney. Whenever there was a problem, she turned to Oney for help. But when Martha became first lady and moved first to New York and then to Philadelphia, Oney vanished. Martha was said to be devastated. The president sent out discreet inquiries, but Oney was never heard from again. They believed she had been seduced and whisked away by one of Lafayette's Frenchmen.

The story of Oney haunts me. In light of the origins of my own family, it was natural for me to wonder whether Oney might have been Martha's half sister and through her related to me. My connection to Martha, however, the First Lady of Whiteness, remains abstract and difficult to digest, a sidebar to my search. I wondered what my father would have said. I am certain he would have been secretly pleased, but I know his last words on the subject would have been: "That's all well and good, but remember you are a Taylor." In the end, I think he would have been correct. The information has little value for me now.

∽

When I learned what I needed to know about the Dandridge side of the family, I turned to the Halyburton ledger. Judge Halyburton's father, William Halyburton, was a physician who had immigrated from Haddington, Scotland (where the family name was spelled with an "i"), shortly after the Revolution. The Haliburtons in turn had come to Scotland from England around 1066, bearing the name Burton. They traced their origin to Tructe the Saxon, a high-ranking contemporary of David I, king of Scotland during the first half of the twelfth century. The Scots added the adjective "haly" after a member of the clan built a chapel on the family estate. Their coat of arms featured a boar, a tree, a sentinel, an elk and a man who has thick lips and looks as if he is wearing a short Afro. I learned later the man was indeed a Moor. Their motto was "Watch Weell." Judge Halyburton, my great-great-grandfather, had that motto and the Haliburton coat of arms on the family silver he inherited.

In 1700, the Haliburton family acquired Dryburgh Abbey, a few miles from the English border, a site considered a holy place by the Druids. One of the most famous members of the clan to be buried there was Sir Walter Scott, whose maternal grandmother was Barbara Haliburton. What a chase this was turning out to be! In the search for my mother's family, I had unknowingly climbed up the other side of the family tree, and in its branches discovered a Founding Mother and a Romantic poet.

How far down does a gene travel before it mutates and becomes kinky hair instead of straight, gray eyes instead of blue, pale skin instead of tan, thick lips instead of thin? When do the chromosomes break and recombine to create genetic changes? As fragments of genetic material move among the chromosomes, how many generations can a family "look" sustain itself? How long do the transposable elements of DNA move from place to place, controlling the expression of genes? When does the genetic information wear itself out completely?

Could Jewelle's large, luminous eyes be tracked back to the dark eyes of Sir Walter Scott? The hook at the end of Pattee's nose resembles Martha Washington's; then again, it looks like the beaked nose of our Indian paternal grandmother. From pictures, Nelly Custis, Martha Washington's granddaughter, could be my sister, or my mother's sister. Are these pure coincidences or are they nature's advisories that blood will tell?

∽

Judge Halyburton taught his son of color how to read and play the piccolo. His teachings were within the law; Virginia had passed a statute in 1705 requiring masters to teach "orphaned, poor, illegitimate, and sometimes mulatto children to read." Later, his father hired him out as a servant in the U.S. Bank of Richmond, where the judge's uncle was cashier. There, the hired slave would learn about the world of commerce. He would also learn about the world outside the bank.

The southern counties of Virginia and Maryland supplied the greatest number of slaves to the Deep South, and Richmond was the region's second largest slave market. Marie Tyler-McGraw, coauthor of *In Bondage and Freedom*, observes, "The purchase and resale of slaves was a highly profitable and visible business. Public slave auctions became increasingly common. Aside from the chains, manacles and treatment of slaves as livestock, there was the daily heartbreak of family separation on view. These vivid and wrenching scenes made a daily impression on all blacks in Richmond. Slaves were vital in Richmond not only for their labor but for their marketability."

But the city required for itself many of the slaves who were brought there to be sold. They were needed for the thirty-one malodorous tobacco factories, the eight treacherous iron factories and the five hazardous carriage foundries. They were needed for the deadly coal mines on each side of the James River. They were needed to feed the unforgiving furnaces and negotiate the hot metals of the Tredegar Iron Works, which supplied major munitions for the Confederate cause. Their limbs, their eyes, their lungs, were expendable. In return for their life's blood, they earned wages, most of which they turned over to their owners.

I went to Richmond to learn more about the life of an urban slave like my great-grandfather.

The citizens of the capital of the Confederacy have taken great pains to keep much of their city as it was before the war. No fewer than nine museums pay homage to the past. The hotel driver insisted I see Monument Avenue, often called the most beautiful boulevard in the South. Grand homes with circular driveways line the broad street. Running down the center of the avenue is a wide, meticulously manicured green strip, dotted at intervals with fifty-foot statues of Confederate heroes, including Stonewall Jackson, Jefferson Davis, Robert E. Lee and J. E. B. Stuart. A recent campaign to add civil rights heroes has not succeeded. The street is literally a concrete glorification of "The Lost Cause." I wondered about the effects that the celebration of these stone men had on the psyches of Richmond's young black children.

Life for the urban slave was vastly different from that of his plantation counterpart. Urban life bestowed urban privileges. Frederick Douglass once remarked that being a slave in the city was close to being a free man. There was independence, learned skills and information, and unsupervised socializing. Some considered these things dangerous. Tyler-McGraw notes, "To maintain near total control over black Richmond meant a level of constant vigilance and supervision that was impossible. . . . Between 1790 and 1860, the Richmond City Council and the Virginia General Assembly passed law after law and ordinance after ordinance to control the activities and attitudes of free blacks and slaves. The ultimate white power resided not in the law, but in the auction block, the slave's greatest fear."

In one of his unsupervised moments, Edward saw Abraham Lincoln when the president came to the conquered Confederate capital during the last days of the Civil War. A self-consciously proud unit of Negro soldiers accompanied Lincoln as he toured the once beautiful city, which had been ravaged by Union bombardment. Groups of slaves trailed the Emancipator through Richmond's ruined streets and visited the Confederate White House, not far from the judge's house. Edward was at the edge of one of those groups.

Shortly thereafter, he found a way to do what many other slaves had done before him: he ran away. Slaves escaped from Richmond in a variety of ways. Many hid in storage spaces in ships. Richmond's most famous slave escapee was Henry Box Brown, who had himself crated in a box and shipped to Philadelphia around 1850. In Edward's travels through the city, he had come upon a Union army jacket and stashed it away. When a Union band billeted in Richmond, Edward put on the jacket and slipped in among them. With the war drawing to a close, none of the weary musicians asked too many questions or looked too carefully at the new recruit. He was six foot two and fourteen years old at the time. Playing his piccolo, he marched out of Richmond. He stopped marching in Washington, D.C. The Civil War ended that same year.

Why did he escape? Perhaps the tall, handsome, light-skinned slave's presence in his father's household was becoming intolerable to his white brothers and sisters. Maybe it was the desire for refuge from the confusion and uncertainty of war-torn Richmond. It may have been his fear of being sold, as so many around him had been. Or it may have been simply as one former slave told an oral history project when asked why he escaped: "I wanted to be free."

In Richmond I stayed at the Linden Row Inn, a group of Greek Revival row houses built in 1847. The guest rooms in the garden, which had been the childhood playground of Edgar Allan Poe, had once been slave quarters. I was only a few blocks from where Judge Halyburton and his family had lived, and where my great-grandfather had witnessed Lincoln's visit.

I did not linger long in the ultramodern Museum of the Confederacy. Hordes of white tourists crowded before J. E. B. Stuart's plumed hat, the coat worn by Jefferson Davis when he was captured, and Robert E. Lee's Appomattox surrender sword. The section on blacks in Richmond and aspects of slavery was clearly no more than a concession to the current reality of the city's black political majority.

Next door was the Confederate White House, the home of Jefferson Davis. Its rooms were furnished with heavy drapes and carpets and uncomfortable-looking chairs. The mirrors and chandeliers were swathed in netting to keep the summer insects from spotting their surfaces. The tour guide told us that all of the Davis children had come to a bad end.

I walked across Capitol Square past the governor's mansion, inhabited by Douglas Wilder, to the Virginia State Archives, which had originally sent me the material about Judge Halyburton and the Dandridge family. All the personnel who assisted me were white, and I did not tell them what my project was.

I completed my research in Richmond at the staid Virginia Historical Society and the newer Valentine Museum. The Historical Society had an exhibit called "Virginia's Children," which featured portraits and artifacts from colonial times up to the Civil War. Black children were nowhere to be seen, on the walls or in the exhibition rooms.

∽

In Washington, Edward Morris lived on the fringe. At first, he slept in passageways and alleys, taking odd jobs wherever they turned up. First records of him in the city turn up in the Washington city directory of 1870, five years after the end of the war. He was listed as a laborer whose residence was on "19th near East Capitol Street. S.E."

When he met Margaret Maher, he was selling goods from a stall at an open-air market. Although he looked white, Edward Morris did not hide the fact that he was part black. Later he would tell Margaret the story of his early life and how he made his escape to Washington. Margaret Maher was attracted to the former slave. She was one of the small number of white women of the servant or companion class who dared keep company with a Negro man. Of course, she had had no other experience with men of any sort, black or white, nor had she any previous contact or experience with black women. She had no context from which to speak ugly words or think ugly thoughts.

In many ways, Margaret Maher's circumstances were similar to Edward's. For twelve years, she had not been free. She had lived in a rigidly controlled, unadorned environment where all of her activity was monitored. Until she was sixteen, someone else had made all choices for her. In a manner of speaking, she too had been an enslaved person.

While they were courting in pre-automobile Washington, Margaret and Edward liked to spend her day off walking in her neighborhood, the fashionable Boundary Line section in the northwest part of the city. Their pattern was always the same. They joined a crowd of other walkers and carriages out for the late afternoon air. To most onlookers in the dwindling part of the day, the handsome brown-haired couple made a striking pair.

But someone else had become familiar with their pattern, someone who must have been watching them and knew that a slave had designs on an Irish girl. One early evening in 1875 as they were walking back to the home of Margaret's employer, a large carriage came bearing down on them. Margaret remembered that the horses were tall and fast. She thought she and Edward were going to be run down and killed. Frozen, she shielded her eyes with her hands and waited for the horses' hooves.

She could not see the driver strain as he brought the animals to a halt, nor did she recognize the two young men who jumped out and grabbed her, or the face of the young woman who leaned out of the carriage and screamed, "We're your family. We want you to leave that nigger and come live with us where you belong." After fifteen years, her half sisters and brothers had come to reclaim her.

Margaret did not know how she managed to escape. She remembered twisting away from the two men. Edward reached for her arms and pulled her out of harm's way. The men jumped back into the carriage, which rapidly disappeared. Margaret's dress was ripped, her gloves were dirty, and her hat had fallen off. Her waist and her wrists were bruised, and she was confused and shaken. But the encounter had been so swift that other walkers barely noticed.

Margaret Maher never saw her half sisters and brothers again. She and Edward eloped shortly thereafter, not knowing who else might come swooping out of their pasts to destroy their future. She was nineteen, he twenty-six.

Margaret told this dramatic story to all her children, who then passed it down until it reached me. I heard it when I was twelve, a wonderful age to hear such a romantic tale. How much elaboration there is I can only imagine. It was one of the stories about my great-grandmother that kept me from hating her.

The union of the young, inexperienced Irish girl and the light-complected mixed-race young man set in motion a complicated legacy, a delicate quadrille of miscegenation, a dance that has not yet ended.

⋐⋑

In May 1992, I went down to Washington to be with my sister Jewelle while her husband, Jim, had surgery. My plan was to spend the days in the National Archives and at Howard University gathering more information about my family. One evening, a few nights after I had arrived, Jewelle told me she had to leave the hospital for an important errand. She was going to pick up pictures of our great-grandparents, photographs that we had never seen. She had requested them from one of the granddaughters of my mother's Aunt Mamie as a present for my mother's upcoming birthday.

She returned in an hour, looking more satisfied than I can ever remember seeing her, and handed me a folder. I sat down and gingerly opened it. I had waited for more than fifty years to see what was inside.

There was my mother's Irish grandmother, Margaret Maher Morris, probably in her fifties, her hair a shocking white. Her blue-eyed gaze was clear, her nose rather broad, her thin lips a straight line. The overall impression was of someone annoyed or impatient that her picture had been taken.

Of more interest to me was the photo of Edward Everett Morris. Small rows of blondish brown curls, neatly parted off center, topped a long, almost noble face. Round-rimmed glasses circled his small eyes. A heavy brush mustache covered his upper lip. His nose was neither narrow nor broad, but he did have flaring nostrils. He looked kind. The military-style uniform jacket he wore was the most arresting aspect of the photograph. Our cousin had been told it was the uniform of the Independent Order of Odd Fellows, a secret fraternity of British origin organized for social enjoyment and mutual aid. I like to think it was an updated version of the jacket that enabled him to march out of Richmond to freedom of sorts.

The photographs were my first tangible step toward recovering my mother's family. The liberation of the pictures was a triumph. For the first time we had on our mother's side faces that we could study, eyes we could read, lips we could trace. We could argue back and forth about who looked like whom. If we wanted to, we could see ourselves and our children.

Chapter Three

You know, 'Rene, I've often wondered why more coloured girls like you and Margaret Hammond and Esther Dawson and— oh, lots of others—never passed over. It's such a frightfully easy thing to do. If one's the type, all that's needed is a little nerve.

—CLARE KENDRY in *Passing,* by Nella Larsen

From mid-morning to late afternoon, I spent my days in the genealogy section of the National Archives, located on Pennsylvania Avenue between 7th and 9th streets. Wandering around that part of town, I was struck by how white a city downtown Washington is by day, despite a population that is 80 percent black. Outside the archives is a massive statue of a seated woman with long hair, a strong nose and currently fashionable big lips. On her lap rests an open book. Inscribed at the base of the statue are the words "Past is prologue."

I found my prologue in Room 401, which houses census material, city directories, passenger lists, data on veterans, passport applications and personnel records. Somewhere among all that paper and microfilm, I knew my family's old stories would be told and new ones would come to light.

I was amazed at the number of people looking for validation of their pasts. Ninety-nine percent of them seemed to be white. Of course, the records of black people are mostly buried in anonymity, difficult if not impossible to ferret out. Late one day as I was watching name after name scroll across the screen, I overheard a white couple sitting behind me. They had been working all day, looking for a relative of the husband's.

"Mary Lou," he said, "I don't understand this. I thought I had him. I found the same name, the same age, the same town, the same street, but something is wrong."

"What do you mean?" Mary Lou asked. "How could it be wrong if all the points check out?"

"This person is black," her husband replied. "It's obviously not the same man. We'll have to start all over again."

I smiled to myself.

❧

"You haven't heard what happened, have you?" My cousin Joyce's face was twisted in anger. We had arrived at her house to borrow a car for the duration of our time in Washington. Jurors in Simi Valley, California, had found four white policemen not guilty of viciously beating an unresisting black motorist, Rodney King. I started exploring the color divisions in my family's past the same day the citizens of Los Angeles erupted in frustration over the verdict and its relationship to color issues that divided their city. As I worked, the smoke and death occurring in the City of the Angels seemed distant and unreal. Room 401 was an insulated channel from the past to the present. But at the end of each day, news updates gave my mission an angry urgency.

Until the census of 1930, all census takers had ostensibly been white. In most cases, the enumerator would determine the race of the citizen by looking at him. When uncertain, he would guess, erring on the side of whiteness. The designation would depend on the circumstances and the neighborhood. If the person was light and surrounded by black people, the taker might designate him "mulatto" or "black." If the neighborhood was predominantly black but everyone in the house was white-looking, the taker might write "mulatto." All of these circumstances seem to have prevailed when they were cataloguing the Morris family.

In the census of 1880, Margaret Maher Morris, the Irish girl from Tipperary, was listed as "white." Her place of birth was also correctly posted. She was listed as "Maggie" and the official "head of family," although her occupation was given as "keeping house." Her husband, Edward, was noted as "mulatto," as were the two children they had at the time, William and Mary, known as "Mamie." Edward was described as a "clerk, Dist. govt." and recorded in the space reserved for "other members of the family." I wondered if the census taker automatically listed "Maggie" as the head of the family because she was white.

For most people below the Mason-Dixon Line, the late 1800s, the post-Reconstruction period, were confusing and difficult. Everywhere was destruction. A region sundered by war was searching for a new identity while clinging to old myths. The new social order called for whites to accustom themselves to blacks as free people. But from the top down, whites held on to the old attitudes. In his 1867 message to Congress, President Andrew Johnson said of Negroes, "Wherever they have been left to their own devices, they have shown a constant tendency to relapse into barbarism."

The new "free people" of color were almost universally segregated in the North and viewed as potentially dangerous in the South. Irish dockers rioted in the Northeast at the prospect of Negro longshoremen, and the restriction of other Negro professionals— including physicians, carpenters, plasterers, barbers and blacksmiths—was the object of petitions, legislation and further unrest. And a new, more sinister belief had developed. The Negro was portrayed as a menace to the genetic purity of the white race. Assertion of white supremacy had become a psychological necessity. Hair-splitting distinctions over racial makeup no longer mattered. Black, to whatever degree, was black.

In 1865 and 1866, most Southern states passed the Black Codes, laws designed to keep Negroes in subordinate positions by regulating the conditions and circumstances under which they could live or travel. The codes were resisted by Negro groups, but they took their toll. Those Negroes who did well were the exceptions; most remained laborers without property. The Panic of 1873, which lasted as a depression until 1878, took a particularly heavy toll on those at the bottom rungs of the economic ladder. Eighteen thousand businesses failed, including most railroads and 420 banks. By 1878, more than three million workers had lost their jobs.

Regarding the progress of Negroes, historians call the period from 1880 to 1915 the "years of accommodation." The doctrine of Booker T. Washington was in full flower. To achieve respectability and recognition, Negroes were urged to get an education, learn trades and find jobs. But sophisticated technology for mass industrial production had only recently been introduced. There was no panacea for those clinging to the smallest particles of a fractured society.

For most of those of mixed race, the times were equally hard. There were at least four hundred thousand mulattoes by the end of the Civil War. Yet the country had a major public blind spot as to their existence, a mass denial of the intimate relationships between the powerful majority and the impotent minority.

Negroes and whites alike scorned, abused or ignored what miscegenation had created. Negroes were especially conflicted about the living, breathing, visible evidence of plantation owners' power. Shamed by their own helplessness, they could not divorce natural sympathy for the victims from anger at those who, after all, possessed the former oppressors' blood.

For the small number of mulattoes fortunate enough to have money and access to power, however, it was a different story. They were in the "upper tenth," the black equivalent of the white Four Hundred that included the likes of the Astors and the Vanderbilts. The lives of the upper tenth are minutely chronicled in Willard B. Gatewood's *Aristocrats of Color: The Black Elite, 1880–1920*. Fewer than one hundred Washington families were included in this group. Family continuity was a prerequisite for admission to their ranks, and a rigid sense of caste prevailed. The idea that all blacks were social equals was laughable to them.

To the white community, some lighter blacks were more acceptable than their darker kinfolk. "They" were like "us." Some even had good manners, knew how to read and played musical instruments. In the end, a fair skin emitted mixed signals. It became a badge of prestige or a mark of disdain.

After the war, Judge Halyburton learned of his son Edward Morris's whereabouts. Family lore holds that instead of turning his back on the boy who had liberated himself, the judge helped Edward secure work in the navy yard in Washington as an inspector of stones used in constructing federal buildings. Records confirm his employment. From 1876 until 1897 the city directories list Edward as a government employee.

With his own small savings and again with his father's help,

Edward put a down payment on a modest home in the Mt. Pleasant neighborhood on the top of 16th Street Hill, outside the official boundaries of the city of Washington. Before the Civil War, Mt. Pleasant had been an area of country estates and the site of the Washington Jockey Club's racetrack. The section was isolated from the rest of the city and had the characteristics of a rural town. As a contemporary observer wrote, "It is the most healthy suburb of Washington, proved by its exemption from chills and autumnal fevers of malarial districts which frequently prevail in the city."

Many of its inhabitants were Northerners who had come south to take jobs in the postwar government, and the neighborhood had a New England primness, austerity and reserve. The residents instituted New England–style town meetings where they "fearlessly discussed all questions grave or gay," as one newspaper put it. According to city historians, the neighborhood at that time was all white, populated by so many low-level government workers that it was called "Clerksville." Records of civic activity in the 1870s reveal a community taken up with minstrel entertainments, balls, weekly debates and literary association meetings. And there were mulattoes in their midst.

In their Mt. Pleasant home, the former slave and the Irish woman had four children. First, in 1876, came William, called Will, my grandfather. Three years later, Mary, always known as Mamie, was born. Edward, Jr., followed in 1881, during the birth of the Jim Crow laws that legalized segregation between blacks and whites in Southern states and municipalities. Eleven years later, Ruth was born.

As Arthur Lubow describes it in his biography of author and journalist Richard Harding Davis, the mood of the country was schizophrenic as the century drew to a close. While "the nation was glorifying youth and energy, it was gripped with anxiety about depletion and loss."

The era of the Gibson Girl, the bicycle and the American Beauty rose . . . was also the time of economic depression that began in 1893 and set off a series of convulsions: Populist agitation in the farmlands, violent labor disputes like the Pullman and Homestead strikes in the cities . . . an obsession with degeneration, exhaustion and depletion. Morals were falling down, nerves were wearing thin, natural resources were running out.

As the country grew poorer, race relations in the nation's capital and elsewhere deteriorated. Jim Crow wiped out gains that had been made by Negroes during Reconstruction. Railways and street-cars, public waiting rooms, restaurants, boarding houses, theaters and public parks were segregated; separate schools, hospitals and other public institutions, often of inferior quality, were designated for Negroes. By the beginning of World War I, even places of employment were segregated. No matter your hue, if you made it known you were colored, your life, your safety, your health, your housing and your employment were at risk.

❧

The father that Margaret Maher Morris had seen little of came back into her life in 1894, when her youngest child was two years old. One day, William Maher made a surprise visit to her Mt. Pleasant home while Edward was at work. His dress and bearing exuded financial well-being and respectability. His business in Georgetown was flourishing.

It was a surrealistic encounter. The young mother lined up her four children to meet their grandfather for the first time. Their fair complexions and straight hair made all the Morris children look white. All had brown hair except for Will: his was jet black. Those who knew them said they looked Irish, like their mother.

With great care and much curiosity, Maher inspected the hair and skin of each child. When he was satisfied they could pass for white, he told his daughter he wanted her to come back to the family. He offered to take care of her and all of her children, to provide them better housing and financial security. His condition: Margaret must leave her husband.

Without giving it much thought, she rejected the offer. Edward had been the only loving person in her life—in her words, "the best man that ever was." Now he was her family. From her experience as a companion, she knew well that to live in the white world would mean a more comfortable, safer life. But it also would have meant a renewed white life with a family that had not been a family to her. Once again, Margaret the white woman chose to live on the black side of the line. In reminiscing about her life in later years, she often recounted with relish that last meeting with her father. She felt it was a victory.

From the Morris home on 15th Street in Mt. Pleasant, there was no public transportation into the city. The one road out, 14th Street, was unpaved, dusty and full of mudholes when wet. Fifteenth Street was a curved footpath into the city. The family could not afford a horse and carriage, so they walked everywhere. On Sundays, Edward, Sr., took the children to the park, the zoo and public band concerts. His daughter Mamie's 1969 eulogy described her as having been "reared in a home environment of the cultured poor" and noted that when she entered public schools the teachers were surprised at the knowledge of the classics she'd gotten "from the books my mother gave me."

The marriage of Margaret Maher and Edward Morris lasted for twenty-seven years, until his death in 1903. He was fifty-three. He left behind a widow of forty- six. At the time of their father's death, Will was twenty-seven, Mamie twenty-four, Edward twenty-two and Ruth eleven. With few resources and a child still to care for, Margaret went back to work at the only job she knew, being a companion.

∞

Most of the census records of 1890 were destroyed by fire. In the fragments that remained, I could not find my great-grandparents. In the census of 1900, the enumerators, like the rest of the country, were more race-conscious. Edward Morris was surely no darker, but had become "black." His wife was still "white," but their children living at home were now listed as black. Edward had been elevated to head of the house, and his job description was "government messenger."

In the same census, my maternal grandparents showed up as adults for the first time. Will Morris was twenty-five and listed as the head of the house. He too had been listed as "mulatto" in the 1880 census, but like his father, by 1900 he had become "black" in the eyes of the beholder and for the record. The change of color designation may have been due to the rising racism of the times, combined with the fact that Will and his wife were living in a neighborhood where many poor mulattos and obviously black people lived. The fact is, my great-grandfather and my grandparents were the working poor of mixed race, and the range of educational and job opportunities open to them was limited. The white-looking children attended the black schools of segregated Washington.

The Morris family were a handsome group. My grandfather Will, the oldest, was said to be charming and feckless. He was over six feet tall and well built, with his father's large ears and a prominent flaring nose and a broad open face. A cleft marked his chin, and sculptured cheekbones gave his face a perpetual smile. Thick black hair with a slight curl framed one of those faces whose features come together in a harmony that is called handsome.

Despite these attributes, which in another time and place might have made him a politician or a rock star, he was called a "white nigger." At that point in his life, he did not try to pass for white. His light color and quick temper triggered frequent fights, and his tendency toward brawling and drinking were roadblocks to becoming a "good" Negro. He dropped out of school to support himself, but had trouble keeping jobs. He loved horses and was said to have a way with them. Most of his employment centered on the livery stables, as a driver or a wagon maker. I find it significant that he associated himself with an occupation concerned with movement. Like his grandfather Tip, Will Morris was a rolling wheel, ready to go wherever the spokes carried him.

In 1894, Will married Rosalind Mae Scott, the daughter of Margaret Everett and Edward Scott. Census records tell us that Margaret Everett was born in Maryland in 1849. Family history tells us that she and her parents, also born in Maryland, were part of the large group of Maryland Negroes who were free. Rosalind could not read or write, however. Of Edward Scott, her father, I could find no records.

Rosalind, whom most people called Rose, brought an infant child to her marriage to William. The child's patrimony is a family mystery. His name, Sumner McCory, and his coloring suggest that his father might have been Irish. His skin color would qualify as well.

Although in two different censuses he was listed as a stepson, Sumner subsequently assumed the Morris name.

Mamie Morris, the next oldest after Will, was a star student. She completed high school, graduated from the Miner Normal School in 1900, and became a teacher in the Negro schools of Washington in that same year. The Miner Normal School was a black two-year college that trained young black women of culture to become teachers to other young black women of culture. Miner graduates formed the corps of the black elementary school teachers in the Washington public school system.

The school's founder, Myrtilla Miner, a frail white woman from upstate New York, had seen firsthand the blight of slavery on both races as a governess to the children of a Mississippi planter. It became her obsession to educate those colored people who had become free. Ignoring the admonitions of friends, she made plans to establish in Washington a school for free colored girls. She went to Rochester to talk with Frederick Douglass about her plan. He advised her against it, telling her she would face much adversity. In fact, he said, it was "reckless, almost to the point of madness."

Myrtilla would not be deterred. Harriet Beecher Stowe gave some of the proceeds of *Uncle Tom's Cabin* to help Miss Miner purchase three acres bounded by New Hampshire, N, 19th and 20th streets. In 1853 she opened her school with six pupils. There were about ten thousand free colored people in the District at that time. There were also thirty-six hundred slaves.

The school survived firebombing and stoning by whites. White men gathered outside to insult and proposition the girls as they went to classes. In 1857, the mayor of Washington threatened to close the school, but did not follow through. Finally, in 1863, by an act of Congress, the Institute for the Education of Colored Youth in the District of Columbia was incorporated. It subsequently became Miner's Teachers College, D.C. Teachers College, the University of the District of Columbia, and finally, Federal City College.

Mamie had inherited her mother's whiteness of skin and marble blue eyes, but she continued to live and work as a Negro woman. At twenty-five she married Bradley Smith, a man whose tan skin left no doubt as to which side of the color line claimed him. Prior to his marriage, Smith had served in the United States Navy for six years. As a colored man in the most segregated branch of the armed services, he was relegated to menial assignments. The navy did give him the opportunity twice to circle the globe. And, at the time of his discharge, his service record enabled him to secure a position much coveted by colored people of the time: porter for the Pullman Company.

In the Negro community, Pullman porters were paragons. Many men who held advanced professional degrees became Pullman porters because there were no other jobs for them. For years the newspaper *The Afro American* had a weekly column called "Porters' Doings" that trumpeted their weddings, home purchases, births, children's colleges, vacations and parties.

Like hundreds of other Pullman porters, and contrary to the servile caricature portrayed in drawings and films, Smith carried out his job with dignity and self-respect. For long stretches of time, private car assignments kept him away from home. When he returned, he painted wondrous pictures depicting the intimate glimpses he'd had of such luminaries as the Prince of Wales, General Pershing and J. P. Morgan. This proximity to wealth and power was at once a powerfully tantalizing and motivating force for the Smith family.

◈

At first, Edward Morris, his father's namesake and second son, fared little better than his older brother, Will, had. He too dropped out of school. Under the Booker T. Washington influence, he learned a trade and became an electrician. He was said to be good at his craft.

Edward was beautiful, the most attractive of all the children. He had thick, wavy brown hair. His dark brown eyes were large and luminous, his lips poutingly sensuous over a cleft in his chin. His unlined skin and smooth cheeks gave him a perennially boyish look. Years later, looking at his picture, I found him poetic, romantic, endearing. His dark good looks reminded me of Lord Byron, or better still, his distant relative Sir Walter Scott. Edward's temperament was reputed to match his looks.

He married Minette Williams, a beautiful high school classmate who, like him, had a parent from each race. She and all of her family looked white but lived as colored people. She played the piano with virtuosity and was said to be socially ambitious. Her brother became the first Negro policeman on the District of Columbia police force, although the white department did not know it at the time. The Negro community knew, celebrated, and kept his secret.

Despite his training and skill, work for Edward was sparse. He could not join the white union. Whites preferred to hire white electricians, and blacks were ambivalent about hiring a white-looking skilled worker. In the city directories of 1911, 1912 and 1913 Edward was listed as a janitor, a laborer and then an electrician. Minette was described as a clerk for the Bureau of Engraving. After 1913, their names vanished from the directory. They had left the city and the race.

Ruth Morris, the youngest of the Morris children, was the dramatic beauty of the family. Over six feet tall and elegant, with long brown hair and a Modigliani nose and neck, she believed she was destined for a better life. Like her older sister, Mamie, she finished high school, but she did not go to college. Instead, she got a low-paying government job, but not being enamored of its rote tasks she stayed out of work as often as she could.

Her confidence in a brighter future was rewarded. In 1916 she went to Chicago and married John Tazewell Jones, another light-complected native who had come from Old Point Comfort in the Tidewater area of Virginia. Jones had graduated from Phillips Exeter Academy and was one of six Negroes to graduate from Harvard in 1904, Franklin Roosevelt's class. His father was an "aristocrat of color" whose fortune had allowed him and his wife to send each of their five children to college.

John had plans to become a civil engineer. But despite the fact that two centuries earlier a colored man named Benjamin Banneker had laid out the drawings for an architecturally splendid Washington, in 1904 there was no hope that another black man would be called on to map out roads or build bridges in the District, and John could not find a position. He took a job as assistant surveyor at a coal mine in Zeigler, Illinois, but soon left on account of "labor troubles." He went to work for the Missouri Pacific Railroad in St. Louis and Arkansas, where he worked as a concrete inspector. Subsequent jobs took him to a railroad construction camp in the lowlands along the Mississippi River, where he got swamp fever, then back to Chicago and on to Wyoming and Minnesota, where he asked his fiancée to join him.

࿇

In 1904 Mamie was forced to resign her teaching position, not because of her race, but because she got married. At that time in the District, the law did not permit women teachers of any color to be married. Subsequently, Mamie's color helped her get hired as a white woman for a clerical job in the Liberty Loans Division of the Treasury Department. She was demoted to a lesser post, however, when her white supervisor discovered she was married to and living with a colored man. The story went that a jealous white worker in a menial job had given the supervisor an anonymous tip.

During that period, many Washingtonians passed for white on a part-time basis, mostly for economic and sometimes for social or cultural reasons. Circumstances and opportunity dictated their behavior. If they wanted a certain job, a seat at the front of the trolley car, or a ticket to a play or concert in the white downtown theaters, they became white for a time. Usually, their temporary race change was successful. For a while, however, theaters and concert halls hired Negro "spotters" to point out the racial impostors. Many a colored socialite of Washington was humiliated in the process. To their credit, the Negro newspapers published the names of the spotters so that the community could deal with them in its own way, usually by social ostracism.

࿇

Will Morris's wife, Rosalind, was a light-complected woman who was said to have Italian ancestry on her father's side. Sometimes Rose worked as a servant for wealthy people. The contrast between her work environment and her home life was stark. She came from one of the many small, poor, half-white families that dotted the Washington landscape, scorned by more fortunate Negroes as "mulatto nobodies." Their relationship with both whites and blacks was unpredictable as they gingerly walked the color line.

I have only one picture of my grandmother, whom other relatives described as quiet and sweet but with an unexpected peppery temper. The camera captured a light-skinned, cheerful-looking, round-cheeked woman who resembles my mother, especially in the precisely defined oval chin. Rose had masses of coiled blue-black hair, an open face, deep-set gray eyes framed by perfectly arched, dark eyebrows, and a pert nose. There is an air of insouciance in her expression and she looks eager and ready for life.

At the turn of the century, large families reflected the country's hopes for bustling growth and, in the face of countless infectious diseases that killed indiscriminately, insured survivors to carry the family name. For most families, birth control was not relevant. In keeping with the times, Will Morris and Rose Scott presented the nation with six new citizens. My mother, Margaret Morris, was born in 1912, the second youngest in a family that included twins and a younger brother who had a slight hump on his back. I remember the year of my mother's birth as the year the *Titanic* sank.

Will Morris housed his brood with his wife's family in a small brick row home on Florida Avenue near North Capitol Street, the geographical boundary between the northwestern and northeastern parts of the city. According to the census of 1910, many of the neighborhood's residents were like themselves, poor and striving mulattoes. Others in the surrounding neighborhood were unmistakably Negro.

Although compulsory education did not become law in the District until 1925, school records and family hearsay indicate the Morris children attended two sets of schools. First they went to the colored Slater School, which had been built in 1890. Later, they switched to the Blake School, a few blocks away, which had been constructed in 1887 for white children. Admission was based on visual inspection. From an early age, the children passed the test.

But for Will Morris's family, education was a luxury. On good days, the children went to school. They had little clothing and few regular meals. Art and culture were abstractions. As members of the working poor, their goal was to survive from day to day. Their mixed race and tenuous economic status made them doubly marginal. Their struggles were played out at the edge of their father's scrapes, drinking bouts and absences.

Things worsened when Rose became ill with cancer and was bedridden for a long stretch of time. There was no counting on Will. Sometimes he was at home, sometimes he wasn't. Often he spent his paycheck before he reached home. Rose's family, especially a cousin named Bessie Clay, neighbors and friends helped with the baby, bought groceries and supplies, and tended the sick woman. The birth of her last child, Michael, hastened her end. In 1916, Rose died, and the family unraveled.

Will withdrew from the family completely, leaving behind Sumner, William, Jr., called Bill, Edward, Eugene, Grace, Margaret and Michael. Sumner was twenty-four and went out on his own. Bill, the twins, Edward and Eugene, and Grace were in their teens and homeless. Michael, two, was taken in by a neighbor, Rebecca Allen, a light tan woman with curly hair, large round eyes and a trim figure who sewed for wealthy white women. She had been married, but her husband was no longer around and she had lost a young son of her own. She welcomed the sweet-tempered child with golden ringlets, round blue eyes and the hump on his back into the small house she shared with her mother and her sister. And Rose's cousin Bessie Clay, who was also Margaret's godmother, took the four-year-old girl with waist-length hair. The family dissolved.

Drifting, Will Morris, Sr., now lived as a white man. Twice he made his home in Maryland. Just after Rose's death, he briefly boarded with a Meyers family, who sometime later took in his daughter Grace. She stayed for two years, working first in a sweat shop and then in the boarding house to earn her keep. She was not yet fourteen. The Meyerses were kind to the frightened, shy child. They could not imagine the life she had before she came to them, nor could she tell them. She had begun to hide it somewhere deep in the vault of unwanted memories.

Her father found work in Delaware, then tried Cleveland, Buffalo and Canada, places where other family members had been or had settled. Finally, he came to the town of Parsonsburg, not far from Maryland's very white, very insular Eastern Shore. Eight years after Rose died, Will married a "fully" white woman. Her name was Nora Rooney, and she was a young Irish immigrant with red hair and a thick brogue. She did not know about Will's colored connections. For a while, the two of them worked for the Marvels of Wilmington, a family that was said to own half of Delaware.

But Will had bad luck with wives. After only three years of marriage, Nora died, childless. Once again Will became a lodger, again in Parsonsburg, Maryland, a few miles east of Salisbury, where he lived and worked as a handyman for the Perdue family on their large chicken farm.

In letters to Grace, Will related that Frank Perdue, the owner's son who would take the business to the big time on national television, was especially kind to him. In 1957 it was Frank Perdue who notified Grace of her father's death and paid for hotel rooms for her and Bill when they came to Salisbury to make the funeral arrangements. After Grace and Bill had buried Will, Mamie notified my mother of his death. That's when she tore his picture into bits and pieces.

∾

Mamie and her husband had three daughters, who were my mother's first cousins. After attending Washington's black public schools, each of the women went on to higher education. The two oldest girls went to Miner Normal School and Howard University. The youngest went to Mount Holyoke, eventually getting a doctoral degree from Western Reserve. They all became educators, two in Washington's public schools and one at Howard. The oldest married a man who became one of America's most distinguished physical anthropologists and the president of the board of directors of the NAACP.

Mamie's other two daughters also married well, one to a teaching physician and the other to an educator. All of their children would go to Ivy League schools, including Harvard and Yale. In their own world and time, these grandchildren of a slave and an Irish immigrant matched the social and educational status of their forebear, the white judge.

Edward's wife, Minette, was frustrated by her husband's inability to find work as a colored man. At her urging, the couple made a decision to try their luck in another city and as another race. In the early 1900s, Buffalo was a good place to be white. For at least six months out of the year, its streets were covered with white snow and white ice. In the sun, Lake Erie shimmered white. Its northern sky was more white than blue. Most of its citizens had pale skins. The Morrises fit right in.

Buffalo in those days was a city self-consciously proud of its broad avenues and distinctive squares. Its major ethnic group was the Poles, and the newcomers from Washington grew accustomed to the Easter baskets that were taken to church to be blessed and the miniature theaters portraying the Nativity that were carried from house to house as the children chattered about Gwiazdor, the Polish Santa Claus. After the Poles had come the Germans, who settled on the east side, then the Italians and the Hungarians, each with their own colonies. Later, in the 1930s, more than thirteen thousand Negroes would be drawn to Buffalo by jobs in the steel mills and packing houses and on the docks. They clustered around Jesse Clipper Square, named for a local Negro hero of World War I.

But Negro lives had little relevance for Edward and Minette Morris. They lived in a house on Elmwood Avenue on the city's west side. Minette turned most of their new home into a boarding house for whites only. Edward worked as an electrician when he was not gambling on the horses.

Edward and Minette had no children of their own. No one in Buffalo knew of their colored past, not their clients, their neighbors, their vendors, their church or their friends.

Those in the family who could pass came to see them. In the summertime, light-skinned Mamie would bring her light-skinned children. Her brown husband, of course, did not go. All the while the Washington visitors were there, Edward and Minette would keep their shades drawn. No neighbors came to be introduced. No outings were taken. The talk centered on Washington and childhood friends. Mamie's children long remembered the visits to the large, airy clapboard home. They thought the rooms must have been brilliant with sun when the shades were lifted. Even though they were all under ten at the time, they sensed the danger their visit brought. My mother and her family never went to Buffalo at all. Minette made frequent trips to visit her colored family and friends in Washington, but she and Edward lived as white in that northern city until they died.

∽

Ruth's marriage created options that lifted her above the rest of her family. John's report to his Harvard class in 1929 noted that he was in charge of the factory sales for the Johns-Manville company in São Paulo. Although Brazil has always had more black people than any other country outside of Africa, when Ruth and John went there, they found it more convenient to be part of the white upper classes than the masses of dark, poor people. To my ear, John's observations sound like those of a white man observing colored people and their world:

Imagine living in one of the largest and most sparsely settled countries in the world, a country with very poor means of transportation, in a city with about only two hundred and fifty Americans and where the language spoken is Portuguese! The most that one can do under such circumstances is to attend to the business at hand, which is to sell American merchandise.

The only excitement is to break away from the monotony of things occasionally and wander around in the vast interior of Brazil. . . . One can travel for days without meeting a single human being or passing a single house. You finally arrive at some little hamlet hidden away in the hills, miles from anywhere.

The most striking thing to me is the extreme hospitality of the people one finds in these small villages. I suppose it is because these people only see a stranger about once a year, but once with them they can never do too much for you. If you want a rest cure par excellence you can certainly find it by living in one of these small hamlets. You are as completely cut off from the rest of the world as if you were living on Mars. But the deadly monotony of it all soon gets on one's nerves: besides, one is anxious to take a bath or to get a decent meal, and then the long trip back to civilization again.

One meets with many strange and curious experiences on such a trip. It is not uncommon to meet with a band of lepers (they run loose down here) begging their way through the country. Some of these lepers are the most horrible sights imaginable. In every little village there are always stories and myths to be told which, if you know the language and have gained the confidence of the people, will more than compensate for the trip. These stories are generally founded on some slight incident of long ago, and grown in the telling to fascinating yarns, a weird mixture of fact and fancy, something like the sagas of the Scandinavian races. The basis of these stories is generally a huge serpent or other mystical beast.

After all, the people are the products of their environment, a land with probably the largest forests in the world, huge serpents, very poisonous snakes, enormous hairy spiders, many of them as poisonous as the serpents, anteaters as big as a young calf. Add to this environment the fact that the people are of Indian, Negro and Portuguese ancestry, with a Latin mentality, and you have the background for their way of thinking and living. Yet, they are lovable, kind and generous.

Like Minette and Edward, Ruth and John had no children. Some in the family say it was because they feared their genes would tell: they might give birth to a brown child.

From time to time, Ruth would come to Washington to visit her family and have dental work done. Her visits were state occasions. Bearing unusual gifts, wearing beautiful, well-tailored clothes, and telling truly exotic stories, Ruth seemed like visiting royalty. While she held court, old friends from all parts of the city would come to visit. Admiring nieces would peek around the doorway at this glamorous aunt who was so unlike anyone they knew.

Ruth told her family that the highlight of her life in Brazil was the invitation to dinner on a ship with John's former classmate, President Roosevelt, during one of his South American visits. He had never forgotten the cultured Negro man in his classes who excelled at Spanish and higher mathematics.

John died on an airplane in 1955, on his way to visit a brother in Boston. But Ruth did not return to her birthplace. She is said to have returned to Philadelphia for a while, probably because her mother was there. That is where her trail ends.

The year my great-uncle John died I graduated from high school. I did not know about this interesting man who liked to catch butterflies and loved books until I began to do research on my family. Once again I felt anger over being deprived of an older relative I would love to have known. It is likely he would not have wanted to know me. He was a loyal American and a loyal Harvard man, but he did not claim his blackness.

I can only begin to understand the edges of this fear, this dread of being black, of being lumped in with the Other. I doubt that I can ever get to the center of it. I wonder if "real" white people understand the terrors that "pretend white" people have of being exposed as black. White author Andrew Hacker believes they would. Unequivocally he says, "No white American, including those who insist that opportunities exist for persons of every race, would change places with even the most successful black American." According to Adrian Piper, white people "recoil" at the thought of being identified as black. To say that a black person "looks white" is assumed to be a compliment, but the converse is not true.

In trying to come to grips with my family's passing, I came upon a scenario from *Children of Strangers*, Lyle Saxon's 1937 novel about life among Louisiana creoles. Joel, a young white-skinned Negro with red hair, tells his mother, Famie, that he is going to California and will not return to Chicago, where he has been living. "I've left Chicago for good and all, and I'm going to California where I don't know anybody at all," he tells her. "I've crossed the line in Chicago, but it's dangerous there. Too many people know that I'm not white. On the coast, nobody will ever know. I'm going, and I'm breaking off clean with the people I've known." When Famie asks him where he is going to live, "he bit his lip, and she understood. He did not want her to know. It was better, safer that way."

I wondered if the severing had been like that for Edward, for Will, for Ruth. Some of my elders who approved of their crossover explained to me that they could be more successful as white people. They could do more, have more, travel more, be happier. Their

light skins would give them the privileges, status and entitlements
of white people, a state of grace that clearly meant more to them
than their connections to the black community. But at what cost,
I wondered. What did such distancing and denial of one's self as
well as of an entire group of people do to the mind and the soul?

❧

Life was neither fair nor generous to the abandoned children of
Will Morris. As a white man, the eldest, Sumner, sold vegetables
and fruit at the O Street market. His home base shifted between
the Eastern Shore and Washington, where the 1920 census listed
him as a white man lodging with a white family named Johnson
on 5th Street in the northeast section of town.

Even now my mother remembers her excitement at being taken
by her mother's dark cousin Bessie to see Sumner at his vegetable
stand. He acknowledged her with a nod. "I could not kiss him nor
act too familiar, for fear of exposing him as a colored person,"
Margaret recalls, but she found every excuse to run errands to the
O Street market. Eventually Sumner purchased a chicken farm in
Landover, Maryland, where he married a white woman and raised
mostly white chickens.

Sometime in the mid-1940s, my family was visiting my father's
family in Highland Beach, a Negro resort in Maryland, when my
mother decided she would like to see Sumner. Her sister-in-law
offered to drive her to Landover. At the edge of the road leading
to the farm, my mother grew nervous. What would she say? What
would she do? What would he do? She could not cope with the
uncertainties. She refused to go further, and she never tried to
locate Sumner again.

❧

Eugene Morris answered the call of the First World War, where
he served and died as a white man. The great influenza epidemic
of 1918 that suffocated the nation and killed more than twenty
million people claimed the life of his twin, Edward. Economic
necessity had forced Edward, Grace and Bill to drop out of school.
Without skills or connections, there was little work they could do.
Persistence and desperation helped Bill land a job delivering news-

papers to each congressional office. With his earnings, he took care of Grace until she went to Maryland, hoping to live with her father.

In the practice of the day, the government reserved its lowest-level jobs for people whose blackness was obvious. They kept the buildings clean, presided over the elevators and provided human locomotion for the streams of missives flowing back and forth between government offices. They were required to use the back entrances of the buildings they maintained.

The family story is that a white manager took pity on Bill, who was no darker than he and jarringly lighter than most of his co-workers. Like his father, he was over six feet tall and handsome, with the characteristic Morris ears and prominent nose. The supervisor convinced Bill that he was working beneath his level. Confirming he could never advance because government records showed he was colored, the supervisor urged Bill to leave town and start a new life. Along with the advice, the boss supposedly gave Bill money. Bill went as far as that money would take him. For a while he lived in Buffalo, where he could be near his grandmother Margaret, and his uncle Edward. East Cleveland was his final stop and the city where he became white.

There is no doubt that Bill was a low-level government worker. Records of his employment are in the city directory and the census. That he relocated to Cleveland is also a matter of record. What is questionable is the existence of the supervisor as *deus ex machina*. The role and motivation of the white Samaritan seem apocryphal to me. But that's the way the family prefers to tell the story.

When Bill Morris arrived in East Cleveland in the early 1920s, it was a quiet, self-contained, ostensibly all-white suburb seven miles from Cleveland's center. Housing and jobs were plentiful. Bill could take his choice between the light industries of East Cleveland or the heavier steel industries of the mother city. He chose the factories, having learned the art of metal plating in his spare time just before he left Washington. He was a hard worker, and over the years he rose to plant manager at the Park Drop Forge Company, which had no black supervisors. Bill supervised the mostly black blacksmiths, who poured red-hot steel into molds to make crankshafts, forges and dies. He was good to the men who worked for him, and they respected him. During the steel strikes of the 1950s, when union workers threw marbles under the hooves of the mounted police who were trying to contain them, Bill was allowed to pass through the picket line each day unscathed.

Shortly after Bill arrived in East Cleveland, his father and Grace came for a visit. Always distant and angry with his father, Bill clashed with him over his drinking. William, Sr., left, but Grace stayed. Just over sixteen, she told the personnel department of the local department store she was eighteen and got a job that paid her fourteen dollars a week. Half of that she gave to Bill for room and board. Inexperienced and without a high school diploma, she began work in the credit department, then moved to other areas of the store. She worked there comfortably for a few years, then took the job she would have until she retired, as a worker in the Sherwin-Williams company.

Like his father, Bill married twice. His first wife was a German woman, Bertha Koch, one of five daughters of a German immigrant. With Bertha he had a brown-haired daughter whom he named Dorothy. From the beginning, Bertha let Bill know there were certain groups of people she did not like, and Negroes were high on the list.

Bill met his second wife, Jessie Breen, at the Park Drop Forge Company, where she was employed as a stenographer. Her nickname was Sunny, and her mother made aprons that Grace took to work and sold for fifty cents apiece. The new marriage produced another daughter with dark-brown hair, Carol. Carol's eyes were slanted, and during the Korean War she was rejected by her playmates because she looked Korean to them. (Years later, when Carol visited Bill and Sunny in Florida, where they had moved to escape the cold, her dark tan got her chased away from the "whites only" drinking fountain.) But in most respects theirs was a normal white middle-class life. Bill was a competitive bowler and a thirty-second-degree Mason, and the family had enough money to do as they wished. They had plenty of friends, but little family apart from Grace.

In 1923, at twenty, Grace met and married Earl Cramer, who also worked at the Park Drop Forge Company. He had come to Cleveland from the farmlands of Wisconsin, where his German father and English mother had a large family and a farm. A year after their marriage, the Cramers had their first and only child, a brown-haired, blue-eyed girl they called Patricia Mae, her middle name after grandmother Rose's. Earl had no knowledge of Grace's mixed heritage.

That is how it came to be that my mother's brothers and her one sister, her father, her father's mother and all her aunts and uncles except one chose to live another life. In the meantime, my mother was still in Washington and its environs, not knowing where her family lived or these details of their lives. Those who were not familiar with the Morrises' heritage called them white. Those who did know kept their secret. Until now.

∞

When Margaret Maher Morris was between jobs, her options were limited. Will was unreliable and Ruth had gone to Brazil. Sometimes she cast her lot with her son Edward in Buffalo or her grandchildren Bill and Grace in Cleveland. With a fondness for travel and varied experiences, the Irish matriarch now known as "Little Grandmother" divided her time between her "white" descendants and her daughter Mamie, who was living a black life in Washington. Every once in a while, in periods of sobriety, Will would visit her, either at Edward's or at a home where she worked for many years as a companion in Silver Creek, a small town not far from Buffalo. Ruth came back to see Little Grandmother in Washington once or twice when she was at Mamie's, and wrote to her from Brazil.

From Buffalo Little Grandmother carried news to Washington. From the District she gathered hometown gossip for Cleveland. When she tired of the heartland, she unpacked her bags on Maryland's Eastern Shore. She had more freedom than her children and grandchildren.

Wherever she was, Grandmother Maher would talk about her smart daughter Mamie in Washington. The grandmother's chatter stirred interest in the family history on the part of one of her great granddaughters in Cleveland. According to a story Mamie told, the girl, then in her twenties, visited Washington for the first time. She carried with her Mamie's address.

Late one afternoon, a taxi pulled up in front of Mamie's house and waited as its passenger went to the door. Mamie answered the bell and saw a young white woman in a pale blue seersucker business suit. The visitor said, "You must be my Aunt Mamie. I'm one of your great nieces from Cleveland." Mamie froze. Without opening the screen door she replied, "I'm afraid you have made a mistake. I don't know anyone in Cleveland." Puzzled, the girl did not persist and returned to the waiting cab. Mamie sat down and thought a long time about what she had done. She had denied her own identity to spare the girl hers.

It was not until she was in her seventies that my mother learned from Mamie's daughters that from time to time her sister, brother, aunts and uncles would quietly come into Washington to visit with Mamie and Margaret Maher. The knowledge of those clandestine visits upset my mother greatly. "Can you imagine?" she said. "They came into the city and never once called me."

On one such visit to see her grandmother, Grace sat in the yard with Mamie and two of Mamie's daughters. Grace was proud to report that her daughter, Patricia, a student at Western Reserve College, was racially free; unprejudiced, in fact. But Grace was bewildered by the fact that Patricia, who knew nothing of her colored relatives, was sometimes attracted to young Negro men in her class.

Grace did not bring her husband to Mamie's home. There was no way to hide the colored neighborhood or Mamie's colored husband.

But in 1931, when she was seventy-five, Margaret Maher eloped again with another man of color, a light-complected man from the Tidewater area of Virginia. The family called him Poppa Griffin. He was said to be a retired gentleman farmer who was well fixed. He took his bride to Philadelphia, where they lived comfortably for about eight years. He would die of a heart attack in Mamie's home while he and Margaret Maher were visiting. Grace's last visit to the Washington family was for Margaret Maher Morris's funeral in 1948. Although she knew about the service, my mother chose not to attend. Later she regretted her decision, because she learned she would have seen her sister there.

It is clear that Margaret Maher Morris had deep reserves of stamina and resilience. As the family matriarch she not only served as a conduit of family news; she, along with Mamie, bridged the color line, broadcasting to both sides. But Little Grandmother did not keep in touch with her namesake, my mother, Margaret Morris. News about Will Morris's younger daughter reached the "white" side through Mamie. They knew where she was, what she was doing, and who she was doing it with. Most important, they knew she had chosen to stay Negro.

To the out-of-town siblings and aunts and uncles, my mother was no longer relevant. For her, there was no wealth of stories. No homes were described; no lives were embellished. There was no prodding to be a dutiful daughter, a concerned sister or an interested niece. There were no requests to write letters or make telephone calls. There were tantalizing if sparing references to Cleveland and Buffalo, Maryland and Brazil. For my mother they were places devoid of faces and feelings, places of whiteness, places of pain.

It is still a matter of speculation as to why my mother's father or one of her much older brothers or her sister did not keep in touch with her and her younger brother. Over the years, Aunt Mamie and my mother's various guardians supplied differing explanations. The times were hard. They were bad for mulattoes and worse for "real" Negroes. There was little money around. Her father drank, drifted and could not keep jobs. Her teenage siblings could barely take care of themselves. At four years old, she was too dependent and would have been an emotional, physical and financial burden. She was too dark, revealing both the Negro and swarthy Italian strains of her ancestry. Her color would give them away in their new white settings. They did not want to separate her from her younger brother.

All of these reasons were plausible. None of them sufficed. None could take away the pain, the anger, the isolation, the questions.

But the abandoned child asked few questions. It was impolite for a youngster to question a family elder. Mamie was her only link to her father's family. The need for affection and a sense of belonging subverted less positive feelings. Early in her life she turned her anger, hurt and rejection inward. It stayed just near her surface, as a layer of melancholy. It glistened at holidays, when she talked about her family. It shone when she empathized with girls who had no mothers. It never left her eyes.

Chapter Four

I can't live inside yesterday's pain, but I can't live without it. . . . How do you get the goodies and strength that come from pain without being consumed by it?

—GEORGE C. WOLFE, interviewed in *The Los Angeles Times*, November 24, 1992

It is stressful for my mother to talk of her background and growing-up years. She either is ambivalent about her color or rejects outright the white part of herself. Some people looked at her and saw an abandoned child blemished by her mixed racial background. Others saw a lucky creature with long, straight auburn hair (which became jet black over time), white skin and a face most people called beautiful. She never thought she was pretty, but she knew people liked her long hair. She remembers that the teachers always made her the Madonna in the school plays.

She grew up in a black Washington rigidly stratified by color and class. Her color allowed her to straddle the top of the light and the well-to-do, who strove to protect and replicate themselves. They practiced pigmentation endogamy. They wallowed in their whiteness. They flaunted their straight hair, their high noses and thin lips. All of her guardians were darker than she and took pride in her light skin. She became a prized possession, a trophy child.

Historian Carter Woodson suggests that a Negro family's prominence originated with "a member who accomplished something unusual and others of his descendants [who] lived up to that record by likewise achieving distinction." Wealth was not the most important factor in belonging. Education was the key. In 1887 a white observer from Baltimore wrote, "A colored aristocrat is one of the most perfect pictures of conscious exclusiveness that the world has ever known."

By virtue of her color, the education of one aunt, the "brilliant" marriage of her aunt in Brazil, the presumed success of her uncle in Buffalo, the length of time her family had been in Washington, and the respectability of her new home life, my mother was a de facto member of the group that would become the apex of the black bourgeoisie of that city. The pluses of the other members of her family outweighed the liability of her absent father, although they would have loved his good looks and light skin.

Aristocrats of little color, members of this group were Negro Saxons of sorts. Eight decades later they would become Afro Saxons, a highly moralistic, in-bred, class- and color-conscious assemblage that believed it held the exclusive deeds to Negro propriety and respectability. Of course they found the word "black" abhorrent. It reflected slavery and ignorance. They called themselves colored or Negro.

In *Aristocrats of Color*, Willard Gatewood calls Washington the "Capital of the Colored Aristocracy." Its members patterned their behavior after upper-class whites: "The District's colored aristocrats surrounded themselves with books, paintings, fine furniture and musical instruments. Among their most prized possessions were family heirlooms, such as the 'free papers' or silver pieces of their antebellum ancestors and mementoes of special occasions." They eschewed Southern-style food. They attended the 19th Street Baptist Church, considered a "high tone" temple of worship "that bore little resemblance to lower-class Baptist congregations scattered throughout the rural South or poor districts of cities."

They formed exclusive clubs like the Kingdom. According to a black society column, admission required fair skin, light eyes, thin lips, a high-bridged nose and an automobile. If the Kingdom was full, they might choose to join the Mu-So-Lit men's club. The club was originally founded for musical, social and literary ends, but "in time its clubhouse became a retreat for upper-class black men to find respite of a purely social variety from the strife of race and 'questions of the hour.' " If not the Mu-So-Lit, there was the ultra-exclusive Monocan Club, whose membership was limited to twenty-six distinguished gentlemen.

There was nothing exotic about this group. Their dress was conservative. They listened to classical music and studied violin, piano and flute. They held tea dances and balls and bought summer houses at Highland Beach in Maryland. They began to send their children to Ivy League and Seven Sisters colleges. When they died, only one "society" undertaker, the handsome Maguire family, was qualified to escort them to the other side.

With each succeeding generation, the group became more insulated and more secure. They were Booker T.'s babies, but they disdained vocations. They sought professions instead. They attained education, property, financial security and, most of all, respectability. But they did not completely turn their backs on their darker or less affluent brethren. Many taught at Howard University and what was now called Miner's Teachers College. They held high positions or taught in the District's black public school system. A good number of them founded or participated in the forerunners of civil rights organizations that were designed to uplift the "masses" of their people. They began to relax and enjoy the lack of color in their skin.

∽

Except that they were free people from Maryland, I know little of the maternal side of my mother's family, the Everetts and the Scotts. The Morris family and the Scott family might as well have lived in different worlds. All of the Morrises were light. Some of the Scotts were medium brown. Despite the relationship through marriage, the two families were not especially friendly. Some said color divided them. Others said it was because Will Morris did not take care of Rose Scott and her children. Her brother Eddie Scott, Jr., had allowed them to live in his house on Florida Avenue but had little regard for his brother-in-law.

From the time she was four until she married, my mother had four guardians and seven different homes. Industrious, aggressive, respectable Bessie Clay was the first and only blood relative who would care for her. Bessie had been an Everett, a first cousin on Rose's side. She was a small, wiry woman with a broad nose, little eyes, a mouth that turned upward, and great stores of energy. When Margaret was born in 1912, Bessie had had her christened at her Foggy Bottom church, magnificent St. Mary's, the first Negro Episcopal church in Washington.

For a while, Bessie, her retired father, Henry, and her new charge lived together in Henry's small two-story house on H Street in Foggy Bottom. Born in Maryland in 1837, Henry was a handsome, dark man in his eighties with high cheekbones and long, straight white hair flowing over a luxuriant silver beard. Some people think he looked like Walt Whitman. A widower, he had been married to Mary Everett, a sister to Margaret's maternal grandmother, Margaret Everett Scott.

During colonial times, Foggy Bottom was a seaport and fishing village. Before the Civil War, it attracted both slaves and freedmen. Then came industries, breweries and waves of Irish, Italian and German immigrants. When Henry Clay lived there in the 1890s, Foggy Bottom was a crowded mixed neighborhood of working-class people. A generation later it had deteriorated into a noxious, dirty slum. Now it has been gentrified and for the first time is an elegant place to live.

For a short time, Henry looked after Margaret while Bessie worked. Bessie worried about them constantly. It was not easy for an eighty-year-old man to look after a four-year-old child. Margaret liked to stroke the old man's soft hair and beard. Sometimes she combed it. Henry had been a horse-and-buggy driver for the White House. He carried guests to and from the door but never went in. When I went to college, my mother gave me a fur carriage robe that he had used to cover his elegant guests. Margaret sat by him as he told her stories of the great white folks he carried in his carriage to the big white house.

The first time I went to the White House, for a lunch in the East Wing in conjunction with a public television series on youth and drugs, I thought of Bessie Clay and her father. There was only one other black guest in the room, a man from another public television station. All of the waiters were silver-haired men the color of caramel, supposedly a carryover from the days when only the lightest blacks were allowed in the big house. They were lighter than Henry Clay.

I asked one waiter if he would bring me an extra book of matches that bore the hallmark "The President's House." Pleased with my presence, he brought me five. When the white woman next to me asked for extras, he told her there were no more. She seemed puzzled as to why the waiter had favored me. I knew.

⟳

When Henry died, Bessie and Margaret moved to a third-floor apartment on N Street in the District's northwestern section. The move had its effect. Margaret developed a severe lisp that prevented her from pronouncing certain words. The new neighborhood was known as Shaw, after Colonel Robert Shaw, who led a Negro regiment during the Civil War. It was filled with historic colored churches, social clubs and community institutions such as the Howard Theater and the Whitelaw Hotel.

Bessie was an activist and a subscriber to Frederick Douglass's calls for equality and social justice, in contrast to the accommodation preachments of Booker T. Washington. Early on, she had given up a teaching post for a marriage that turned out to be short-lived. An early feminist, she shed her married name as easily as she shed her husband.

In addition to her full-time government job, Bessie involved herself in numerous social causes. She would become one of the founders of the first black YWCA in Washington. She worked side by side with Mary McLeod Bethune and was one of the godmothers of the National Council of Negro Women. She became a confidante and close friend to Mary Church Terrell, a key figure in the desegregation of Washington's public facilities.

As Bessie moved up in the world, she found more luxurious surroundings for herself and her charge. They moved again, this time to 2nd Street and one of the elegant boarding houses that dotted LeDroit Park, one of the most desirable areas for colored people. Originally designed for whites, the first homes there were large structures in styles that ranged from Queen Anne to Gothic Revival. Handsome brick townhouses were added in the 1880s and 1890s. It was a fitting setting for the Negro poet Paul Laurence Dunbar, who described the area in an essay on "Negro Society in Washington" for the *Saturday Evening Post*.

Here exists a society which is sufficient unto itself—a society which is satisfied with its own condition, and which is not asking for social intercourse with whites . . . [the] homes [are] finely, beautifully and tastefully furnished. Here comes together the flower of colored citizenship from all parts of the country. . . . My house is very beautiful and my parlor suite is swell. . . . [There are] dark green plush and cherry-colored inlaid wood . . . polished floors . . . fine big Morris chair . . . and a study off the parlor.

෴

During the 1920s and 1930s, LeDroit Park was also home to such luminaries as Oscar De Priest, the first black congressman since Reconstruction, pioneer in black adult education Anna J. Cooper, and poet Langston Hughes.

෴

Although she was warm and loving to Margaret, Bessie had little time to give to an active preschooler. When projects consumed her schedule, she farmed Margaret out for short periods to Annie Duncan and her mother, Ida, cousins of Bessie's neighbor Mitt Jackson. Margaret loved her visits to the cultured Duncans.

Reluctantly, Bessie understood that Margaret needed to be in a more stable home situation. She put Margaret in the care of the Nashes, an elderly couple who lived on a farm in Culpeper, Virginia. Beautiful but isolated, the rural environment held no comfort for a motherless child. The house was silent, and there were no neighbors nearby, let alone other children. The farm animals, especially the horses, were Margaret's companions. There was a pony that Mr. Nash said would be Margaret's special pet. Each day when he was through with his chores, he lifted the little girl up and placed her on its back. Then he led her around the perimeter of the farm, telling her about the animals and the creatures in the woods. Although my mother remembers the Nashes as kind, she also remembers that every day she cried for her Washington home and family.

To her credit, Bessie was sensitive to Margaret's unhappiness and sympathetic to her needs. But her second attempt to give Margaret a loving home was even less successful. This time the surrogate parent was a Mrs. Edwards, an elderly spinster who lived in Anacostia, then an outlying, rural district of Washington, close to the Maryland line. She and Margaret lived alone among the somber rooms and heavy silences. Margaret remembers that she was kept dressed in her Sunday best. She was not allowed to play outside, alone or with other children. She was terribly unhappy there.

Bessie visited Margaret in Virginia and then Maryland on weekends and holidays. As often as she could, she would bring Margaret to the city for a visit with her brother Michael. Aunt Mamie sent the child clothes and money, as did her uncle, Eddie Scott. On special occasions Margaret would visit Mamie and her three daughters. Aside from her brother Michael, these girls were the only young relatives on her father's side whom she knew, and their ages were close to hers. "Those were like holidays for me," Margaret remembers. But she was depressed and unhappy when she returned to the cold, loveless woman in Anacostia. "I began to ask God why he had made me so dark, so ugly or so terrible that my father would leave me, and my family would not love me."

When I was eight or nine, I remember being close to tears when my mother told me about her years in Virginia and Maryland. I could almost see the apparition of the woman she said came into her room nightly and sat on her bed whenever she cried. "It was like a mist in the form of a woman with long dark hair. She moved toward the head of my bed and seemed to rest there. I was not afraid. She seemed kind. She never said a word. It was as if she were trying to comfort me." She was sure it was the ghost of her mother. I had no doubt that it was. It was probably then that I began to plan to find her family someday.

❧

At eight years old, Margaret was not yet in school. Her lisp had worsened. Her Aunt Mamie was horrified, and she insisted that her niece go to school. Cousin Bessie balked. Mamie called Bessie a "pigtailer," implying that her nappy hair made her less worthy or credible. Since Bessie was the primary financial supporter of the child, she believed she had the right to determine how the little girl should live. But Mamie claimed her direct blood tie to Margaret took precedence and threatened legal action. The cousin rethought her position.

Bessie told Mamie she had been approached by a childless couple, a well-to-do doctor and his wife, who wanted to adopt Margaret. The doctor, whose name was Brown, had in fact delivered my mother. But Mamie insisted that Will Morris's permission be obtained, and he was nowhere to be found. The adoption plan was dropped. In the end, Mamie won out. Bessie returned Margaret to Washington to begin school.

On the recommendation of the Duncans, Bessie settled her cousin in a white frame house back in the Shaw district, near 6th Street and Florida Avenue. The home belonged to Mary and James Jackson, cousins of the Duncans. Mary Jackson, known as Mama Mitt, would be an eccentric and distant mother figure for Margaret for more than ten years, as she traveled from childhood to womanhood. They were not wonder years.

Mitt was a talented seamstress. She took great interest in fashion and was always immaculately dressed. Each season she would survey and make line-for-line copies of the fashions in the "five-million-dollar window" of Garfinkel's, Washington's most elite store. For some years, her stately posture and fashionable clothes made her a stunning figure in her neighborhood, her church and her circle of friends.

Shortly after Margaret became part of the Jackson household, the couple purchased a large brownstone at 6th and Q streets, a section known as Shaw's "Quality Row." The move meant still another change for Margaret. But she was happy to start her first classes at the Mott Street School, not knowing it was favored by "the best" colored families in Washington.

Along with the new location, however, came a radical personality change in Mitt. If Bessie had hoped for a normal life for Margaret in the Jackson household, her expectations were unfulfilled. Mitt no longer paid any attention to her appearance. For months on end she wore the same dirty, shabby, shapeless clothes and heavy men's work boots. Finally she just wore flour sacks. She rarely bathed.

She also had a color complex. Both her first and second husbands were mulattoes who looked like white men. Jackson, the second husband, had light skin, straight hair and blue eyes, and in fact passed for white to hold on to his government position. So great was Mitt's aversion to dark-skinned people that she would not allow Margaret to associate with anyone darker than herself. If Mitt saw her walking to school with darker classmates, she was scolded and punished. Despite the ban, my mother kept her dark-skinned chums.

There was little conversation between Mitt and her husband. Mitt dominated him as she prevailed over everyone else in the house. They slept in separate bedrooms. Mitt's bedroom was spacious and she had Margaret sleep there in an adjoining bed, although the house had five bedrooms.

Some months after Margaret's arrival, Mitt took in another nearly white girl with hazel eyes, Thelma Burt. Her mother suffered from a chronic illness and had been placed in an institution. Her father, a dark-skinned tailor who made uniforms, went to live in Hartford, Connecticut. Margaret was excited about having a "sister" at last. Thelma was a few years older and quickly established herself as the big sister. Thelma had no sisters or brothers of her own, but she had several blond, green-eyed aunts who lived in the District and sent her money and clothes. They referred to Thelma's father as "Old Black Burt," a nickname Thelma deeply resented. But their occasional visits to the aunts were special events for Thelma and Margaret.

Mitt would not give the girls their own rooms. Instead, Thelma joined Margaret in Mitt's bedroom. All the practical information the girls had about life they got from each other. They became allies against Mitt's angry outbursts and repressive ways. In each other they found affection and emotional security. Thelma began to work on Margaret's lisp. Every time Margaret would mispronounce a word in Thelma's presence, Thelma would go over and over it until the younger girl got it right. She did not relent until the lisp was gone, almost a year later.

Thelma was an excellent student who loved to read. Mitt would not allow her to read at night, on the grounds that it would make her mind go bad, so Thelma would take a candle into the bathroom and read as long as the candle burned. She became the valedictorian of her Dunbar High School class.

From time to time, Mitt took in other roomers, including her alcoholic son from her previous marriage, who mostly stayed in his room and slept. Then there was Henry Lewis, a dwarf who worked as a dishwasher in a hotel. He was a dark man with a severe limp who had to stand on a chair to work. He was the girls' favorite lodger. After his work was done, he liked to sit in the cozy, warm room behind the main staircase and make small talk with them, the little girls who were no taller than he.

For my mother, the most memorable roomers were the two beautiful show girls Mitt took in while the all-Negro musical *Shuffle Along*, by Eubie Blake and Noble Sissle, had its run at the Howard Theater. It was the most famous colored musical of its time, and it brought chorus girl Josephine Baker to public attention.

Mitt's beautiful boarders took a liking to the pretty young girl with long hair whose eyes followed their every move. They invited her to see one of the performances, and afterward they took her backstage. My mother had never seen so many beautiful colored girls. Decades later, watching my daughter Melissa star as Josephine Baker at the La Mama Theatre in New York brought the entire memory back to her in vivid detail.

❧

When Mitt's bachelor brother, Jack Cooper, was terminally ill, Margaret nursed him. Jack was at the far end of Mitt's preferred color spectrum but he was a beloved exception to her prejudices. He was coal black, with straight, heavy hair. His hawklike nose, thin lips and high cheekbones suggested Indian ancestry.

The girls' household duties expanded to include Jack's care when they came home from school. One afternoon, as Thelma held him, ten-year-old Margaret gave him his last glass of water. It dribbled from his mouth and down his chin. The moment is vivid in my mother's memory. Mitt was coming up the stairs and Margaret called to her, "I think Uncle Jack is gone." The coroner came to the house. He told Mitt that the girls would have to undergo some tests. Jack had died of tuberculosis. For a year my mother was sick and did not go to school. Thelma, too, was sickly. Mitt did not believe in doctors, so they never knew for certain what the illness was, but it was probably early-stage tuberculosis.

Friends and neighbors often asked Mitt to come to their homes and prepare for the undertaker the bodies of relatives who had died. The ritual included undressing, bathing, redressing and combing the hair of the dead. Mitt often took my mother with her on these ghastly errands. Once when they entered the room of a middle-aged woman, the stench of decaying, putrid flesh made my mother's eyes water. When Mitt undressed the body, Margaret saw that an area the size of a hand had been eaten away at the base of the woman's stomach. My mother began to cry and asked to go home. She never again went with Mitt to anoint the dead.

&

   In addition to her pattern-making and sewing, Mitt had many practical talents. She knew how to refinish and upholster furniture. She could make electrical and plumbing repairs. And she was proficient at carpentry. She shared with the girls her papering and painting skills. They would know how to take care of a home, if they ever had one.
   Mitt's eccentricities did not obscure her good taste or her talents. Although she never entertained, she crammed her brownstone with beautiful furniture and an astonishing range of decorative objects. There were Chinese urns, gold-leaf chairs, gilt portraits, bronze sculptures, china figurines. Carefully wrapped and stored away were fine linens, china and silver. She was "saving" all these things for Margaret and Thelma.
   Mitt kept the house dark and cold. Every surface had to be spotless. She made the girls scrub hard-to-reach areas with a toothbrush. All year long she kept the shades drawn and her furniture covered in white sheets. Twice a year, at Thanksgiving and Christmas, the sheets came off. Under her supervision, she allowed the girls to put up decorations that no one else would see. Otherwise, it was a somber, dark, unwelcoming group of rooms.
   In the house, there were no toys or other things that young girls usually have, although they were allowed to have cats. Even after the girls became teenagers, they could not bring friends home. The liberating currents of the 1920s did not penetrate those walls. Parties were out of the question. No one sat on the beautiful furniture or ate from the heirloom china. They were for the special occasions that somehow never came.

Outside, Mitt created gardens so beautiful they were photographed by the newspapers of the day. It was my mother's job to water the flowers. She was proud when her schoolmates stopped to admire the profusion of blossoms encircled by intricately worked red-brick pathways. It was the closest they were allowed to the house in which she was as much a captive as her grandmother had been in the orphanage.

In this grim environment, some normalcy was provided by Mitt's husband, James, whom Margaret called Poppa. He was a rotund, dignified-looking man who wore three-piece suits with jackets that did not quite close. Even though he worked every day, Poppa did all the cooking. In contrast to Mitt, he was warm and affectionate. He gave my mother spending change and talked to her as she stood by the stove watching him cook. After the evening meal, he would go to his room and not appear again until the next morning.

The house on Q Street became a repository for other abandoned and unable-to-be-cared-for children. There was a little blond boy named John whose mother, an unmarried Howard University student who was determined to finish her education, had left him there and never returned. He died when he was just over two, the same year that Jack died. My mother cradled him in her arms as he slept his life away.

The infant daughter of another unmarried Howard student came to the house. The mother promised to reclaim her daughter at the end of the term, but she never did. The baby's name was Eloise, but Mitt changed it to Sara Lou, Lou for short.

Mitt was strict, punitive and inconsistent. Sometimes she was capricious, sometimes petty. Apart from admonishing them and giving orders, Mitt had little to say to the girls. For minor infractions, she slapped them and beat them roughly with an electric cord, inflicting bruises and welts.

Mitt's craziness did not obliterate her preoccupation with the vagaries and minutiae of social class. To ensure that her charges could navigate in the right circles, she taught Margaret and Thelma the rules of etiquette and how to dress properly and well. She showed them the socially acceptable ways of sitting, walking and speaking. She told them to wear gloves and hats whenever they left the house for social occasions. While she continued to dress in rags, for them she made beautiful clothes of fine silk, velvet, moiré and lawn. Having "daughters" who were well bred and light and had long hair fostered her false sense of membership in the highest echelon of Washington society, even though her own color was enough to ban her.

It is no wonder that the girls did not like to spend much time at home, and that my mother began to run away on a regular basis. She was getting older, and she realized she did not have to live like this. She would bring her troubles to the Duncans or Cousin Bessie or Aunt Mamie, but she always returned to Mitt's. Sometimes she got out of the house and made a little money by working as a clerk for Annie Duncan, who was then the principal of a night school.

Mitt was a rigid, cold, dominating woman who grew progressively more eccentric as she aged. The girls did not understand until they were older that her eccentricities were more than that. They were mental aberrations. Her strangeness has obliterated everyone's memories of her looks. No one who knew her can describe her now. Partly obscured by hair over her eyes, her agitated face must have been constantly in motion. Despite all the years in her home, my mother saw Mitt's face clearly for the first time in her coffin. The troubled features were clean and serene in death.

I can remember being taken to see Mitt when I was six. I recall a slender figure and a pompadour of unpressed hair, with scraggly strands snaking down her forehead. Although in my storybooks all the witches were white, Mitt reminded me of a colored witch in shapeless clothes. The house was still dark and musty, and the sheets remained in place over the furniture. Although we had come all the way from Connecticut for our annual visit and had called ahead, she had not removed the sheets. We all acted as if it were perfectly normal to sit in a dark room with curious odors, in the middle of a hot August day.

A skittish girl-woman dressed like a younger version of Mitt darted in and out of the room. Her unpressed long hair was shaped in Gibson Girl style. On her feet she wore heavy work boots. Sometimes she hid behind the tall wing-backed chairs. Sometimes she came and touched my hand. She wanted to be with the company, but she would not sit down. She talked funny. Her pixilated behavior fascinated me. Her name was Lou, the little girl left behind more than a decade before.

Ten minutes before we left, Mitt asked me to come upstairs with her to help retrieve something she wanted to give to my mother. I did not want to go, but with a pinch from my mother, I followed Mitt up the tall staircase adorned with a curved mahogany banister and down a long hallway that was even darker than the parlor. Odd shapes covered in dusty sheets seemed poised to move toward me from shadowed alcoves and unlit crannies.

The walls of the upstairs hall looked like a shoe store. They were lined with hundreds of boxes neatly stacked up to the ceiling. From a vertical row of containers, Mitt selected an ancient-looking box and asked me to carry it downstairs. In the parlor, without explanation, she gave it to my mother. My mother made a happy fuss over the gift and opened it. Inside, carefully wrapped, were several exquisitely embroidered damask tablecloths that had never been used. These were some of the things Mitt had "saved" for my mother for more than thirty years.

⌘

My mother was fourteen and living with Mitt when she saw her Irish grandmother for the first time since Rose's death. The visit is her earliest clear memory of Margaret Maher. It was not a happy occasion. Michael had died of spinal meningitis. To his grandmother, his death was more important than his life. She had not visited him while he was living.

Margaret hoped and expected that the father, brothers and sister she had not seen in a decade would come to the funeral service as well. She did not think about her brothers much. It was her sister she longed for the most. She had no idea where Grace was, but she thought about her constantly. She cut out pictures of older girls from magazines and newspapers and wondered if Grace looked like them. When she was old enough, she went downtown to look at the young women on the street, peering at faces, hoping somehow to find her sister under someone's dark hair and light skin. But the rest of the family did not appear at the funeral, nor did they send word.

Emotions tend to run close to the surface when there is a death in the family. The adolescent Margaret did not hold hers in check. Hurt, angry and disappointed, the little colored girl confronted her white grandmother in the receiving room where the coffin lay. She quizzed her on the family's whereabouts and their reasons for not coming, and blamed her grandmother for their absence. At least her family could write to her. "The postman cannot tell the color of a person's skin by her handwriting," she said.

"You are old enough to understand," was her grandmother's response, in a tone that made it clear the subject was closed. Mitt slapped my mother. A clock chimed. The grandmother left. Margaret can still feel the stinging blow and the heavy silence of that dark parlor whose centerpiece was a small white box. It was 1926.

❧

Mamie made it her business to be a presence in my mother's life. When Mamie bought clothes and school supplies for her three daughters, she included a few items for her niece. From time to time, Margaret went to visit her aunt and her cousins. She wished for a life more like theirs. They had a white cloth on the dining room table, a mother who cooked and a home that was bright and warm, where friends were welcome. A family and home of her own would become Margaret's most important goals.

The other close living relative who took a special interest in my mother's life was her uncle Eddie Scott, her mother's only brother. Scott was a widower who worked as valet and butler for the Glovers, the family who founded Washington's "Bank of the Presidents," the Riggs National Bank. Most of the time he lived in Westover, their vast Georgian mansion on Massachusetts Avenue. In summer Eddie traveled with the family to Bar Harbor, Maine, and in the fall, to Europe. The Glovers led the grand life of the very rich in the early part of the century. They were an institution in Washington, their home the scene of major social events. Charles Glover, the family patriarch, was the moving spirit behind the development of Rock Creek Park, Glover Park and the National Cathedral.

Some of the white rich of Washington preferred immigrant help or white-looking black people. Eddie looked like those he served. Those who saw him might have taken him for a WASP. His hair was full, brown and straight, his features patrician, his eyes gray and his clothes and bearing impeccable. He could have been a retainer to the aristocratic English gentry. In some ways, he was.

Eddie was a man of property, with two homes in the District and one in Maryland. His life of exquisite service to others left him little time for a young niece without parents, but he sent Margaret generous gifts of cash and clothes on a regular basis. His other niece and nephews had gone out of his life.

When he could arrange it, he invited my mother to visit him in the mansion. By the time she was ten, she would take the bus up tree-lined Massachusetts Avenue. Usually she rode in the back of the bus reserved for colored patrons, but when she was feeling defiant, she would ride up front. It pleased her that she could fool people who put so much stock in skin color. She enjoyed looking out the windows at the stately mansions. The bus stopped near the cul-de-sac that marked the beginning of the Glover property. Margaret walked the long curving driveway, overhung with ancient trees. Bushes stood like green sentinels. She had entered another world.

She remembers her uncle as brusque but interested. He always asked my mother the same thing: "How are you doing in school?" He saw that some of the other help fixed her a sandwich and milk. Then he gave her some money and sent her on her way. It was a rare glimpse for a colored child of the insulated, pampered life that money and white skin could achieve. Later, she would bring her children to the mansion to give us the same glimpse.

Eddie was engaged for years to the first maid of the mansion, a tiny little light woman, Rosa Alexander. For her ears and fingers he gave her diamonds, and for her hope chest he presented her with linens, china, crystal and silver. They saved their money, that they might enjoy their marriage in retirement. It was a goal they would not reach.

෩

In 1870, the first public high school for colored students in the United States came into existence. Its founders named it the Preparatory High School for Negro Youth and it was located in the basement of the 15th Street Presbyterian Church. After several moves, it found a more permanent site at 1st and M streets. Then it became simply the M Street High School. In 1916 it moved again, to a brick and stone Tudor-style building on 1st Street. With the move came a change of name, to Paul Laurence Dunbar High School.

Dunbar stressed classical education, Many of its graduates became this country's black leaders in science, the arts, politics and law. Pictures of its faculty show a neurasthenic lot with center parts, bobbed hair, cameos, pearls and a pinched upper-class white look. Scattered among the light faces is an occasional brown one. Most were brilliant graduates of the Ivy League and Seven Sisters. Many had advanced degrees. Teaching was one of the few routes open to respectability for them. Their status in the community was unparalleled.

Aware of the limited career options for Negroes, the teachers tried to steer as many students as they could to their New England alma maters. Degrees from those schools at least ensured a place on the lowest rungs of a very tall ladder. Dunbar catered to the children of the wealthiest and oldest Negro families of the District. Students with lighter skins and comfortable economic situations were favored and even propped up academically. Every once in a while the undeniable brilliance of a gifted darker student broke through the barriers. Those darker scholars won recognition against great odds.

Although she was light and in spite of Mitt's admonitions, my mother gravitated toward her darker classmates. In her life, those who had provided her the most comfort and security were dark. There was something else at work as well. Because she had been abandoned by her white family, she perceived herself to be darker than she was.

School was a great liberation for Margaret. The color and drama of the assemblies, pageants and school plays offered relief from her troubled, cloistered home life. She was more interested in the extracurricular activities and socializing school offered than in studying. She entered every dance contest she could, and the Charleston was her specialty. But there was no doubt in her mind that she would go to college, because it was expected of her. She wanted to be a nurse or a dancer. Her plan was to attend the alma mater of both her Aunt Mamie and her Cousin Bessie, Miner Normal School.

Thelma was the first to leave Mitt's. As soon as she finished high school, she married the son of one of her aunt's neighbors, Horace Lazenberry, a quiet, reserved man eight years her senior. Horace was in the contracting business with his father, and both were members of the tradesmen's union, for which white skin was an absolute prerequisite. All of the Lazenberry family passed as white on their jobs and married people with skin color like their own. When Horace's brother married a medium-brown woman, his father did not speak to him for twenty-five years.

Mitt found rooms for Thelma and Horace on the top floor of a home four doors from her house. Margaret had a new refuge. Thelma became pregnant soon after marriage and had a daughter with long, straight red hair and green eyes like her own. Margaret loved to baby-sit for this beautiful, dimpled child.

❧

In 1931, my mother's senior year, Eddie Scott dropped dead on a busy downtown street at the age of fifty-four. When she learned that the Glovers had sent their limousine for her, Margaret knew something was wrong. She was surprised that her uncle's employers were aware of her existence. But their dead servant's papers had disclosed that Margaret was his only living relative. In gratitude for his long service, they must do right by her. She was taken to the morgue to identify the body.

Eddie died intestate, leaving behind more than one hundred thousand dollars and several pieces of property. For middle-class whites or blacks in 1931, that sum was a small fortune. The Glovers offered their lawyers and their services to my mother. Since Eddie had been sending money to Margaret for her support, the court arranged for her to collect and keep the rents from the estate until its disposition was settled. This unexpected infusion of money allowed her a kind of freedom and independence she had never before experienced.

Then as now, lawyers had a way of finding anyone, anywhere, anytime. Through Mamie, they had no trouble tracking down Margaret's brothers and sister. All of Eddie's nieces and nephews were to share equally in their dead colored uncle's estate. My mother was nervous, excited and frightened at the prospect of seeing her brothers and sister after seventeen years of absence and silence. She asked the lawyer if he would arrange a meeting in his office after the official proceedings were completed.

Sumner came from Maryland and Bill from Cleveland. My mother saw their names and Grace's on the form she was obliged to sign. Decades later she would learn that Grace had not come to Washington. Bill had picked up Grace's check for her and signed her name to the documents.

Her brothers did not stay to meet her. The Glovers' white lawyer did not offer her a real explanation as to why her relatives left his office just minutes before she arrived. He suggested that they had to catch a train back to Cleveland. My mother was devastated and angry. She cried so hard she could not go to the bank that day. She went home to bed instead. Almost sixty years later she would learn from one of Mamie's daughters that her brother Bill had stayed and spent the night at Mamie's.

Initially, the estate paid Margaret her share of the money. But the affairs of the estate were taken out of her hands. Sumner, as the eldest, was named executor. Once again the "white" relatives prevailed. Although Margaret had been declared an equal heir, she was never given any of the proceeds from the sale of Eddie's three properties. She did not seek legal recourse. But she kept their addresses.

The pain and humiliation of this second rejection is still with my mother. For years she had accepted the fact that her siblings had chosen to live another life. She had wanted to believe that it was for economic betterment and social acceptance. She thought that when the time came and she met them under cloistered circumstances, they would talk with her and learn who she had become. Nothing could have been further from the truth.

She told the inheritance story often when I was growing up, clouding up each time. She used it as a reminder for her children to love one another, to stay together and to keep in touch. She did not want history to repeat itself. Hearing the story heightened my resolve to search for the Morrises. I wanted to see what kind of people would reject their sister. I wanted to see if they would look any less than normal.

The next day, recovered from her crying bout, Margaret went with Bessie to deposit the inheritance check. She told Bessie she would like to stop and pay one bill. They went to the District tax office and paid several thousand dollars of Mitt's back real estate taxes. When she got home, Mitt put the receipt on a shelf and said nothing.

Charles Dickens could have made a great novel out of my mother's Washington years. The missing, rejecting relatives, the numerous guardians, the moves, the madness, the cruelty, the death and dying, the strange house and its even stranger mistress. It is likely that my mother's memory has expunged the worst of times. I wonder how she stayed sane, how she survived, how she became loving and able to give. Then I think there must be a gene for resiliency.

∾

With beauty, charm, sweetness of personality, the "correct" color and now an inheritance to boot, my mother had many suitors. She rejected the son of a prosperous owner of a taxicab fleet because he was too light. Another admirer of cinnamon tone was too possessive. Then, with Mitt's blessing, she had an "understanding" to be engaged to the scion of one of Washington's most prestigious black families. It was said that his family had been free and prosperous since Revolutionary times.

Annie Duncan advised my mother to think carefully before she married the handsome heir, because there was a history of insanity in his family. His mother, his aunts and his grandmother had all been institutionalized. Hoping to get an answer to his marriage proposal, he invited Margaret to join him and his family for an intensively chaperoned week at their summer home on Highland Beach. Margaret wanted to go, but Mitt did not think it proper and would not allow the trip. My mother and her intended were parted for eight weeks.

It was that very same summer that Margaret met Julian Taylor, gave him the pre-engagement ring she was wearing, dumped her taffy-colored boyfriend and pledged her allegiance to the dark son of an even darker Baptist minister. It is likely my mother was attracted to my father because he represented a stable, older figure from a large, close family. He also had color. In the future, Margaret thought, there would be no mistake about who or what she was.

The courtship did not rest well in a number of circles. Margaret was nineteen, Julian twenty-nine. Mitt thought Julian was too dark, too old and too married. Although separated, he was not yet divorced. Her sister Thelma thought Margaret was too young and too naive for him. Aunt Mamie thought Julian was too dark and without prospects. The Duncans also questioned his age and his color. On the other side, Julian's father did not want his son to repeat his mistake of marrying a light-skinned woman who had no family. Only Cousin Bessie approved.

In spite of the disapproval, the courting couple grew close. Julian was not allowed to come into Mitt's house, and in those days there was not a wide range of entertainment available to young colored people, but once they met, the pair saw each other every day. They went to house parties, movies, and shows at the Howard Theater and took countless walks. They made visits with Thelma and Horace special events. They went to ice cream parlors and visited friends from school. Julian had a portrait of himself made for her. In a matter of time, they were engaged.

Although Margaret had her own money and had planned to go to Miner Normal School, getting married and having her own family was far more important to her than finishing school. What she wanted was a stable home and someone who would look after her for a long time—someone who would not leave or reject her because of her color. In 1933 the couple eloped to New York and from there to Connecticut. Bessie gave the couple their only wedding present, a set of six sterling teaspoons, monogrammed with "M" for Morris.

That first year of marriage was an endurance test for my mother. It was the middle of the Depression. She was a new bride, in a new place, about to be a new mother. No close family was nearby to offer support. The weather was cold, the town was rural and the people were really white. Margaret cried every day. The journey from Washington to Connecticut was as traumatic for her as had been her grandmother's journey from Ireland to the United States.

The newlyweds lived briefly in a room in a church member's house in Stratford until they found a small bungalow with a large yard and a tree-covered stream. After a while, a small group of attractive colored people from several surrounding towns became their friends and invited them to lawn parties and card games. Margaret consoled herself by spending some of her inheritance on her new husband. There was a new Studebaker, a black velvet smoking jacket, and to protect him from the unaccustomed New England chills a long raccoon coat. Years later I remember seeing that raccoon coat hanging in an attic, scruffy and moth-eaten. I did not appreciate its significance as a buffer against transition and deep pain until long after it disappeared from the family consciousness and artifacts.

In an attempt to lift my mother's melancholy, more than once my father suggested she try to contact her family again. It was difficult for him to understand a family so different from his own. Using the addresses on the inheritance papers, he composed a letter to each of his wife's siblings, for her signature. He explained that she would like to reestablish contact with them. Recognizing the delicacy of the situation on their side, he did not mention visits or any other type of personal commitments. All the letters were returned to her with the identical notation: "addressee unknown." Margaret sank deeper into despair.

For three years, Julian kept the letters in his file. In 1936 he called the chief of police in Cleveland. He told the official he was a minister who needed to get in touch with his wife's family because of an emergency. He gave the chief the last known address for Will, Grace and Bill and asked if they could send someone to the house. The chief agreed. Later he called back and said his officers had found the parties in question, but they all denied knowing a Margaret Morris Taylor. Julian asked him to put it in writing.

I still have the tissue-thin, ice-blue letter written in the ice-blue April of 1936. It reads:

Dear Madam:

In reply to your letter of the 22nd inst. permit me to advise you that persons named William Morris Sr., William Morris Jr., and Mrs. Grace Morris Cramer were found to be residing at 1347 East

142nd St. East Cleveland, Ohio (suburb of Cleveland), but all stated that you are not known to them.

That was the next to last time Margaret tried to find her family.

In my own attempts to piece the story together, I have often wondered about my mother's grandmother, Margaret Maher Morris, the Irish immigrant. The symmetry and parallel of her life to my mother's early years is startling. When they were four, their mothers died. When they were four, their fathers left them. Each left a familiar culture for an alien one. Each married men of color against the wishes of their families. It would seem that those parallels would have created bonds, but it didn't work that way.

The symmetry in the lives of my mother and her grandmother would take a further twist. The grandmother's relatives abandoned her when she was four and came into her life again briefly when she was seventeen. The granddaughter's relatives abandoned her when she was four and returned to her life briefly when she was nineteen. Once again, the results of those encounters were defined by color. Reclamation was the goal on one side, renunciation on the other.

I used to dream of reuniting my mother with her sister, her brothers, her nieces and nephews. It was a nice dream, a dream of love and warmth and acceptance. As I got older, the dream became more of a dark fantasy, at times a nightmare of vengeance. I wanted to punish by dramatic exposure the family that had left my mother behind. In some bare room where judgment would be written, I wanted to show them that despite their abandonment, my mother had survived. I wanted them to twist and turn and sweat as they learned she had created a successful, caring family of her own. I wanted to shout at them that she had no need of their emotional involvement or their white lives. I wanted to white them out of my consciousness.

Chapter Five

Ashamed of my race?
And of what race am I?
I am many in one.
Through my veins there flows the blood
Of Red Man, Black Man, Briton, Celt and Scot.
In warring clash and tumultuous riot
I welcome all,
But love the blood of the kindly race
That swarthes my skin, crinkles my hair
And puts sweet music into my soul.

—JOSEPH COTTER
"The Mulatto to His Critics"

I must have been very young when I first heard about my family's variegated bloodlines, including at least three different Indian strains. Until I was old enough to understand how the heart continuously pumps blood through veins, arteries and capillaries, I used to look at my hands, arms, legs and feet and wonder which held my Indian blood, my colored blood and my white blood. I would look in the mirror and see my Indian nose, or was it Italian? I was said to have English ears, Irish eyes and black hair. I understood that my roots grew in many gardens.

And so I was conditioned to be pleased with the idea of being part Indian and having reservation rights. The fact that I had an ancestor named John Fortune and another named White Cloud always put me on the side of the men we called red in the childhood games of summer afternoons. Although I could not know whether my prominent nose was a genetic gift from the Indians, the Irish, the English or the Italians, I ascribed it to the Indians. I was happy to look like the people whose profiles were on the pennies I saved.

Before the resurgence of black pride in the 1960s, Negroes doted on their Native American heritage. They were much less ambivalent in claiming their Indian blood than in parading their white connections. I suspect there were two reasons for this. As Andrew Hacker observes in *Two Nations*, "America imposes a stigma on every black child at birth." It was more acceptable to be Indian than Negro. And it was often easier to trace one's Indian roots than one's African connections.

Writing in the *Journal of Negro History* in 1920, noted black historian Carter G. Woodson mused, "One of the longest unwritten chapters in the history of the United States is that treating of the relations of the Negroes and the Indians. The Indians were already here when the white men came and the Negroes brought in soon after to serve as a subject race found among the Indians one of their means of escape."

At least 80 percent of the black population has significant Indian ancestry. Crispus Attucks, given the dubious credit of being the first Negro to fall in the Revolutionary War, was a black Natick Indian. Paul Cuffee, a Negro Dartmouth Indian, was the wealthy Massachusetts merchant and ship owner who in 1815 became the father of America's Back to Africa movements. His ship *Traveller* carried thirty-eight settlers whom he had subsidized to Sierra Leone. Frederick Douglass was part Indian, as was Langston Hughes, who believed that Pocahontas was one of his ancestors.

In *Black Indians*, William Loren Katz suggests that African slaves and Indians came together because, "A common foe, not any special affinity of skin color, became the first link of friendship, the earliest motivation for alliance." Katz notes other commonalities between the two cultures: the importance of family and the elderly, religion as a daily part of life, and an emphasis on economic cooperation over competition.

∽

Long before the English explorer Raleigh twice tried to settle Roanoke Island, on the Outer Banks of North Carolina, aboriginal

Americans roamed its piney forests and sandy trails. Raleigh was unsuccessful at both of his colonization attempts. After the second time, disease and skirmishes left fewer natives, but, with members of nearby tribes, they were able to maintain continuity.

According to family stories, descendants of the Roanoke Indian survivors gave birth to one of the earliest members of the Taylor clan, my father's great-grandmother. She was born around 1852 on Roanoke Island into the Weapomeoc Indian nation, local remnants of the Algonquins. Her American name was Anna, but her father preferred to call her by her Indian name, White Cloud. One of her parents was said to have been part black, part white and part Indian. White Cloud married John Fortune, a Cherokee whose family had migrated from the western part of North Carolina to Virginia, where he was born. He was one of the thousand or so described by James Mooney, a chronicler of Native American history, as "principally of the mountain Cherokee of North Carolina, the purest blooded and most conservative of the Nation," who evaded the 1838 government roundup of sixteen thousand Cherokees for removal to Oklahoma. On that forced march west, now called the Trail of Tears, four thousand Cherokees died.

One picture of White Cloud survives. With great dignity and her head cocked, she sits in a photographer's studio. She is light-skinned, with a broad flat face, dark curving eyebrows, a long nose with slightly flaring nostrils, and full lips. Her eyes have an Asian cast. Her grandsons, including my father, remember them as green, and there are several green-eyed cousins on my father's side. Her long, straight hair is rolled up on each side of her cheeks. She wears a hat that might have been seen in Sherwood Forest. A satin blouse with sleeves edged in lace, and what looks like a long velvet jumper, cover an ample body. Around her neck is a choker, and a brooch rests in the vee of her wide lapel. Her eyes and hair look Native American, her mouth black, her skin white, her nose a mixture of all three.

John and White Cloud left Roanoke Island and came to Washington, where John became a bricklayer. I know little else about their life except that they lived on V Street in the Shaw district. They had fourteen children, most of whom died young. Early death claimed White Cloud as well, and Fortune would marry again, to a woman named Pinky. They had four more children, and a dwelling in Goat Alley large enough to accommodate five lodgers. According to the 1900 census, Goat Alley was one of the most populous of the District's crowded residential alleys that housed many of the blacks streaming into the city from the South. The same census counted four hundred dwellers there, all but one family listed as black.

One of their children was my grandmother, Roberta Fortune, born in 1878. A short, plump, pleasant but stately woman, Roberta looked as if she had never been young. She inherited White Cloud's dark eyebrows and mouth. Unlike her mother's straight tresses, Roberta's hair grew in short and rough. Her skin was a medium tan. A woman of unadorned dress, she wore perfectly round glasses and little jewelry. Her sons described her as quiet, shy, sweet and compliant, a good foil for the dominant black man who was to be her husband. She died before I was born.

∽

A long time ago, some of my ancestors lived in Africa. Most Africans who were enslaved came from West Africa, but I do not know which country or tribe claimed my people. I do not know the circumstances of their capture and enslavement. I do not know the date of their forced departure. It might have been as early as 1619, when the first slaves landed in Virginia, or as late as 1808, when the slave trade was abolished. I do not know which ship brought them to America, nor the port at which they were forced from the filthy holes into air that was clean again. All I know is that their children and grandchildren eventually settled in North Carolina, and in my mother's case, Maryland and Virginia. As much as they might want to, they would never be African again. They would remake themselves into Americans. They would distill drops from the American dream to water their minds and flood their souls. They would become Negroes, mulattoes, colored, black and African-American. They would become me.

The ghosts of my African forebears haunt me as much as my missing white relatives. When you do not know about your past, you tend to romanticize it. What pictures can I paint of my ancient black family? Were they farmers or nomads? Did they balance huge silver-sheened fish on their heads as they gracefully walked along some roiling seashore? What patterns did they weave or dye? Did they mine gold or carve the faces of their ancestors in masks of wood or bronze? Were they tall and slender or short and squat? Did they cut beauty marks into their faces or dramatize them with painted lines? Did they let their hair grow or did they make themselves bald? Were they warriors or chiefs? Which of their traits did they pass on to me? The manner of their coming to America obscures such knowledge. But I struggle to find clues that will unlock the answers.

In 1983 I was among a group of six people involved in public broadcasting who journeyed to Dakar, Senegal, to meet African film-makers and explore ways of bringing the African experience to the American television screen. About that same time, Bo Derek was showing on African screens in a new version of *Tarzan*. I found the coincidence embarrassing. Senegal enveloped and enchanted me. The look of the people and their dialect reminded me of the Virgin Islands, where I had lived. Indeed the Isle of Goree, a few miles off the shore of Dakar, was an important export center for slaves, and one of the major trade routes from Senegal was to the West Indies.

We went to Goree to see the slave pens. The place was quiet, like a great stone church. Was it my imagination or did I sense sorrowing presences? How could so many bodies fit in so little space? Their waste raised the floor by many inches. No words were left behind, just scratches and stains on the stone walls. There on the rocky Goree beach, I imagined how some of my ancestors might have stepped on those same rounded stones. My paternal great-grandmother, Chanie Robinson Taylor, was the face I could place there.

In 1991 my sister Jewelle had a party for all the Taylor cousins in Washington in the elegant Capitol Hill town house she and her husband, Jim, were occupying during a sabbatical from their respective positions at Berkeley and Stanford. At the party I saw not one but two incarnations of my ancestor Chanie Taylor in the faces of my cousin Eleanor and her daughter, Aaronette, whom I was meeting for the first time. The women did not realize how much they had fulfilled my dream of seeing another great-grandparent's image. They had never seen a likeness of the woman their chromosomes had copied, gene for gene.

Chanie's was not a picture that I had lived with from my youth. My father's youngest brother Percy had given it to me a few years before. The image allowed me to gaze beyond the horizon of my grandfather Taylor's life. There sat Chanie, undoubtedly born into slavery, with two of her grandchildren, my uncles. In an elegant long printed dress, she holds her head slightly to the side. Her skin seems to be mahogany dark. She wears her hair parted and close to her head. There is a long, prominent Indian nose—or could it be West African? High, sculptured cheekbones shadow a thin upper lip pursed over a full bottom one. Her eyes have a familiar Asian cast, but she looks like a beautiful sculpture from Benin.

~~~

In 1830, a year before Nat Turner led a slave revolt, Southern states enacted laws to outlaw Negro ministers. Laws also existed that forbade teaching Negroes to read. In 1864, General Sherman issued Field Order 15, giving confiscated plantation land to newly freed slaves. Later, President Andrew Johnson rescinded the order. Houses and jobs that had gone to Negroes after the Civil War were soon taken by whites.

When the great financial panic swept over the country in 1873, the North turned its attention to money matters. The white Southerners coalesced and formed a solid Democratic bloc. Some colored people who had purchased their masters' homes were falsely charged with delinquent taxes. Employers refused to pay for service rendered on plantations. The South had new hopes for Negro disfranchisement. Negroes were kept from going to the polls, and lynchings and beatings became commonplace. In 1879, about sixty thousand colored people left the South. Beginning in 1890, Jim Crow laws were enacted.

My grandfather's dark-complected family challenged and overcame the color barriers of the times. Over the course of the next four generations, they acquired college educations, forged professional careers, established families, bought homes and bettered their communities.

In the eighteenth and nineteenth centuries, much of the northeastern part of North Carolina where my paternal ancestors lived was a terrain of swamps, forests, lagoons and rivers. It was a good place to hide. Fog and mist and Spanish moss were beneficent camouflage. It was also the site of many slave rebellions, from the early 1800s to Emancipation in 1863. Contrary to the preferred mythology, which fostered images of complacent, passive slaves, hundreds of slave revolts were recorded in the newspapers, letters and journals of that period. The fact is, slaves outnumbered whites and the slaves were not content with their lot.

Their discontent was foremost in the minds of Southern whites. Frances Anne Kemble, a well-known English actress who was mistress of a large plantation in Georgia, gave voice to Southern fears when she wrote in 1838, "I know that the Southern men are apt to deny that they do live under a habitual sense of danger, but a slave population, coerced into obedience, though unarmed and half-fed, is a threatening source of constant insecurity, and every Southern woman to whom I have spoken on the subject has admitted to me that they live in terror of their slaves."

Brutality against rebellious slaves was unbridled. The author Herbert Aptheker reports in *American Negro Slave Revolts* a case so heinous that it was brought to the highest court in Virginia in 1851. A master had ordered a slave to "cob Sam with a shingle" and apply "fire to the body of the slave; about his back, belly and private parts." Then Sam was washed in hot water in which red-hot pepper had been steeped. Finally he was kicked, stamped and choked with a rope until he died.

Despite such antidotes, rebelliousness persisted. Economic depressions, industrialization and urbanization contributed to the revolts. But as Aptheker notes, "The fundamental factor provoking rebellion against slavery was that social system itself, the degradation, exploitation, oppression, and brutality which it created, and with which, indeed, it was synonymous."

In eastern North Carolina in 1825, Aptheker reports, a slave plot was uncovered and crushed. Slave preachers were blamed, for having told the slaves "that the national government had set them free in October and that they were being unjustly held in servitude." Five years later, again in northeastern North Carolina, slaves were restive and plotting. It was reported that "a very general and extensive impression has been made on the minds of the negroes in this vicinity that measures have been taken towards their emancipation on a certain and not distant day." In 1835 in the same area, slaves believed that a liberator was on his way from the North to lead them in their struggle for freedom.

My ancestors came from or lived in all the areas where revolts had occurred—Bertie County, Elizabeth City, Windsor, Plymouth and Hertford. Family history and geography suggest that they were part of or certainly influenced by the widespread slave restiveness. I like to believe that the independent thinking, leadership and political advocacy in my family are the results of tendencies passed down from those oppressive times through more than six generations.

❧

When black people try to trace their families, they generally come up against the anonymities and gaps created by slavery. My grandfather's family Bible and some of his archives provided me with some clues about his heritage. Census records and city directories added a little more information. Stories my father and uncles told me provided a personal perspective. Nonetheless, there are spaces and blanks I would like to fill. I will keep trying.

The earliest black presence I found in our Taylor family records was that of Mary Shaw, listed in the family Bible as my great-great-grandmother. She was born in the early 1830s in Bertie County in that infamous northeastern corridor of North Carolina. Mary's mate, whose name was Isaac Taylor, was said to be part Indian. Together they produced Ned Taylor, my great-grandfather.

Issac told his son Ned that he had planned to take part in "a great slave upset" near his home in 1860. Other slaves from a nearby plantation asked him to join them. Ned told the story to his own sons, my father and uncles, and they passed it on to me. I believe it is the one documented in Aptheker's book. Records indicate that in 1860 about three hundred slaves from different plantations were going to march down from Hertford, Elizabeth City, Windsor and Bertie County to a town called Plymouth. Aptheker says their plan was to "murder and destroy all they might encounter on the road, set fire to the town, kill all the inhabitants that might oppose them, seize what money there might be, also what ammunitions and weapons they might acquire, then take possession of such vessels as they required for their purpose and go in them where they might think proper." The slaveholders' discovery aborted the plan. My great-great-grandfather lived to tell the tale.

Ned Taylor, like his parents, was born during slavery. Unlike his parents, he became the owner of tobacco lands and seven small houses. He married Chanie Robinson, and seven children were born to them, the first of whom was my grandfather, William.

William Taylor was born in Windsor, the seat of Bertie County, in July 1870, seven years after the Emancipation Proclamation and five years after the end of the Civil War. The town was surrounded by plantations that grew cotton, tobacco and peanuts, and small as it was, it had sawmills, barrel mills and tobacco warehouses. But Ned and Chanie were anxious to leave the plantation memories behind, and, with the deed to a significant amount of tobacco acreage, they moved to Hertford, a picturesque town situated at a bend in a river. Nearby was Dismal Swamp, a 2,200-square-mile tangle of trees and undergrowth. George Washington surveyed Dismal Swamp in 1763 as a member of a company organized to drain it. The drainage did not take place. The swamp became the setting for Harriet Beecher Stowe's *Dred*, her second novel about slavery.

William spent much of his early life in a large three-story frame house graced with an ample front porch on King Street, facing a park. He went to high school thirty miles away in Elizabeth City at the Roanoke Institute, one of the dozens of Negro private schools that dotted the state, drawing as its brochure suggested "children of the state who did not have the advantage of an adequate education in their local communities." After sleepy Hertford, Elizabeth City, a trade center for the northeast part of the state, must have seemed busy and colorful.

In the late 1800s, upward movement was foreordained for only a few colored faces. In a family of many children, there was usually no more than one star. Although all his siblings went to college, my grandfather, the firstborn, was clearly the glowing orb of the group. The tenets of W. E. B. Du Bois and Frederick Douglass formed the bulwark for his life. He would forever be influenced by their calls for social equality, justice and the uplifting of the black race.

By the end of the nineteenth century, there was a long list of Negro colleges generally supported by Northern philanthropy. Most of them were denominational schools for Methodists, Congregationalists, Baptists, Presbyterians, Episcopalians and Roman Catholics. William selected Shaw University in Raleigh, founded for Baptists in 1865 and considered to be one of the best schools for Negroes at that time.

In 1892, he was among the tiny percentage of Negroes who attended college. (Eight years later, only 4 percent of the entire population between eighteen and twenty-one went to college.) He graduated in 1896, the same year that the Supreme Court upheld *Plessy v. Ferguson,* ruling that a Louisiana statute mandating segregated railroad carriages did not violate the equal protection clause of the Fourteenth Amendment. The decision opened the way for Jim Crow laws to be adopted throughout the South, not to be overturned until 1954.

Upon graduation William was immediately appointed principal of Hertford Academy in Hertford, another private school. He subsequently returned to Roanoke Institute, this time to study theology.

William was interested in the ministry early in life, and missed no opportunity to develop himself as a preacher at the same time as he continued his education. In a history of the First Baptist Church of Hertford prepared for the 1976 Bicentennial, there is a turn-of-the-century picture of William and six other well-dressed, unsmiling black men. The picture is captioned "Early Leaders" and in it, my grandfather, who was probably in his twenties at the time, wears a superbly fitted double-breasted, velvet-collared morning coat as he holds an open Bible.

The brief biographical paragraph on William's life in the 1927 and 1928 editions of *Who's Who in Colored America* is a bare-bones outline. In 1894 he married Roberta Fortune, six years his junior. Starting the next year, they produced seven children. My father, Julian, was the fifth child to be born, among five boys and two girls. Only the boys survived. One girl died at birth, and the other at seventeen, from tuberculosis. The biography also reports that my grandfather was a compiler of the Standard Baptist Hymnal, which is used every Sunday by millions of people in most Baptist churches, a national officer of the National Baptist Convention, a teacher at several colleges, including Howard University, and a member of the NAACP, the Equal Rights League, the Masons, the Odd Fellows and the Republican Party, which he joined because of its historical antislavery platform.

∽

In Windsor, not far from the site of the slave rebellion, is a church called Cedar's Landing. It's a small, quiet place, sitting deep in a pine grove. While a member there, William Taylor preached his first sermon in the warm spring of 1899. In recognition of his faithful membership and his message, pastor J. A. Frank wrote him a letter of recommendation.

> This certifies that Brother W.A. Taylor is a member of the Cedar's Landing Baptist Church in good and regular standing and is held by us in high esteem. We believe him to have been called of God to the work of the gospel ministry, and do hereby give him our entire and cordial approbation in the improvement of his gifts, by preaching the gospel, as Providence may afford him opportunity. And we pray the Great Head of the Church to endow him with all needful grace and crown his labors with abundant Success.

In the 1940s and 1950s, my father would carry on his father's work in Cedar's Landing, traveling from Connecticut to conduct revivals.

The census of 1900 shows my grandfather living in a house he owned on Hyde Park Street in Hertford. His occupation was given as teacher. He and his wife had a lodger who was also listed as a teacher. According to that record, the neighborhood was black, and the neighbors worked in the brickyard or the sawmill. One was listed as a house carpenter. The two teachers were the only professionals noted on the page.

History was the Reverend Taylor's first love, and he named each of his children after a historical figure. There was William, Jr., after William the Conqueror; Henry Clinton, after Sir Henry Clinton, a Revolutionary War general; Blanche, named for Blanche of

Castile, powerful queen of Louis VIII of France; my father, Julian Augustus, after the first Roman emperor and nephew of Julius Caesar; Robert E. Lee, after the Civil War general; Percy, for one of the Knights of the Round Table. Mary, who died in infancy, was the namesake of Mary Queen of Scots.

In 1903, when he was thirty-three, my grandfather became pastor of the Sycamore Baptist Church in Greenville, the first of a series of important posts. My father was a year old at the time. Shortly thereafter, William took on an additional congregation, the Cornerstone Baptist Church in Elizabeth City. He ministered to his two flocks on alternate Sundays. During the week he was the principal of the Tar River Institute, a private black high school in Greenville. To be both a teacher and a preacher was to be a figure of double prestige in the community.

While pastoring, William completed his studies, earning a doctorate in divinity from the Virginia Theological Seminary and College at Lynchburg in 1908. Later, he took courses at Howard and Columbia universities. His educational achievements seeded a garden that has proliferated over four generations.

I often feel bad that my grandfather died before I was born. I know him only from his photographs and the stories told by his sons and many others who knew him. In pictures he is dark, handsome, imposing and confident. His expression is always pleasant. He had a broad face, a high forehead, a strong nose and full lips. Some would say he had "bedroom eyes."

Evidently my grandfather had what psychiatrists like to call a high "transference valence"—he got to you. You either loved or hated him. There was no room for neutrality. People who knew him said he had a quiet voice and talked just above a whisper. This restraint was in itself provocative. In hushed tones, he called the women who constantly fluttered around him "sugar," "honey" and "baby." His contemporaries described him as refined, cultured and eloquent. His colleagues compared him to William Jennings Bryan, the silver-tongued orator. His handwritten sermons, which my father saved and used for reference, were at once intellectual and full of the colorful images known in Baptist circles as "picture painting."

My grandfather lived his life with little reference to white people. He had a black doctor, a black lawyer, a black banker and a black piano teacher and at one time owned his own grocery store. His income came from his black church and from his property, which he let to black tenants. He lived in black neighborhoods and the people who were important to him had black faces. In addition, he preferred women who did not look white. None of his wives had light skin.

Whenever I asked my father or his brothers about their father, they invariably mentioned his seriousness, his sense of propriety, his impeccable style and grooming, his intelligence, his faultless elocution, his soft voice and his charm. His sons claimed he was exquisitely aware of what he thought was his special position in life and was too proud to carry a package outside the house. He believed his image should be that of a gentleman and a scholar.

From North Carolina William moved to the First Baptist Church in Newport News, Virginia, whose history dated back to 1864. The census of 1910 listed his occupation there as teacher and minister. His new neighbors included blacksmiths, a barber and shipyard workers, all black. When I was young I heard my father talk about Ophelia, a housekeeper who lived with the family in Newport News. I thought he might have exaggerated. But in the census I found Ophelia Hassel, a seventeen-year-old girl the family brought with them from North Carolina, listed as the Taylors' servant.

In 1913, black world heavyweight champion Jack Johnson, once considered the epitome of the "new Negro," was forced to leave the country for taking a white woman to his bed. That same year my grandfather, another new Negro, became the founding pastor of the Florida Avenue Baptist Church in Washington. This position was to be the apotheosis of his ministry. The Florida Avenue Baptist Church flourishes today and has become one of the city's historic institutions. It was born after a simmering dispute by twenty-two members of the Vermont Avenue Baptist Church led to an open rebellion. Eighteen women and four men held meetings in their homes for a period of fourteen months, at first seeking a reconciliation with their home church. Hope for a gathering back into the fold faded, and the twenty-two stalwarts decided to start a new church and buy a new building.

Located at the corner of Florida Avenue and Bohrer, the building had been the all-white Gurley Memorial Presbyterian Church. The

Negro group bought it in 1913 for $25,000. The initial payment was $2,000 and each member was asked to contribute at least a dollar toward that amount. In a ceremony of recognition, the church received its new name on January 15, 1913. Anticipating that the minister from Newport News would bring in a substantial new membership, six of the founders decided to build and install a baptismal pool before his arrival so that the sacrament could be performed within their own building.

Eight committees were formed to plan the new pastor's introduction to the church. An "Installation Programme" chronicles "a Week of Preaching, Commencing May 26 and ending June 2, 1913 with a Banquet." At the installation service itself, Rev. W. Bishop Johnson, an advisor to the founding mothers and fathers, preached from the text "Draw the bow and the venture. Let the arrow fly." Sixteen other ministers wore out the crowd.

But it was my grandfather who was the star of the event. He instructed that his inaugural sermon of fifteen pages should be bound and printed for the service, along with his picture and a picture of the church. "Curiosity," it began, "is a very great thing, and I have never had any ambition to satisfy curiosity or to come up to expectations. My only ambition is to deliver a simple gospel message. I come to you, dear friends, tonight, to deliver no great sermon, but a simple message, characteristic of the kind that I hope to deliver from time to time."

Of course his message was not simple. It was a great sermon, replete with heroic phrases: "When the sun rises in the morning, dashing its golden beams over the eastern horizon and kissing creation with a refulgent smile . . . Let me call on the soldiers to fall in line, keep step with the beat of the drum and as your humble servant I shall blow the trumpet and strive to hold the banner high. I call on the church to support me and stand by me and if we fail I shall report to Heaven the reason why. . . ." And so on. His theme was "Meet for the Master's Use" from 2 Timothy 2:21, from which, if they listened carefully, his members would know that he was saying he was there to lead and that everything else was secondary.

On the next evening, starting at eight o'clock, there were "Short Addresses" by R. C. Bruce, the assistant superintendent of the public schools, George W. Cook, a professor from Howard University, W. Calvin Chase, the editor of *The Bee*, Washington's major Negro newspaper at the time, Robert Terrell, the judge of the municipal court, Nannie H. Burroughs, president of the National Training School, and seven heads of fraternal organizations. "Three Minute addresses by the Clergy of the City" brought up the rear. For those who made it through the program, a reception followed.

It was a who's who of Negro Washington's social, cultural and political elite. Superintendent Bruce was the Harvard-educated son of Blanche K. Bruce, the politician from Mississippi who was a U.S. senator in 1874. A well-known educator of the day, Nannie Burroughs was the author of an often-quoted treatise on Negro color-consciousness, *Not Color but Character*. ("Many Negroes have colorphobia as badly as the white folks have Negrophobia. Some Negro men have it . . . some Negro women have it. Whole families have it, and . . . some Negro churches have it.") Her comments did not apply to Florida Avenue as a whole: its membership spanned the full range of colored people.

Judge Terrell was a graduate of Harvard College and Howard Law School. He taught Latin at the M Street School and was appointed to the bench by Theodore Roosevelt. He married Mary Church, who would later become the queen of Washington's colored aristocrats and a significant figure in my mother's life.

❧

My grandfather had a bounteous quiver of arrows. His missiles flew sure and straight. Within three years he had paid off the first and second mortgages on the church. Frugality was one of William's well-known traits. If anyone in the family asked him for money, he would turn his back and open his wallet, so that no one would see how much it contained. But he was not shy about asking other people to give up their funds. When he felt the church collection plates were not full enough, he sent them back. His ability to raise money for the church became legendary.

The Taylor homestead, a roomy brownstone purchased in 1912, was at 2021 13th Street in the heart of Shaw, where the black intelligentsia flowered during the "new Negro renaissance." Not far away lived the poet Georgia Douglas Johnson, whose literary salons often featured her friend Langston Hughes. Johnson had written a book of poetry called *The Heart of a Woman*, about black women's thoughts on freedom.

On the streets of the Taylors' neighborhood might be seen Jean Toomer, the writer Countee Cullen, or NAACP founder W. E. B. Du Bois. Howard professor Kelly Miller may have been thinking specifically about the Shaw neighborhood when he wrote, "Washington is still the Negro's heaven and it will be many a moon before Harlem will be able to take away her sceptre." Just behind the Taylor house was the Lincoln Theater, a Negro entertainment center that featured live productions and weekly talent shows. It was a magnet for young people, and the Taylor boys were no exception.

Hand in hand with William's pride in self was his pride in his race. Negro history was central to his teaching. From him his sons learned the messages of Du Bois, Frederick Douglass, Ida B. Wells and Booker T. Washington. They knew all the black biblical figures and were schooled in the black figures of ancient history. My grandfather's primary message at home was to bring honor to self and family and uplift the race. His sons took heed. They learned as much at home as at Armstrong or Dunbar High School, where my father, dark though he was, was the valedictorian.

In addition to intelligence William and all his sons were gifted with diverse musical talents. Each played the piano and sang. William, Jr., the eldest, called Bill, also played the bass fiddle and the saxophone. All were visible in the musical programs of the church. Three sang in the choir, another was the choir director, and still another the organist. They formed a group called the Taylor Brothers and performed the light classics and spirituals in music halls and churches up and down the East Coast. Admission to their concerts was twenty-five cents. The slogan printed on their tickets read, "You have admired them singly, now hear them together." My father branched out and for a while had his own weekly radio segment on which he sang popular love songs.

His brother Clinton, whom his friends called "Breeze," was the pianist leader of his own jazz band, the Harmonizers, during his years at Dunbar High School. It was one of the two most popular black bands in Washington at that time, playing the leading hotels, parties in private homes and local radio stations. The leader of the other band was a contemporary, a neighbor and a friendly competitor, Duke Ellington, with his Serenaders, forerunners of the more famous Washingtonians. Clinton was also gifted artistically, and a letter of commendation he received from William Harding for his portrait of the president helped get him into Syracuse University, where he studied art. Ellington, who had received a scholarship to the Pratt Institute of Art in New York, chose music instead. He too left Washington for New York and a fabled life in the world of jazz. Later, Clinton would also go to New York, to study art on a special scholarship at Columbia.

Julian's sister Blanche, the only Taylor daughter to survive infancy, had been sick with "consumption," most likely tuberculosis, for several years. She slept apart from the rest of the family, in a room on the third floor. Her parents knew she was not likely to get better. Yet even as a teenager she remained hopeful. In the spring of 1917 Blanche told her mother she was going to get well in time for Easter Sunday service. She asked for a new dress to wear to church. Roberta bought the dress, a ruffled, sashed pastel affair. When Easter morning came, Roberta looked in on Blanche before she left for the sunrise service. Blanche appeared weak but told her mother she wanted to get dressed for the eleven o'clock service. When William and Roberta returned, Blanche was lying on her bed, fully dressed in her new outfit, dead. She was seventeen. The room was sealed for several years. On the third anniversary of Blanche's death, her mother's heart stopped beating. She was forty-two.

❧

William was not a simple man. From his churchly forum he held sway over hundreds of loyal and loving parishioners. Some were too loving. His reputation as a ladies' man was no secret. According to his sons, their mother showed no obvious resentment at William's philandering. Yet I wonder if her feelings settled heavily in her heart, which gave out years before it should have.

The reverend married two more times. He had become attracted to Alice White Thomas, the dignified, comely wife of one of his ailing parishioners. He made many visits to the bedside of the sick man. After his death, William barely waited a decent interval before he married the widow, known as Miss Alice in the Southern fashion, in 1921.

With his second wife, William acquired a stepdaughter and stepson, Marjorie and Waddell Thomas. Their father had been a hatter to elite white Washington by day, by night the leader of an all-black string quartet that played the White House on a number of occasions. Marjorie, a talented musician in her own right who became the church's pianist, entered the Taylor household as the second new sister. Earlier, William had taken in his younger brother Jesse's child Thelma, known as "T.T.," after the death of her mother when she was twelve years old. Her father had to divide his large brood so that they would all be well cared for. William was pleased to have two girls in his household again.

Waddell Thomas was approaching his twenties when his mother married Reverend Taylor, but he did not follow his sister into the house. In exchange for the security and amenities of a new home, my grandfather wanted Waddell to take the name Taylor. Waddell refused, and went to live with Miss Alice's mother, Sarah White.

When she was a little girl, Sarah, a white-looking mulatto and ex-slave, lived on a farm in Bowling Green, Virginia. The land abutted Garrett's farm, where John Wilkes Booth hid in a barn for two weeks in April 1865 after assassinating President Lincoln. After a hysterical fourteen-day search by the army and secret service forces, Booth was found. The pursuers fired a fusillade of bullets at the barn. One traveled through a crack and shot Booth in the spine, paralyzing him. The barn caught fire. As the barn burned, the captors dragged the assassin to the porch of the farm, where he died.

Sarah White stood among the crowd that gathered when word spread that Booth was in the barn. Someone began to cut Booth's hair and sell it to souvenir hunters. When there was no more hair to cut, the entrepreneurs grabbed the frightened young Sarah, took her behind one of the other farm buildings, and cut her waist-length hair to just below her ears. They scissored it further into dozens of sections and continued to hawk Booth's hair, threatening to punish Sarah if she gave them away. In a sad irony, the hair of the black-but-not-black Sarah White had been transformed into the white hair of one of this country's whitest villains.

My grandfather could be very much the autocrat. He insisted that the family eat together every day. He would not allow his "daughters" Marjorie and T.T. to wear heavy makeup or silk stockings, which he considered common. Despite the ban, the girls wore the stockings and sneaked out, even after he threatened to wrap their limbs in paper. When the girls had gentleman callers, William elicited their detailed biographies before he would permit the girls to leave the house. If they did not make the curfew, he would wait up and lecture them for at least an hour.

Subscribing to the fundamentalist doctrine of the Baptist church, Reverend Taylor forbade theater, but his sons and daughters went nonetheless. Once daughter Marjorie won a bolt of material in the Lincoln Theater talent show for playing the piano. When she told her stepfather how she'd acquired it, he literally cast it out of the house. Another time, when he discovered that Marjorie and T.T. were in the theater, he had them paged and marched them home. Liquor was not supposed to cross the threshold, but the young Taylor men kept bottles hidden in their bedrooms.

William was a fast and reckless driver. Once, while out driving with Miss Alice, Marjorie and T.T., he and Miss Alice argued about his growing attentiveness to a pretty young church member. He was so perturbed by their discussion that he crashed into a wall. No one was hurt. Often he would take the girls with him when he was supposedly going on official church errands. They would remain in the car while he visited with one attractive church member or another.

My grandfather had one son that his family knew about outside the bonds of his marriage. His name was Peter Moore and he lived in Baltimore. It was rumored there were other children as well. My father recognized Peter as his half brother and went to see him whenever he stopped in Baltimore. They exchanged letters and greeting cards. My mother and I met him just once. He was taller and darker than my father, and in my view looked like my grandfather. I did not know until I was in college that he was my grandfather's love child. When he died, my father made the trip from Connecticut to Maryland for his funeral.

∽

After taking ill in Connecticut at Julian's church installation, Alice White Thomas Taylor died of heart trouble in 1933. For a while, the widower William vigorously pursued the beautiful young wife of one of his nephews, both active members of his church. His open attentions generated widespread gossip. The nephew finally left the church, taking his errant wife with him. In an open act of retribution, they became regular members of a rival church.

William's third and last wife, Rosetta Hyman, was a beautiful woman half his age. It was plain that his grown sons were not thrilled with the match, and he tried to win at least one of them over by inviting my mother to visit while Julian was away at a revival. "Rosetta and Margaret are having a lot of fun," William wrote to my father. "The old homestead seems like a real one again."

In any event, the marriage was short-lived; after three months, William died of a heart attack. Funeral coverage by the Washington press was extensive and gossipy. *The Afro American* ran a full page, under the headline "100 Cars in Funeral Cortege." There were three photographs, one of the reverend lying in state in an open coffin, one of the twenty-six presiding ministers leading the funeral procession into the church, and one of the "widowed bride" being supported by two of her stepsons. More than three thousand people were on hand for the funeral service, which was conducted at Vermont Avenue Baptist Church because Florida Avenue could not accommodate such a crowd. Playing to the crowds, his eulogist described Reverend Taylor's life as "tempestuous." Taylor, he said, was "maligned, admired and hated but had pursued his way unafraid until he came gloriously to the end of his career. There was a grim determination about the man who was in every way remarkable."

William's sons idolized him, and agreed that Julian was his favorite. Whatever Julian wanted to do he supported. My mother remembers my grandfather as quietly controlling and demanding of his sons, even after they became adults. He advised and fathered them well into their middle age.

Bill Taylor went on to Howard University Dental School and became a practicing dentist in Raleigh and then in Washington. He married twice and had two sons and a daughter. Clinton returned to the South to teach art at North Carolina Agricultural and Technical University and ultimately became head of the department. He married and had a daughter. Robert Taylor went to Miner Normal School and Howard University. After serving as a first lieutenant in the army, he became a journalist. At one point, he was an assistant to Walter Washington, the first black mayor of Washington, D.C. He married and had a daughter. The children of my uncles were the only first cousins I had.

Percy was the baby of the Taylor family. He studied at Howard University and then at Juilliard. He became a teacher of voice and piano, and an accompanist for soloists and choirs. My father married him to Marguerite Walker, a perky Dunbar High School classmate. With the inheritance from his father's death, he bought a new home in Washington for himself and his bride. We went there once. All I remember were bright white walls, one of which my brother christened with crayons. Percy did not invite us back.

The marriage did not last longer than two years, but Percy and Marguerite remained lifelong friends. He moved to New York, and often came to visit my family in New Haven, bringing an enormous suitcase for a few days' visit. He loved to show us his new jackets or ties or boots. An avid reader, Percy kept up with everything around him. He especially liked to gossip about entertainment figures and their scandals. His behavior was so youthful that we regarded him as an older brother rather than an uncle, a perception he encouraged.

William's stepson, Waddell Thomas, married Irene Lee, the beautiful daughter of a jet black woman and a white man. Irene inherited her father's color. She and Waddell would make a successful life together, he in real estate and she as a much sought-after hostess of Washington's black society. For many years, they lived next door to my uncle Bill, across from Rock Creek Park in the northwest section of Washington known as the "Gold Coast" because of its affluence. Waddell's sister Marjorie worked in his real estate firm, married and had a child, but remained the organist at Florida Avenue for more than forty years. The other Taylor "sister," Thelma (T.T.), also married and remained a lifelong supporter of her uncle William's church.

☙

Just after completing high school, in 1919, Julian married a beautiful, white-looking, strong-willed classmate named Viola Thompson, the daughter of a black woman and a white man. Viola was sixteen and Julian only a year older when they eloped, but the marriage certificate gives his age as twenty-one. Having no money for wedding flowers, he scaled a churchyard fence in Rockville, Maryland, to gather a bouquet of lilacs for his bride.

After their marriage, they went to live with Julian's brother Bill and his first wife, Antoinette. The newlyweds quickly had a son, who died in infancy, then two daughters, Mauryne and Doris. To support his family, Julian took a series of jobs, including insurance salesman, dance teacher, radio disc jockey (he was known as "The Lonesome Lover"), concert soloist and evangelist. He also enrolled at Howard University, where his father taught courses in religion and preaching. Whenever he could, Julian assisted his father in the Florida Avenue pulpit.

Julian's first official ministerial "call" came from Ebenezer Baptist Church, a small congregation in Martinsburg, West Virginia. A practicing Catholic, Viola accompanied him reluctantly. There were continuing conflicts over finances, what Julian was going to do, and where they were going to live. The couple were separated more than they were together, and they finally divorced when the girls were on the verge of adolescence. Viola took and held for years a job that was considered a plum for colored people of that time. She was an elevator operator in one of Washington's premier department stores, Woodard & Lothrop, a position awarded only to light-skinned Negroes.

Julian lived with various friends, touching base frequently at the family home. Despite his failed marriage, he still wanted to follow in his father's ministerial footsteps. He continued his studies and, probably because of the congregation's response to his separation, left Ebenezer to become a full-time assistant pastor at Florida Avenue. Under William's tutelage, Julian expanded the ministerial career that he had begun in West Virginia. His father made certain he was exposed to other ministers and their congregations. It was on one of their joint pastoral duties that he met my mother, in the hot summer of 1932.

It is not often that a wake is the site of the beginning of romance.

In that drab year, Margaret Morris was twenty. She was slender and well formed, and her voice was soft, with a trace of a Southern accent. Thanks to Mitt, her manners were those of a boarding school graduate. In Thelma's large black picture hat and an unadorned black dress, she resembled Merle Oberon. Among those who found the beautiful girl in the parlor's front row alluring was the son of the presiding minister. Julian slipped a note into a hymnal inviting her to join him in the funeral cortege to Arlington National Cemetery and passed it to her. She accepted. Her new romance started amid stately trees, white tombstones and American flags on land that had once belonged to her ancestors.

Chapter Six

I suppose too my family directly and my people indirectly have given me the kind of strength that enables me to go anywhere.

—MAYA ANGELOU, quoted in *Voices of Struggle, Voices of Pride*

The first seventeen years of my life were bounded by my parents and siblings, the white working-class town in which we lived, and the black churches that nourished us. I thought that our life was ordinary but we did extraordinary things. Now I understand that we did indeed live extraordinary lives. My childhood was a place without shadows. There really were white Christmases, bright blue Octobers and jars of fireflies in July. Some would say it was an idyll, and it almost was.

In the spring of 1992, when I was looking through some of my father's papers, I came across forty-seven small books filled with his notations. They were his diaries, dating from 1934 to 1981, which my mother had saved. Each year the color of the book changed. He kept them in his inside jacket pocket, and I remembered seeing him write in them daily, but I never thought much about them. I looked to see what was there.

In the muted rainbow of those slim volumes, my father had documented his own history. A meticulous but terse diarist, he recorded the events of his life and often his thoughts about them. There were notes on his meetings, appointments, purchases of clothes and household items, movies, births of his children, family illnesses and deaths. Much could be read between the lines.

As reflected in his diary, there was little comfort anywhere in

1937, the year Ansonia's Macedonia Baptist Church welcomed my father as its new pastor. The church facing the river had eighty names on its membership rolls. There was no savings, no bank account and no credit. Julian had negotiated a salary of twenty-five dollars a week, which turned out to be an elusive sum. Each Sunday eighteen or nineteen dollars, mostly in change, barely covered the smooth green-felt bottom of the silver collection plates. Sometimes the deacons thought gifts of cakes, pies, fried chicken and chitterlings would satisfy the deficit.

To his congregation and other Negroes that he met, Julian sold life insurance that covered the cost of a decent burial and gave the beneficiary a handful of change. In the black community, it was important to go out in style. So many colored people lived such hard and meager lives, they were determined to be well talked about, well turned out and well put away on the day of their death. It was a steady way for Julian to earn pocket change. When his parishioners died, they rarely left wills. He was generally named executor of their estates, which brought another supplement to his fluctuating salary.

Instead of waiting for people to come to the church, Julian took his ministry to the streets. In his creased fedora, tailored suits and highly polished shoes, he strode down Main Street and through the Negro sections of the town, touching his hat to the ladies, cajoling every colored person he met to come to Macedonia. He exempted only the bars. He knocked on doors and introduced himself, made himself at home, drank tea and ate whatever was offered. He had the special gift of being able to listen to people as if their every utterance was profound. If they were not members of his church, he invited them to come. And people did come, if only out of curiosity or embarrassment at first.

He had his hair cut and shoes shined in the one black barbershop in town, a center of news, gossip and humor where he never missed an opportunity to proselytize. The Masons and the Elks invited him to join their lodges, giving him new fields to furrow. From the very first he left no doubt that he wanted to assist the Negroes of the town in gaining more education, better jobs and better housing. He introduced himself at city hall, and made sure he was informed about or invited to work on community projects that involved better opportunities for his people. In a short time, he had the reputation of being dignified, educated and accessible.

Older colored men, sometimes in soiled work clothes, sometimes in rumpled, ill-fitting suits, would regularly come to see my father, carrying school books in hands soiled from a day's work. He would escort them into his study where they sat for an hour or more in private, reading the Bible or a first-grade primer together. Through the walls I could hear their murmuring voices hesitating and stumbling over word after word. I thought it strange that these grown-up visitors had such difficulty pronouncing easy words like "the" and "men."

I did not understand until I was about six years old that my father was in fact teaching them to read—and especially to read the Bible. He explained that I should not belittle them because of their illiteracy, telling me how hard their lives had been in the South, how they had been forced to leave school early to help support their families. He continued to have students at home until his death, quietly teaching scores of black men to read.

He succeeded in establishing a line of credit for Macedonia. Then he began a fund-raising campaign for improvements to the church and for a parsonage. His first target was the owner of one of the foundries that employed most of his congregation. Soon thereafter, down from one of Ansonia's few mansions in the hills came a check for stained-glass windows.

To be a successful black Baptist minister, one must be a consummate politician. There are members to please, deacons to stroke, trustees to reign in and many women to fend off. My father ran a "preacher's church." He selected the deacons and the trustees and they followed his agenda. He reported to no one. From the womb he understood the importance of music in the Negro church, and among his first tasks were a revitalization of the senior choir, the formation of a junior choir and the development of a gospel chorus. He also organized a drum-and-bugle corps, which the church outfitted with gray and blue uniforms and full instrumentation. He formed clubs for every age and interest, including a Negro History Club, under whose auspices he presented an annual Emancipation Day Address, to which he invited the entire community.

He remained pastor at Macedonia for forty-two years, not only building a spiritual home of more than five hundred members, but also creating a powerful political and social base. He was the first black to serve on many of the town's boards and commissions. He became the chairman of the Town Planning Commission, an important locus of power.

He quietly integrated the local YMCA. With great hoopla, he brought Jackie Robinson to speak at the local high school. He encouraged the young people of his church to go to college, often giving them money out of his own pocket for applications and entrance exams. When the teenage son of one of the congregation families was arrested and falsely charged with raping a white girl, my father raised the money for his defense and got him a white lawyer from New Haven who successfully defended him. Knowing the importance of organized group pressure in such cases, he formed a local chapter of the NAACP, over which he presided for thirty-five years.

He was the first Negro to run for political office in Ansonia, and on the Democratic ticket at that. He was so confident he would win that he did not campaign, and his loss staggered him. For weeks he did not venture out into the community except to go to church, until finally my mother said, "Get up out of that bed and go act as if nothing happened."

Like many other Negroes, my father felt a deep kinship for FDR, whom he had met on a number of occasions. He hosted an event for Mary McLeod Bethune and her friend Mrs. Roosevelt. He was an advisor to Roosevelt's "Shadow Cabinet," the group of Negroes who counseled the president on racial issues. On a warm April day my mother called me in from the sidewalk in front of the house, where I had been practicing cartwheels. I saw my father slumped over in his chair, his knees pressed together. I was amazed to see tears rolling down his long nose into his handkerchief. No one had told me that fathers cried. I thought one of his brothers must have died. My mother told me it was the president. She said we all had lost a good friend. I patted my father's arm and told him I was sorry about his friend.

My father was a tireless campaigner for causes and candidates, and on occasion for hire. "Nothing wrong with it," his father wrote to him about his attempts to secure a commitment as a campaign speaker on one occasion. "Everyone who can is endeavoring to get a little rake off during this political campaign. If you can get anything, go to it. I have been appointed to the Republican committee, but I have not done anything about it yet, well, your man Roosevelt went over for another term. Maybe your address last Sunday night helped to put him over." My father's favorite story was about how he came to campaign for John F. Kennedy. He had met and worked with the senator on several occasions. Just before the West Virginia primary in May 1960, he was conducting a week of nightly revival services in Chicago. On the last day of the revival, he was in Chicago shopping for a new suit for himself and a dress for my mother when the manager of the store came up and asked if he was Reverend Taylor from Connecticut. Governor Ribicoff was urgently trying to reach him. Senator Kennedy had asked the governor to see if my father would go to West Virginia and campaign for him among the Negro groups. He was on a plane the next day and Kennedy won the state. My father always concluded the story, "For me the joy and wonder of the event was that a Jewish governor had asked a Negro minister to work as hard as he could for a Roman Catholic Irish senator who wanted to be president of the United States. I believe that's the way our country should work."

As a result of his work for Kennedy, my father became Connecticut's first black delegate at large to the Democratic National Convention. We watched him on national television when Kennedy's victory was announced, smiling broadly and yelling at the top of his lungs in an uncharacteristically undignified moment of pure joy.

❧

My father's private persona was quite different from his public image. At home he was a reserved but dominant presence. My earliest and constant memory of him was in his dark red armchair, reading the paper or a crime story and listening to the news on the radio. There was always a Philip Morris cigarette hanging lightly from his thin, well-manicured left hand. We learned early not to disturb him when he was listening to the news. With an ear for future sermon material, he avidly digested the commentaries of

Gabriel Heatter and Edward R. Murrow. He spent most of his spare time reading. There was always a newspaper, magazine or book in his hand or on his lap. He had inherited a library of several thousand books from his father. He read the Bible, history, the classics, philosophy and other literary sources when he was preparing a sermon. When he tired of reading, he sat at the piano, softly playing and singing songs like "Indian Love Call" and "The Chocolate Soldier" in his clear lyric tenor. He played just well enough to accompany himself. Sometimes he whistled his songs instead of singing them. His whistle, like his voice, had a tremulous vibrato that made us children laugh.

Words to my father were like jewels to be set out, turned over, polished and studied. His extensive knowledge of Latin and Greek made him precise in his use of language. His enunciation and diction were flawless, carryovers, he said, from his father's oratorical style. There was no trace of his Southern upbringing in his speech. He had a habit of speaking in a soft, measured way as if he were weighing what he was going to say, even about humorous things. His humor was subtle and dry, and he had a cackle rather than a laugh. Rarely, when he was exceedingly angry and only at home, my father used one curse word, "dammit." He said it quickly and precisely, so that you mostly heard the "damn" part with the "it" coming out as if he were clearing his throat.

His speech was always formal, but it seemed natural, without pretense. He was fond of archaic words and British modes of spelling. Entertainment for him was "intertainment." He "motored" instead of drove. When he had had enough to eat he would say, "I have had a gracious plenty." If he felt a woman's behavior or dress was not ladylike, he referred to her as a "strumpet," rolling the "r" in his low deep voice. We loved to hear my father say both "dammit" and "strumpet," because he pronounced them with exquisite articulation, grave dignity and utter disgust. His next best and more frequently used epithet was "devilish." From time to time, people, things, our behavior and our German shepherd, Queenie, were "devilish."

Although he always seemed occupied, my father took time to answer my questions. He enjoyed my curiosity as much as the opportunity to be an authority, and he used the Socratic method of asking questions to teach. The fact that I liked to read as much as he did brought him enormous satisfaction. When I needed it, he helped me with my homework. As I got older, he took particular interest in how I handled my writing and English assignments. From him I learned that ideas had little worth if they could not be communicated clearly and well.

In the pulpit, he tailored his sermons to the occasion and his audience. His homilies were a mixture of the homespun and the intellectual, and the congregation was always amused when he used a current slang expression appropriately. Unfailingly he wove the events of the day or the trends of the moment into his message. Once in 1954 when I was a junior in high school, I came home to find my father weeping and writing at the dining room table. He was using a fountain pen and his tears were creating blotches on the lined paper. My mother was sitting across the table from him with a pleased expression on her face. The juxtaposition of their moods confused me. She said my father had just received word from the national office of the NAACP that the Supreme Court had overturned *Plessy v. Ferguson* in favor of school desegregation. He was writing his sermon for Sunday: "The Moral Choice: The Only Choice."

Image as well as substance were important to him. He projected the languid yet formal persona of an upper-class British gentleman. His slender, elegant frame never carried more than 140 pounds, and he tended a large wardrobe of expensive, tailored suits, including half a dozen white ones for summer. He had his size-six-and-a-half wingtips shined once a week at the barbershop, and buffed them himself each morning, fastidiously and with great ceremony. He completed his outfits with an array of hats, from Russian toques to wool berets. Regularly he would drive to a hat factory in Danbury, where he bought expensive headwear at factory prices. The top of his neatly arranged closet was crowded with gray and cream-colored oval boxes that protected his felt fedoras and Panama straws.

He was only five foot nine, but his erect posture and uplifted chin added the illusion of several inches to his stature. He had an unusual, determined, slew-footed gait like that of a dancer. Because he thought it demeaning, common and ungentlemanly, he would not carry packages in public. He insisted that groceries be loaded into his car. Often he reminded us that his father never carried anything heavier than a letter.

In harmony with the rest of his form, his hands were small and expressive. He frequently rested them together at the tip of his nose or the bottom of his chin, as if in prayer. He was especially proud of his handwriting, an even, backward-slanting script that looked like calligraphy. When I married, he spent the better part of a week carefully inscribing names and addresses on five hundred invitations. Although proficient at the typewriter, he wrote many of his sermons in longhand. Carrying on his father's tradition, he took pleasure in writing letters to his brothers, colleagues and friends. Whenever he went away, he would send each of us a post-card. Even as a grown woman, I looked forward to seeing that distinctive, oblique handwriting in the mail.

No matter the occasion, my father always wore a suit, a fresh shirt and one of the hundreds of silk ties he collected. The only time I saw him roll up his sleeves, and then with finicky neatness, just a little above the wrist, was when he painted or cooked, the only physical labor he ever did. He looked incongruous at the stove in a white shirt, a tie and dark pants, wearing one of my mother's aprons, but he made wonderful biscuits, stews, neck bones, scrambled eggs and liver, the foods of his native North Carolina.

Many Baptists with Southern roots believe that dancing and drinking are the tools of the devil. My father did not subscribe to that type of religious fundamentalism. In spite of his own father's remonstrations, he had been a ballroom dancer in his youth, and he cut a graceful figure on the dance floor. In a few rare moments of abandon, he dropped his reserve and gave me professional demonstrations of the Charleston and the Black Bottom. He also taught me to waltz, telling me to imagine that I was a leaf being blown in patterns around the dance floor.

Nor did he consider it a sin to enjoy a glass of brandy or wine with my mother. Ansonia was no place for him to drink publicly, but in a few clubs in New York or at restaurants out of town, he might have one—just one—drink. The only time he ever allowed himself to become inebriated, to my knowledge, was at the wedding of Governor Ribicoff's son. After he had drunk several glasses of champagne, he said to my mother, "Margaret, I do believe I am a trifle tipsy."

Although he had played baseball in his high school days, my father did not fish, play tennis, golf or attend sporting events. But he had a group of friends, mostly ministers or politicians, with whom he shared more contemplative pursuits. One minister always began his phone calls with a Latin quotation for my father to identify. With other friends he discussed the Great Books, politics and Sherlock Holmes.

Although generous on his own terms, my father did not like us to ask him for money. He gave us a weekly allowance from the time we started school to the end of the twelfth grade. I remember that mine started at twenty-five cents. By the time I was in high school, I got three dollars a week. He did not keep up with inflation.

Like his own father, my father loved driving and cars. Both the activity and the machine were extensions of his persona, but he was not interested in mechanics. His was one of very few Cadillacs in the town. As soon as vanity plates were created, he installed REVT on his bumpers. No one else in the family was allowed to drive his cars until he was well into his sixties. When I was small, I was proud of the big shiny cars I rode in. As a teenager I found them ostentatious. By my twenties, I had come full circle. Once again I was proud of the big shiny cars.

༄

When I was around ten, I came home from school one day to a quiet house and a church member dressed in white, who explained that my mother was at the hospital because my father had had a heart attack. I had no idea what that was. Late that night, my mother came home and told us my father was going to be all right, but we would have to be quiet and good so as not to upset him. After a week in the hospital, he came home and rested in bed for another two weeks. We had never seen him sick or in bed so long. Everything in the house revolved around his illness. He recovered, but he would suffer from a heart condition for the rest of his life. We never got over the fear that he might suddenly leave us.

Even before his illness, there was a distance to my father that kept him unknowable; a secret hidden, a transgression harbored. I felt I could never get to his center. For my father, as Shakespeare said, it was not an easy thing to play on the instrument of the soul. Many years later I would learn that a scandal haunted him, although its details had been expunged from the family's memory. It happened before he met my mother, and he had closed and locked the door on that dark corner of his life.

Whatever was in my father's past, it is clear that his marriage to my mother dramatically altered the course of his life. Nor would my mother's story have taken its unusual turns, or been as sharply etched, without the deep and lasting influence of my father's family.

❧

When I first read about Irene, the heroine of *The Forsythe Saga*, I thought of my mother: someone I experienced mainly through my senses. Although she was often tentative, diffident and even shy, her physical presence—her looks, her scent and sound—enveloped me and made me feel safe.

From the time I was very little, I thought my mother was beautiful and kind. I remember watching her as she put Pond's cold cream on her face each night. In the morning, she would rinse it off, put on a light red lipstick and powder and be ready for the day. A prominent dark mole accented her large, sad dark eyes and set off her soft, unlined ivory skin. She never wore eye makeup or rouge. Her skin mirrored the emotions below its surface, without reservation. Her hair was fine, with a natural curl, and she never took much time with it.

Her voice was soft and girlish. Unlike my father, she had a hint of a Southern accent. If you listened carefully, you could hear an elusive sadness in her voice. When she was provoked, the Furies burst forth, but they did not stay long. She rarely held a grudge.

With her agreement and at her request, my father selected my mother's entire wardrobe, Pygmalion to her Galatea. He shopped for her in New Haven, Waterbury, Bridgeport, Hartford and New York. When he traveled, which was often, he would always return with a large box. I loved to sit on my mother's bed as she unwrapped a beautiful dress or hat from some glittering emporium in the city my father had conquered. He bought her vibrant prints, expensive tailored afternoon suits, luxurious satin, velvet and silk cocktail dresses. He especially liked to present her with large picture hats of straw, wool, fur, velvet, flowers and feathers. Hanging in her closet, her clothes were redolent of her favorite perfumes, White Shoulders, My Sin and Lavender.

There was an innate elegance about her slender frame and photogenic features that made her a couturier's vision. Even housedresses looked good on her. She sometimes said she would like to dress less dramatically, but her desire to please my father was more important to her than her own needs. From my father's point of view, dressing my mother well was his way of telling her, "You are beautiful; you are special; you are loved," words she had never heard when she was young. In addition, he saw her as an extension of himself. She could not look less than perfect.

In all her outfits, despite their drama, my mother appeared beautiful, fragile and ladylike. But when she was feeling uncertain, tired or insecure, or when too many eyes were on her, her posture drooped and she seemed to cave in upon herself, as if she were shielding herself from some ancient hurt.

∞

My mother was always at home with us. As a motherless child, she had vowed never to leave her children. Her vision of us was idealized. No one else was as smart, pretty and talented as her children. She wanted us to be well bred, well educated and successful. As we grew toward adolescence, she did not require us to do household chores. If we volunteered to help, she was delighted, but she told everyone she was not raising her daughters to be maids. She herself, however, took great pleasure in keeping our clothes clean. Before we had a washing machine, she laundered everything by hand and kept us spotless.

On steamy summer days after lunch, until we were fifteen or sixteen, Jewelle, Pattee, Brother and I had to rest and be quiet for a part of the day. When we got up just before dinner, my mother insisted that we put on the outfits she'd freshly ironed and starched. When I saw *Gone With the Wind* for the first time, I was surprised that Scarlett and her friends had to rest after lunch like I did.

A minister's wife automatically becomes a hostess and a church leader. The role brought out my mother's natural friendliness and warmth, but she could also be fierce when the occasion warranted. Once, as a favor to a congregation mother who was ailing along with several of her children, she went to see the school nurse, a giant of a woman who was infamous for her rudeness and said to be particularly unkind to colored children. Without identifying herself, my mother attempted to explain the children's absence from school. The nurse was dismissive, then irate. When she attempted to push my mother down the stairs to her office, Margaret turned and kicked the giant solidly in the shin. Outraged at the behavior of the "fresh young upstart" she had taken for a white teenager, the nurse agreed to drop charges only after the local paper ran the story under the headline "Minister's Wife Plays David to School Nurse's Goliath." The congregation was thrilled.

As with her children, my mother never doubted that my father was the smartest and most clever man she knew. She expected him to take care of all business and budgeting matters and do the food shopping. After she spent the inheritance from her uncle, she had no money of her own, and my father did not give her an allowance. Entries in his diary reveal small disbursements of cash to her.

In 1945, my mother unexpectedly received another inheritance, from Rebecca Allen, the woman who had been her family's next-door neighbor before her mother's death and caretaker to her younger brother, Michael. It included a small house, an insurance policy and some cash. My mother sold the house and cashed in the policy to help my father buy a frame apartment building that housed eight white families on our street in Ansonia. The apartment building was the first of a number of properties that my parents acquired that supported a comfortable lifestyle and paid for costly educations. Whenever white tenants moved out of the building and there were Negroes we knew who needed an apartment, my father rented to them.

My mother held only one paying job during her life, as a part-time census taker in 1950. The person who hired her listed her race as white, which my mother corrected before he could lift the pen from the page. She enjoyed getting out of the house and finding out about other people's lives. My father looked upon the assignment as an important civic duty, a federal responsibility and a step forward for the race. But later when she was offered a part-time position as a saleswoman in the town's only dress store, he became incensed. "No wife of mine," he said, "would work in a department store." That was the last time my mother sought work.

About the time I became a freshman in high school, I began to chide my mother about her acquiescence to my father. He had taught his children to be independent, assertive and freethinking, but we lived in the house with a woman who did his every bidding. I would tell her she should make up her own mind and do what she wanted to do. Sometimes she would commit a contrary act in laughing conspiracy with me, although it was always so insignificant that my father would be unlikely to know the difference.

The older I got, the more aware and less accepting I was of my father's dominance over my mother. But I could push her only so far. I finally understood that he could not dominate if she did not willingly submit. In many ways, he was the father and older brothers she had lost. She would offer to him all the things she had not been able to give them.

Mother's love of animals was famous. In addition to our resident dog and cats, she took in stray cats, dogs, birds, turtles and chickens. She also acquired a neighbor's parrot, which was said to be seventy-five. The bird talked in spurts and had an extensive vocabulary of obscenities, learned from one of its previous owners. When church members came to the house for meetings, the door to the kitchen where the parrot was kept remained closed. When it got angry, its yellow eyes would turn dark, it would ruffle its feathers, and just like my father it would say "dammit" very quickly. The only way to stop the bird from talking was to cover its cage or feed it ice cream, which it ate from its own silver baby spoon that it held in one claw, while balancing on the other scabrous leg. Reverend Taylor's swearing parrot was a town legend.

Once, while visiting an animal farm in Liberia as part of a delegation negotiating for land on behalf of the National Baptist Convention, my father made the mistake of saying that he loved animals. Months later, he received a crate containing a pair of Liberian monkeys. There were no instructions with them, so we decided to let them loose in the garage until we could build a cage for them. The next morning, while we were dressing for church, the phone rang. It was a neighbor, calling to say that there were two monkeys on the roof of the garage, and she had not been drinking. Armed with bananas and what I thought sounded like monkey noises, I managed to retrieve them. We named them Cain and Abel and they lived happily with my parents for many years.

∽

During the years my father was becoming a citizen of note, my mother devoted most of her time to raising her family and supporting my father's work. Outside of the church, her social life was geared to the Negro circles of New Haven, Waterbury and Bridgeport. She founded the Southern Connecticut Chapter of the Links, a national Negro women's civic organization. In her life at home, in the church and in her community, my mother had found a comfortable, safe place at last.

Beyond the church clubs and auxiliaries, my parents had another social life. With their friends the Keyeses they saw the exhibits at the New York World's Fair of 1939. In summer they went to the horse races at Saratoga or visited friends in Cape May, New Jersey. Fall took them to New York and shows at the Cotton Club. They had friends in all of Connecticut's larger cities. I thought their life was glamorous and exciting.

Despite their sophistication, my parents shared a bent toward the mystical. My mother talked about her mother's ghost. My father spellbound us with the tale of his familiar. The first time I heard it, we were sitting around the table after dinner on a late winter's afternoon. There had been an ice storm, and the rime-wrapped branches scraped against the window and glittered in the waning sunlight as my father spun out the story in his soft, precise voice.

He was a young man in Washington, D.C., driving alone at night and extremely tired. He knew he was nodding, but thought he could make it home. Suddenly a small hand on his shoulder gently shook him awake. His car had crossed the divider into oncoming traffic. Veering in time to miss the grille of a taxi, he pulled the car over to the side of the road and came to a stop outside the wall of the cemetery where his mother was buried. He knew it was her hand that had awakened and saved him. Later in my life, I came to understand that my father had a flair for the dramatic. Nonetheless, I believed the story then, and I believe it now.

Why, I have since wondered, has my family always been attracted to ancient spirits and beguiling ghosts? Is it that we are obliged by some barely remembered covenants to carry around our ancestors and their lives in our psyches? Do we project their essences onto restless souls that lurk in corners looking for company? In short, do the wraiths know that we will welcome them? Or have we simply inherited the genes of fantasy, imagination and tale-telling from our mingled roots?

∽

In the late summer of 1942, when I was five years old, my father's church was finally able to buy a parsonage in Ansonia. The century-old frame house a half block from the church would be our home for fourteen years.

The parsonage sat about fifty feet above the west bank of the Naugatuck. It was one of two houses that had been built on Clifton Avenue for the first managers of the mills, a homey, modest structure. On one side was a porch crowding a small yard. On the other was a tangle of trees and weeds rising out of a deep gully, a runoff to the river. I thought our location was exciting, almost dangerous, because of the way the land behind the house dropped precipitously toward the water. My mother and I looked at the river every day from the kitchen or dining room windows. We knew the way the light played on its pools and eddies. We knew where the large rocks were, and where the pools of oil would form at the edges.

One cold February week, there was a new configuration of light and shadow in the middle of the water. A large pale blue hump caused the water to part around it. My mother asked me if I saw it. She thought it looked like part of a body, but she was not certain. I thought it looked like a woman lying on her side. We went outside to get a closer look, but we were too far away to see what it really was.

My mother called the police. They waded out midstream with hooks and grapples. From the water they lifted an old white woman's rigid body. She wore only a pale blue dress and a gray sweater. We did not know her. Her body had evidently washed down from a town farther upstream. How sad, I thought, that an old woman could lie there dead in the river, and no one had been searching for her. What kind of family, I wondered, could she have been from?

∽

Our new home faced a cluster of one- and two-family frame houses that sheltered black, Irish, Czechoslovakian, Italian, Polish and Greek families. Ansonia was a magnet for immigrants, and there was no getting away from mixtures.

This was the geography of my childhood. Three wiry white women with curly white hair and pale, pink-rimmed eyes lived next door. They moved and looked like large white rabbits. To me, all three appeared to be the same age and never seemed to get older as long as we lived there. They were the Hazzards, a mother, her sister-in-law and her daughter, Irish descendants of the early mill supervisors who had been the first inhabitants of their house. They were helpful and gracious to my parents, although they never had them over to dinner.

Next to the Hazzards were a black couple, Miss Hattie and Dave Antrum, who looked after Dave's pretty nieces, Evelyn and Corrine Tucker. Miss Hattie was a stolid little woman who wore tiny hats on the side of her head and carried large pocketbooks high under her arm, moving so deliberately that she gave the impression of someone three times her size. She passed our house each morning at six o'clock and like an alarm clock called out, "Good morning, Rev." Up from the Antrums were the Spaders, a Polish family with two blond sons. Their mother wore a babushka and cotton dresses all year round.

Directly across from the parsonage, from the second-floor porch of her dark red shingled house, grizzled, chocolate-colored Mrs. Randolf kept watch on her taciturn son, Buster, and the rest of the street. Her parents had been among the group that founded Macedonia, a legacy that made her one of its most important members. Buster was dark like his mother and wore his hair conked. He wore a black leather jacket and a motorcycle cap and rode enormous black motorcycles, a fleet of which bordered the house.

The Tinneys' land flanked Mrs. Randolf's. The Tinney family looked more Indian than the black they were called. Their hair was straight, their noses large and prominently curved, and their skin the color of red clay. Good-looking and solid, Howie Tinney was one of Jewelle's classmates and my childhood heroes. His head was permanently tilted as if listening to music that only he could hear. His handsome uncle, Nornie Tinney, walked briskly by the parsonage each morning at seven with his Indian-straight hair slicked back. "Get up Shirl and Pat, it's time for school," he bellowed in passing.

Beyond the Tinneys', the land became rocky, steep and wooded. At its end, half a mile away, perched the Russian Orthodox church, looking like something out of a fairy tale. Bricks the color of pumpkin formed its walls and turrets, which were capped by aqua-colored minarets and spires. I was intensely curious about what went on in the church, but I never went inside.

Down past Mrs. Randolph's, toward our church, lived Mrs. Nugent, a white-haired Irish widow with the septuagenarian parrot she later gave to my mother when she moved. Over Mrs. Nugent lived the Hodios, a ruddy-faced policeman and his mother who never failed to remind me how much they admired my father and liked my mother. Between the Hodios' and the church was the neighborhood grocery store, owned by the immigrant Russian family who lived above it. We had a charge account there, which I freely used for essentials like chocolate milk, small pies, Devil Dogs, gum, candy and potato chips.

Beside the church was an apothecary that had been there since the 1920s. Musty and dark, McQuade's filled prescriptions and carried greeting cards and boxes of candy as well. Its most attractive feature was its infrequently patronized soda fountain. Thin, gray-haired Mr. McQuade was a kindly, gentle man with watery blue eyes and a neat mustache who prepared prescriptions and made ice cream sodas with equal lassitude. Next door was Muzzi's, a luncheonette run by Mr. Musante, a little sallow Italian who always wore a soiled tan apron and was full of gossip for his patrons.

Across the street was my favorite neighborhood store, Fitzi's. Mrs. Fitzgerald was a plump woman as pleasant as her husband was dour. Fitzi walked with a deep limp, dragging one leg and cradling one arm, which was paralyzed from elbow to fingertips.

His stock-in-trade was comic books, magazines, cigarettes, newspapers, candy, small gift items and perfume. After Sunday school we'd gather at Fitzi's lunch counter to drink cherry Cokes or eat chocolate nut sundaes before the regular church service. My father bought his newspaper at Fitzi's, and I stopped there most days after school to browse through the comics and movie magazines.

Next door was Bogen's, a murky little candy store whose owners were an old, quiet immigrant couple. Barely distinguishable from each other, the Bogens wore shapeless cardigans and shuffled around their shop. They reminded me of people I had seen in the newsreels leaving the bombed villages of Europe. There was never very much in their display cases. Over their store lived the family of two of my closest childhood friends, some more Tinneys, Judy and Sissie. Their father, Babe, would become the town's first black policeman.

My play area extended to Wooster Street, which sloped down into the sandy flat land that bordered the river. At the top of the hill was the other candy store in the neighborhood, which was operated by Phil Lipman, one of the few Jews in town. Because he specialized in baseball cards and adventure comic books, the neighborhood boys were in and out of his store in running clusters. Phil's was not a must stop on my itinerary.

The trees on Wooster Street seemed taller and greener to me. The inhabitants of that leafy street were mostly Negroes. If the road had been unpaved, it would have seemed like a neighborhood in a small Southern town. Midway down the street, the Douglas family ran one of the town's two black-owned retail establishments, a small grocery store. On Wooster Street I traded comic books and early romantic crushes with Nummy and Lennie Mayo, the tall sons of Charlotte Johnson, the church's short, dynamic choir leader. They lived next to Agnes Hartsfield, a chunky, studious girl with thick glasses, with whom I shared secrets and movie magazines in her deep green backyard.

By an S-shaped curve in the river, just a few hundred yards down from and in back of the parsonage, there was a wide, sandy embankment that stretched for almost a mile alongside the railroad tracks. We called it the Sandbank. There the neighborhood children would gather every afternoon. In the Sandbank's tall brown grass, the younger ones would play cowboys-and-Indians, cops-and-robbers or hide-and-seek until snow covered the ground, while older children and teenagers played softball.

By day, the Sandbank was considered a safe haven. At twilight, however, the Silver Man appeared and roamed the barren fields and their environs until dawn. His legend was based on a series of incidents that had supposedly occurred in our neighborhood. A white man had covered himself with luminous silver paint and run naked through and near the Sandbank at night. It was said that he'd molested several young children. He was never apprehended.

My mother was equivocal when I asked her whether the stories about the Silver Man were true. The possibility of his arrival was a strong motivator in emptying out the Sandbank at dusk and keeping children from playing too late on the street. For many years, just before I went to sleep, I would peer out my window across the low rippling water, hoping and hoping not to catch a glimpse of him. Later I realized that in my way of thinking the Silver Man came to stand for the white man and the bad things he could do to black children.

☙

Originally, what is now Ansonia had been part of the town of Derby. In 1800, Derby was the site of the annual statewide Negro "election" that had formerly been held in Hartford. Negroes gathered from all parts of the state to elect a "governor" and to parade, feast and dance. The governor, who usually claimed direct descent from an African king, had authority to settle disputes and to impose fines and other punishments for flagrant misconduct.

In 1864, Anson Phelps put his brass and copper mills on Derby acreage. A new town, named for him, grew up around them, populated by the first Irish labor he imported to build the dam that would drive the mills. From then on, Ansonia's history was recorded in its mills. First they produced clocks and textiles, and, later, heavy machinery. Farrell Foundry and American Brass squatted in the town's center, large and dour, dominating its life economically, physically and spiritually. Around the clock their chimneys spewed soot and ashes that covered nearby houses and stores. Out from the bellies of the blast furnaces lumbered machinery to be shipped to Cuba, South America and other exotic places where few Ansonians ever traveled.

Almost all the men, Negro and white, worked in the mills. Some of the women also found jobs there, doing light assembly tasks. But the majority of colored women were relegated to work as domestics for the small group of white people who were merchants, professionals or middle managers in the mills. There were two black professionals, one a heavyset, placid dentist, Dr. Foeman, who worked but did not live in Ansonia. The other was a tall, handsome metallurgist who worked in Farrell Foundry but lived in New Haven. He did not speak to the other Negro workers, nor to my father.

The Irish controlled the town's politics, the school system and the police department. The Italians came next in the ethnic pecking order, then the Poles, the Russians and finally the blacks. There were several churches and numerous taverns for white people. In addition, there were Polish, Irish, Italian and Russian social centers. It was not until the 1950s that these places gingerly opened their doors to blacks. Years later, I would be feted with a baby shower for my first child in the Polish Hall. There were two movie houses and one of everything else: high school, newspaper, ice cream parlor and library.

The two movie houses were the Capitol and the Tremont. The Capitol presented itself as a modest version of an old-style movie palace, with velvet curtains and a brass-enclosed balcony. It was a far cry from the Palace in Waterbury. The Tremont had no such pretensions. It was a much smaller, odorous, poorly maintained auditorium in the heart of the Negro community.

When I was eight, my brother took me to the Tremont to see my first Frankenstein film. He had told my parents we were going to see a Betty Grable musical at the Capitol. We had to cross the town's main bridge and travel several blocks to reach the theater. It was an icy Saturday afternoon. In that ill-smelling theater, the images of the misshapen giant terrified me. I wanted to leave, but my brother said I would have to walk home alone. We stayed for the second picture, which was Lon Chaney, Jr., in *The Wolf Man*. By the time the double feature was over, the sunny day had turned into a dark, chilly evening. My brother kept running ahead and teasing me that Frankenstein was following us across the deserted bridge.

Meeting and recreational places for blacks in Ansonia were few. For Negro men, there were two popular, modest bars, Bing's Tavern on Main Street and Collins' Grille on Tremont. My father never went to bars, but in the middle of one night, he was summoned to Bing's. Bing's beautiful wife, Milly, of the long hair and wide Lena Horne smile, had had her throat slit by a former boyfriend, nearly decapitating her. The event made me uneasy about bars in general, which I linked with glamour, unrequited love, murder and death. When I was twenty-one, however, Bing called and told me he had a wedding present for me. Heads turned as I came in, because it was known that the Taylor girls did not go to bars. I sat down with Bing at a nondescript table in the big, dimly lit room, and without asking, he ordered a Shirley Temple for Shirley Taylor. He told me he could not attend the wedding, but he handed me an envelope that contained a hundred-dollar bill.

Besides the bars, for Negro men there was a dark, dingy room, elegantly named the Southern Men's Club, an Elks Hall and the barbershop. There were no meeting places for Negro women, not even a beauty parlor. Women had their hair done in people's homes. If they wanted and could afford the luxury of a Negro salon, they had to travel eight miles to New Haven.

When we first moved to Ansonia, the local YMCA did not allow Negroes to use its facilities. There was nowhere for Negro children to learn to swim except for scouting programs, and few Negro children joined those groups, whose activities, interests and costs were at odds with their essentially rural Southern culture.

When I was six years old, my father took me to the annual Sunday school picnic, held at a small, murky pond and wooded area on the town's eastern slope, the unofficial recreation spot for black people. There was no lifeguard, and very few of the church members knew how to swim. As I stood at the edge of the water, I heard yelling and saw picknickers running back and forth on the far side of the pond. Two teenage girls had stepped into a hole over their heads. Transfixed, I watched as one managed to propel herself to the shallows, while the other bobbed up and down before disappearing under the surface. Tom McDuffie, the Sunday school superintendent, walked quickly into the pond, fully dressed. He did not know how to swim either, but because he was tall, he thought he could reach the girl without falling into the hole. He miscalculated, floundered, flailed about and went down.

Then my father, who also could not swim, began to wade out to the spot where the girl and Tom had disappeared. Several other adult men went after him, to keep him from going deeper, and he wept loudly as he struggled to free himself. By this time, the fire department had been called, and the town's emergency sirens were shrieking along with the picnickers. I remember that when they brought Tom out, his long, dark frame almost dragged the ground. His was the first dead body I had ever seen. My father stood for a long time by the edge of the pond, his white pants turned a grayish brown by the brackish water. He held his face in his hands and wept quietly. I was not frightened, just deeply curious. Someone finally took me home, where my mother was frantic. She had heard the sirens and the news about a double drowning, but not the names of the victims.

The twin funeral was one of the largest and saddest my father ever preached. I did not know then that the young people had died because they were black and poor. I did not understand that race and economics could determine mortality. All I knew is that a colored man and a girl drowned because they did not know how to swim. Thereafter, the church's summer gatherings were held fifty miles away, under the watchful eyes of white lifeguards at Ocean Beach on Long Island Sound in New London. Not long after, my father met with the director of the YMCA, who agreed to accept the membership applications of two teenage parishioners, and without fuss or fanfare the Y was integrated.

❧

My sisters, and brother and I walked about a half mile each day to Willis School, an old, rambling, two-story gray wooden building on top of a steep hill in a neighborhood of Irish, Italians, Russians and Poles. Through the seventh grade, there were only three or four other Negro children in my classes. Most of the Negro children went to school on the other side of the river. For my entire twelve years of school, there were no Negro teachers in the Ansonia school system. Other than the students, there was no Negro anything in our school: no coaches, no cafeteria workers, no maintenance staff, no janitors. I joined the Girl Scouts and was one of two brown Brownies. The Scout headquarters was a large Victorian house near the town library in the eastern hills. I had to walk two miles to use the library or go to a Scout meeting.

One of the few events that brought the entire town together was the annual operetta put on by the junior high school. Its preparation took a year of rehearsals, costume making and scenery building. Girls with names like Primavera and Barbieri usually got the leads, while the Negro children were relegated to the chorus. For my two junior high years the operettas were *The Belle of Barcelona* and *Huldah of Holland.* In the first I donned a long black straight-haired wig. The next year it was flaxen braids and straight bangs. For me having silky hair that did not come from a hot comb was a novelty.

Parents and friends of the cast filled the auditorium. Differences were put aside for the night as the town's black and white children joined hands, danced together and partnered one another. Mr. Porell, the director, tried to make certain that the pairings were ethnically correct, but invariably some white child ended up dancing with some black child. It could be overlooked, if only for the night.

At the eighth-grade socials, the black children usually danced with one another, except when they played the polka. Then, race magically disappeared, probably because the dance was more like a sporting event than a mode for sexual contact. We had no black music at our socials or proms then, even though we had it on records at home. Instead we danced to Patti Page's "Tennessee Waltz" or Bobby Vinton's "Blue Velvet."

Another event when blacks and whites mingled was the Memorial Day Parade, when each school paraded its students from the third to the seventh grades. Everyone in town turned out. At dawn we woke up to check the weather. Dressed in white and carrying small flags, we assembled at the end of Main Street and marched behind our school bands to the cemetery. There, seated with the town's officials, my father was one of the ministers who offered prayers for the fallen soldiers.

In the fifth and sixth grades, I played the fife in the school band. But in the last grade of elementary school, the principal chose me to be the drum majorette. There had never been a colored majorette at Willis before. Sarah Keyes, my parents' fashionable friend from Waterbury, made my white satin uniform. As I led the band down Main Street, I felt as if all of Macedonia's members were marching beside me.

❧

Although I had dozens of friends at school and we did many after-school activities together, few of my white classmates invited me to their homes. I did not think much about the disparity between in-school and after-school friendships then, perhaps because my life was so full at home.

I loved school, and burying my head in a book was my favorite pastime. After I had consumed every volume of the *What Every Child Should Know* series, I started reading some of the books in my father's library. It was there that I first became familiar with the works of Langston Hughes, Phillis B. Wheatley, Frederick Douglass and Ida B. Wells. Leather-bound volumes of Dickens and James Fenimore Cooper were favorites.

When I was around nine, I thought the line from the song "Summertime"—"Your daddy's rich and your momma's good-lookin' "—was written for me. I knew my family was special and I thought we had lots of money. I was not yet privy to my parents' financial struggles in the early years of their marriage. I knew we lived in a five-bedroom house that had a guest room and a study. I rode in the new black cars my father purchased every two years. I saw the beautiful clothes and jewelry he brought my mother. I wore the dozens of dresses and shoes he bought for me every season.

It did not escape me that my father owned property from Maine to Washington. Unlike other men in Ansonia, my father took a month off every summer and we went on a family vacation. I think the only things I ever requested that I did not get were a horse and a swimming pool. And that, I thought, was because there was no place to put them. By the time I was twelve, I still knew we were special, but I had learned that we were not rich, just "comfortable."

When I was growing up, in order to be considered truly cultured, the children of middle-class black people were subjected to a wide range of musical instruction. In our family, the expectation that we should know music was even greater than usual, because of the abilities of my father's family. I also had a cousin, Billy Taylor, who was beginning to make a name for himself in jazz.

Brother had a trumpet that stayed in its case more than at his lips. Jewelle had already taken up the violin in Waterbury, but her prowess did not match her enthusiasm, so she switched to the piano. Every other week my father drove Jewelle and me to the home of Mamie Hope, a well-known black piano teacher and church accompanist in New Haven, and waited outside in the car reading while we had our lessons. Later he would also take Pattee. On the alternate weeks, he went for his own private lesson.

Mamie Hope lived in a crowded second-floor apartment on Dixwell Avenue, the heart of New Haven's Negro commercial district. For as long as I knew her, she wore the same black wig, most often askew. Its rigid sides peeped out from under an array of riotously colored turbans. Her vast collection of tarnished dangly earrings framed a sinewy, chocolate-brown neck, bobbing frantically from side to side in time with the music. Long, elegantly thin fingers with bright red polish, invariably chipped, revealed dirty fingernails. Her unusually large teeth brought to mind a horse's grimace, and she had terrible halitosis. At the end of each lesson she flashed a wide, toothy, gold-filled smile of praise and encouragement. Mamie presented her pupils in a formal recital in New Haven once a year, where her flamboyant outfits were more entertaining than the program.

I secretly dreamed of playing like Philippa Duke Schuyler, a composer and piano prodigy of the 1940s and daughter of the well-known conservative Negro journalist George Schuyler, who was a colleague of my uncle Robert, the editor of *The Pittsburgh Courier*. Philippa was the first colored girl I knew about who had achieved national prominence at a young age. She had even been on the cover of a Negro magazine. One summer night at the Keyeses' new home in New Haven, I heard Philippa perform. Wrapped in a ruffled, pastel organdy dress, with a big organdy bow perched like a giant butterfly on her shiny brown hair, light-skinned Philippa resembled Jewelle and me, but I relinquished my dream of emulating her there and then. Learning and memorizing all of those notes seemed an impossible task. I decided I would be a doctor or a lawyer instead.

At the reception that followed, Philippa was aloof. Much later, I learned that her mother was a white Southerner who had passed on her conflicts about race and color to her daughter. In journals and letters, Philippa admitted that she did not like black people and would prefer to be white or Hispanic.

Our cultural excursions in Ansonia were few. They were usually led by Mabel DaCosta, a painfully proper middle-aged Negro who had married a black Portuguese. Plump and self-assured, she wore her hair in ringlets around her face and could be seen all over town sporting youthful frilly sashed dresses and large, elaborate hats that she proudly let you know she designed herself.

Mabel taught piano, voice and elocution. Each year she produced a colored children's pageant at the Opera House on Main Street. Her programs included turn-of-the century verse, songs and tableaux. She recruited me for her "Alice Blue Gown" pageant. As usual, she designed and made all the costumes. Mine was a blue organdy confection of curved petals and ruffled sleeves. She tied a blue silk ribbon around my waist and a matching one around my forehead. I carried a tall white stick with a curved end that looked like a shepherd's crook, from which she had hung blue satin streamers and artificial daisies. My assignment was to move across the proscenium in a series of stylized poses while Mabel sang the title song in a trembling vibrato.

The stage was tiny and had long since lost its curtain. Hoping to add some production value to the event, each year Mabel devised a different curtain and hung it from a clothesline. This year, of course, it was filmy blue nylon. During the song, somehow, one of the other poseurs became entangled in Mabel's curtain. Before the actor could release himself, it fell, draping several of the other participants, who began to laugh hysterically. That was my first and last DaCosta pageant.

As a teenager growing up close to New Haven, I often went to the Shubert Theatre, where I saw musicals such as *Kismet* and *Pajama Game* before they hit the Great White Way. In the summer we went to the pop concerts at Yale Bowl. They were dignified, staid, middle-class and very white events, featuring stars like Ezio Pinza, Howard Keel and Fred Waring. Looking across the vast sea of white faces, I was keenly aware of my doubleness. I knew that those people had no idea that when I went home, I would tune in to the colored music station from Baltimore hoping to hear "Lawdy Miss Claudy" or "Work with Me Annie."

My father made sure we talked with the luminaries who stayed in our home. Many of the faces in *Ebony* looked at me across our dining room table. Chicago congressman William Dawson, NAACP head Roy Wilkins, federal judge William Hastie, the first black governor of the Virgin Islands, and Jackie Robinson, with whom I fell in love, slept in the guest quarters across the hall from my room. We met famous Negro people wherever we went. My father introduced me to the towering heavyweight champion Joe Louis, who was visiting one of our relatives in Washington. He pulled my braids and said he would wait for me. In Washington we also met Adam Clayton Powell, Jr., and General Benjamin O. Davis.

Although my father only used the word "Negro," I considered it scientific and fancy and secretly felt "colored" was more real. I did not like being called "colored" by white people, however. There was something wrong with the word when they said it. They made it sound soiled and undesirable. From white people I wanted the dignity and respect that "Negro" conferred.

I did not think a great deal about white people growing up. Some were friends; none that I knew personally were enemies. Our enemies were those we saw on-screen in the war movies: the Japanese and the Germans. Nice white people were just that: nice white people, nothing more, nothing less. In general, white people were the backdrop and audience for the drama of our lives, aside from the special group that made up my mother's family. For me, they were in a class by themselves.

I knew we were different from white people, but beyond color I was not sure how. In our scheme of things, there were degrees of whiteness. I knew that my mother and father thought "poor white trash" was lower than a snake. A snake was the only animal my mother did not love. My parents sometimes talked about "Tobacco Road" types. I asked them what they meant. They said they were dirty people with stringy hair, unkempt clothing, legs bowed by rickets, rotting teeth and white skin. I looked hard for those types when we went south. The first time I heard my mother talk about "crackers," the term made no sense to me. I could not fathom how a saltine could be dirty and mean. Then I figured out that crackers were first cousins of poor white trash. With "rednecks," my nomenclature of disdain was complete.

❧

Sundays we would wake to the sound of hard-to-find gospel or sermons coming from the radio beside my parents' bed. If we were lucky, we would hear the voices of the Douglas Brothers, members of our church who sometimes sang on a station in Bridgeport. My father dressed while my mother fixed breakfast. Poached fish, grits, softly scrambled eggs and biscuits was a favorite.

I knew that Sunday was my father's workday, and that it was important for me to demonstrate the same respect for the church and for him as the rest of the congregation did. It was also a day that brought much of the black community together. There was gossip, fussy new babies to fuss over, and the latest in small-town fashions to admire. In church black people were honored as deacons, trustees, church officers, club presidents, ushers or missionary ladies. We gave our reports, turned in dues and made plans for the future as if we were running a giant corporation. In church, we were somebody. Even more important, church was where as a people we nurtured our survival and organized our resistance, where we developed and then articulated group consciousness.

For my father, the most special Sunday of the year was Easter. The holiday represented a set of living principles that guided his life's work, and a celebratory mood equaling that of Christmastime filled our home Easter week. On Good Friday, my father would join with the white ministers of the town in an interdenominational service. With our hair freshly pressed, we spent Saturday night in the kitchen coloring eggs while my father prepared his sermon and Mother prepared Easter dinner. Early on Easter Sunday, my parents would get up and go to the six o'clock sunrise service, where my father would baptize new members of the church.

The baptismal pool lay under the pulpit and ran its entire length. The membership candidates wore the traditional white muslin robes. Girls did not like to get baptized on Easter morning because they did not want to muss their hair. With the help of a deacon, my father would immerse the mostly male supplicants in the water. Many were terrified because they did not know how to swim. We always held our breath when an especially rotund member went under; on several occasions my father and the deacon dropped one of the fleshy faithful and there was much scrambling and splashing to bring him back to the surface.

When they returned home, my mother would help us get ready for the eleven o'clock session. We had new Easter outfits, from underwear to black patent leather shoes, that we were determined to wear no matter how cold it was. The church was so full that extra chairs had to be put in the aisles. My father insisted that each member come to the front of the church and leave his offering at the collection table. Row by row, in their new straws and silks, the congregation complied, giving those still sitting ample opportunity to discuss the fit, style and suitability of the passing fashions. The senior choir presented a ragged but earnest rendition of "The Palms," and following his sermon, my father sang "Jerusalem." After church the children would compare pocketbooks, hats and shoes outside of Fitzi's, amid much posing for pictures.

Other than on Sundays, there was little overt religion in our household. My father did not wear a clerical collar. My mother did not dress like a missionary. Except for my father's study, there were no religious pictures on the walls. There were no regularly scheduled family prayer sessions, and we did not have to read the Bible or memorize its verses. My father said the same short grace at every meal, and a longer one on holidays. Visiting ministers were sometimes surprised at our lack of familiarity with the Good Book.

My mother, my siblings and I were the lightest members of the church and the rest of the colored community. Even now, it almost seems a betrayal to say that. We did not talk about it then, and we worked at making it a nonissue. I knew my father considered his color an asset, and I liked my color best in the summer, when I got a dark tan with red undertones.

There was one other light family in the town, but they kept to themselves. They did not attend the church or frequent any Negro social activities. They tried to pass for white, but the colored people knew they were black and generally ignored them. Their attempt to be white did not seem to bring them any advantage with either group. Other blacks in the town ranged from medium tan to dark brown, with the majority being dark brown.

Surrounded by this cloak of color from infancy, reinforced by my father's pride in his blackness and the almost heroic presence of my dark uncles, for eighteen years I saw myself as a dark tan person. It never occurred to me that I would be mistaken for anything but what I was, a colored girl. If I was favored, I assumed it was because I was Reverend Taylor's daughter, not because I was light.

In retrospect, I can see that our special family status may have shielded us from unkind comments. As a family, our relationship to the church members was at once simple and complex. We were "the minister's children," and along with that label came an unstated yet clear sense of responsibility. It may be that part of what we sensed was the unspoken challenge of having to prove ourselves worthy of the mantle of blackness. My father told us to be proud of our family and aware of our role. On the other hand he said we could only be successful in life if we treated all people as equals. He often used the expression "having the common touch and being able to walk with kings." He was confident that he was able to do just that, and that if we followed his precepts we could learn the same route.

We were a family of "firsts" and "onlys," and the "first family" of our tiny Negro community, at a time before notching "firsts" became incorrect and embarrassing, a reminder of how far we still have to travel. Borrowing the title of George C. Wolfe's play, I can see now that much of my family's history belongs in the "colored museum," but at the time it generated genuine respect and affection for us.

The congregation became our extended family. They filled in some of the gaps created by our absent relatives. As the years passed, they expressed pride in our good grades and other achievements, and in the respect that the white people of the town gave us. Those who worked as domestics told us how their employers spoke of the minister's family with a mixture of admiration and curiosity.

In 1945, my father added another church to his pastorate, the Union Baptist Church in Norwich, Connecticut. Every Sunday for eighteen years he drove the fifty miles of dark, wooded road to the picturesque, hilly coastal town near New London. The town had a colorful, romantic past. In colonial times, it suffered an infestation of rattlesnakes, which local legend has it was cured by not a pied piper but a violinist. The Methodist church had been lifted off its foundations by a flash flood and swept down the Thames and out to sea, candles still burning brightly in its windows. But the rattlesnakes were gone and all the churches securely anchored to their foundations by the time my father came to Norwich, and to me it was a quiet, peaceful, Sunday evening place.

Blacks had been in Norwich for a long time, and during slavery days the colored population, as in Derby, had elected their own "governor." The members of the small Negro church, however, were descendants of the black Portuguese who had been fishermen and sailors in the Cape Verde Islands, a Portuguese colony off the west coast of Africa. They came to the New World to work in the whaling industry and later, as it declined, learned blacksmithing, shoe tanning, tailoring and other trades. Some had intermarried members of the Pequot Indian nation.

They were handsome, industrious and conservative people. Their level of education and sophistication was higher than that of my father's Ansonia constituents. Home ownership and higher education were goals most achieved. Despite their nutmeg skin tones, which were similar to those of Native Americans, their manners and mores were those of white people. They even sounded white, singing the Baptist hymns off key and off beat. They shunned gospel and anything bordering on emotionality. They enjoyed the quiet, thoughtful sermons my father delivered, quite unlike the picture-painting, emotional messages he preached to his flock in Ansonia.

I went to Portugal for the first time in 1990, to attend an international meeting of film archivists, at which I was the only black person in attendance. I was greatly looking forward to seeing the beautiful red-brown people of my childhood, but from the time I got off the plane in Lisbon until I left, they were nowhere in evidence. The Portuguese were white and unfriendly and looked like the middle Europeans I had grown up with. At the summer palace of a Portuguese king, we were served a formal dinner by white servants liveried and bewigged in eighteenth-century costume. I had not known that the last of the blacks had been driven out of Portugal in the twelfth century.

One winter, traveling alone on four successive Sundays, my father spotted a woman in white at the side of the road. She wore a thin garment with an uneven hem and seemed to be in distress. Although it was dangerous for a colored man to stop for a white woman late at night on a dark road, my father pulled over. But each time he approached the spot where the woman seemed to be, she had disappeared. On the fifth Sunday, he took Jewelle with him. As they approached the spot where the woman usually stood, Jewelle said, "Daddy, stop, there's a woman waving at us." Again he stopped, and again there was no sign of the woman. He drove directly to the Norwich police headquarters, where he was told that there had been numerous reports of the same sighting. The preceding summer, he was told, a young woman had been in an auto accident at that curve, on the eve of her wedding. She had died of a broken neck.

Late one Sunday night when I was ten, we were returning from Norwich when we saw two teenage girls standing near the side of a dark, deserted road at the crest of the eastern hills that lead down into Ansonia's center. The girls recognized my father's car and we recognized them. They were members of the church.

They flagged us down and told my father they were running away from a man with whom they had had an argument. As the girls got into the car, the man pulled up behind us in another car. We drove down into the valley with the stranger's car following closely. We turned off Main Street onto a darker, smaller street, where my father stopped the car and got out to see the girls to their door. The young stranger who had been following us jumped out and struck my father, who fell beside the car. The girls screamed in unison. The man had a knife.

Frightened, we got out of the car with my mother as the girls ran hysterically down Main Street, yelling, "Reverend Taylor has been killed." Within a few short minutes, hundreds of black people had crowded into the street in their nightclothes, looking for the murderer. They carried brooms, shovels, pipes, baseball bats, guns and knives.

The attacker did not have the presence of mind to leave the scene quickly and was immediately hemmed in by the crowd. Dozens of hands pushed and pulled him roughly. They started to beat him and kick and pull his hair. Angry voices on the edge of hysteria threatened and cursed and taunted him. The police, whose headquarters were a block away, barely arrived in time to rescue him from being lynched.

I remember the curve of my mother's back as she kneeled in the street and cradled my father's head. The stranger did indeed have a knife, but the glancing blow had only pushed my father to the ground. The blade itself had cut through his jacket, shirt, and undershirt, missing his skin.

❧

Ours was a fungible family. In addition to caring for her own children, my mother was a stepmother to my half sisters, Mauryne and Doris, who came up from Washington as soon as school ended each summer for a six-week stay. Later, they lived with us while they finished Ansonia High School. Both were light-skinned and had straight hair. Mauryne was willowy and beautiful in an elusive, turn-of-the-century manner. By the time she was seventeen, she was the most beautiful girl in town, black or white, of which she was keenly aware. She had a small waist and ample hips and long, dark hair that cascaded around her parchment-colored skin. She had the idealized nose of a Greek statue, and her dark eyes were large and round. Her walk was a sensuous, feminine exaggeration of my father's undulating gait. Her persona and good looks were sweetly sexual, like Ava Gardner's. She looked like a dark-haired white girl.

Walking down the street with Mauryne was an exercise in attraction. Cars honked and stopped, men catcalled, women stared and teenage girls pointed. She pretended not to notice the havoc she caused on the streets. Stubby and shapeless in my shorts and braids, I was dazzled and proud that this beautiful creature was my big sister.

Mauryne was an honor student and the class poet, but she wanted a career in show business. Hollywood would not find a place for her, however. The studios told her she was too light and beautiful to be black, and too "exotic" to be white. Independent producers wanted to take her to Europe, but she resisted and turned her attention to the Negro films called "race movies" at that time. She landed the female lead in two back-to-back, identically cast black Westerns, *Come on Cowboy* and *Ride 'em Cowboy*. The pictures were filmed on a ranch in Rahway, New Jersey. A dozen real black cowboys were imported from the West to provide, literally, the "color background." Mauryne shared star billing with two actors who had made the transformation from vaudeville to the big screen. Mantan Moreland was well known for his role as Birmingham Brown, Charlie Chan's chauffeur. Flournoy Miller had been half of a popular song-and-dance act, Miller and Lyles, and had appeared in *Stormy Weather* with Lena Horne.

Mauryne persevered. She had the lead in an all-black play called *Maryann* that toured by bus and truck below the Mason-Dixon Line. She also found work as a leading actor of the New Faces Guild in Washington, D.C., which produced musicals at the Howard Theater. After their run, the shows were performed for Negro military men at bases throughout the South. Mauryne's odyssey took her to New York as well, where she sang in jazz clubs on 52nd Street and at the well-known Harlem club Wells, with her cousin Billy Taylor, who was in the early stages of his jazz career. While in New York she wrote lyrics for Arnold records.

She returned to Washington, and appeared on a weekly radio show called *Americans All*, for which she wrote and read what she called topical poetry. Later she would publish a book of romantic poems. She married, had three children, and was twice a widow. To help support her artistic forays, she worked for many years for one of Washington's preeminent Negro attorneys. At seventy, she retains much of her former beauty and continues to write poetry and give readings of her work.

Doris was shorter, plump and pretty. She spent her summers reading true-life romance stories. She married DeWhit Keith, who became one of the first Negro photographers for the State Department and the White House. He was the family photographer as well. Doris later became a commissioner for the D.C. police. DeWhit died blind at forty-nine, leaving behind a son.

My mother became a surrogate mother for at least eight other girls, who lived in our home for periods ranging from two to nine years. They became our older "sisters" and were treated as members of the family.

Margaret Jackson was the short, dark, lively child who came into our family when she was nine years old and stayed until she was eighteen. At first, she would take food from the table and hide it in her room. An orphan, she had seldom had enough to eat. Ethel Johnson was a voluptuous, medium-brown teenager who liked to smoke and listen to the saxophone and Sarah Vaughan. But her favorite was Billy Eckstine, whose "I Surrender Dear" she played over and over.

Ethel's beau was a soldier, and Margaret dated a sailor. Sometimes they let me sit and watch them as they got ready for their dates. Often they would dab me with Evening in Paris, which came in a royal blue bottle shaped like a minaret. They wore dresses with snugly fitting bodices and pleated or full skirts that swirled from the hips. Ankle-strapped platform shoes and upswept hairdos added several inches to their height. They put on layer upon layer of costume jewelry and usually scattered rhinestone poodles, umbrellas or fruit on their shoulders.

It was a thrill for me to answer the door for their handsome young men in the uniforms of war. They would give me a quarter and pretended to flirt with me as they waited for the girls to come downstairs. I imagined their dates were like those I saw in the movies on Saturday afternoons, where the girls and the servicemen would dance around the lampposts and drink from the same tall glass at the soda fountain.

Margaret married her sailor, a black Portuguese, and had three children. Her life did not turn out like a Saturday matinee. Her handsome serviceman was a wife beater and child abuser whom she eventually divorced. For more than twenty-five years she worked at Yale University in biological research. When she died of cancer at fifty-six, a Nobel Laureate who was one of her colleagues gave one of many eulogies. Ethel, too, married her soldier, a slant-eyed, saxophone-playing young man called Chink, and had a son and two daughters before her wartime romance also ended in divorce. She became the head chef in a home for the elderly.

Tall, brown-skinned Althea Jackson joined the family as our sister when she was in high school. She had a flippant manner, but she was determined and serious, and knew that she wanted to do something important in her life. Years later, when she was New Haven's deputy registrar of voters, I managed her campaign for registrar. For 125 years the deputy had routinely succeeded the registrar, but for 125 years the registrar had been a white male. Long controlled by the Italian political machine, the local Democratic Committee endorsed Althea's opponent, a secretary in her office, and the campaign for a rather minor position took on real fervor. We won the backing of the city's major newspaper and formed a coalition that included Yale students and professors, black high school students, white neighborhood groups and labor unions. Althea garnered massive media attention and got enough signatures to get on the ballot, despite the foot-dragging of black politicians reluctant to go against the machine. She lost the election narrowly, but the campaign established her as the "Rosa Parks of New Haven" and laid the foundation for the election of the city's first black mayor the following year.

My parents nurtured all the girls who lived with us as if they were their daughters. Later they took in several boys from Liberia, but they were not a successful addition to the household. Once they settled in, the boys showed little interest in my parents or the household. Like typical American teenagers, they stayed in their rooms or watched television. My father expected my mother to take charge of the boys, but she was not keen about them. After three tries, my father concluded that the experience would not bear fruit. Once again, outside of my father, the men in my mother's life proved to be disappointing.

∽

Test scores showed that my brother had the highest IQ among us siblings and an ample aptitude for learning, although his pragmatism sometimes overrode his ethical concerns. Once he took the wheels off my new bicycle to create a delivery wagon he needed. He was clever with mechanical things, and his high energy level and pleasant personality led him to frequent part-time work running errands or plucking chicken feathers in a local poultry market.

When Brother was twelve years old, somewhere near the Sandbank, he was sexually molested by an older white man. He did not tell my parents about it right away, and they did not tell the rest of us until years later. The man was apprehended and eventually served time. But in the meantime, Brother began getting into fights and stealing small items from local stores. Notes from my father's diary of 1948 outlined part of Brother's early story. "Juvenile court with Brother—case closed. . . . Drove Brother to Washington." He stayed there with Doris for almost a year before he ran away. By the time I was twelve, it seemed as if Brother was not as much a part of the family as he had been.

My father sought counseling for him, and professionals recommended he be placed at a live-in treatment facility for troubled boys. But he did not improve there and returned home only to get into more trouble. For the next five years or so, he was in and out of scrapes. My mother was always ready to excuse him and put blame for his actions elsewhere. My father protected him and paid what he had to, but the behavior of his only son was a source of embarrassment to him, although most in our community were kind about it.

Brother continued to cause tension in the household. He stayed for a while with my parents' undertaker friends the Keyeses, and then decided to go into the air force. One night, my father, my sister Jewelle and her young man of the moment arranged to accompany Brother back to his base in Massachusetts, from which he was absent without leave. Brother was at the wheel. Everyone else was asleep. The car hit a center divider and was totally demolished, but no one was injured. For the next three weeks, my father stayed in bed, listless and covering his head with a pillow as if to shut out the world. Sometime during that period he asked my mother if she thought Brother had been trying to kill him or to kill himself.

After being discharged from the service at twenty, Brother married Lessie Butler, a quiet, plump black girl who already had one child. Because of Brother's age and incomplete schooling, my parents tried to dissuade him from the marriage, but he was determined. Lessie's family was poor and mostly uneducated. She was brown enough that her race was not in question. I often wondered whether Brother hoped Lessie's color might make him a more desirable male in the Taylor family circle.

Over the next thirty years, however, Brother married four more times, each time to a white woman. He ultimately fathered five children, completed high school and college and held a series of jobs ranging from male nurse to mortician. His most enduring marriage, like his great-grandfather's, was to a quiet Irish girl, Maureen Kelley, from Malden, Massachusetts. With Maureen he had two children, Jeffrey and Julie, and seemed to spend his most productive years.

Brother constantly reinvented himself and left behind his different identities as if they were sets of keys. He was in and out of prison for charges usually related to money, forgery or stealing checks. My father, who was a longtime board member of the state reformatory system, found Brother's incarcerations painful and humiliating and visited him infrequently in jail, but my mother faithfully brought him news, small gifts, food and money. I visited him at least twice, wanting to leave as soon as I arrived. In college I took courses in abnormal psychology and criminology, looking for clues to my brother's behavior. The criminology course required field trips to a penitentiary in Massachusetts. I did not tell my classmates that I had already taken mine.

On at least four occasions that I know of, Brother tried to commit suicide. The attempts were never life-threatening, but we understood they were cries for attention. Although we tried in different ways, none of us could fill Brother's needs. And I deeply resented the pain and embarrassment his behavior continued to cause my parents and me.

When I lived in Cambridge, Brother stayed with my husband and me for almost a year. He was working at a hospital then, and used our house to sleep and eat. Sometimes he would baby-sit for us, and he was a patient, attentive nurse to the two daughters I had by that time. We got along well, except when he drank. His tolerance for liquor was low, and he would turn silly, mean, violent or crazy.

One night around two in the morning, after we had had a long, emotional talk with Brother about his life and his future, there was a knock on our door. My husband answered and I heard his lengthy and firm discussion with the visitor, who turned out to be a mortician's assistant from a well-known Cambridge funeral home. Responding to a telephone request, the undertaker had come to pick up my body. Harold called me to the door to confirm that I was indeed alive. The next day we asked Brother whether he had made the call. He vigorously denied it. We could not imagine anyone else we knew to play so macabre a prank.

My father bought Brother a house and a funeral home in Hartford. He managed the house well, but resented the mortician my father hired to oversee the operation of the business because Brother did not have an undertaker's license. After a fire extensively damaged the business, the funeral home closed.

Wherever I lived, Brother would visit. When I lived in the Virgin Islands he came to stay for a week. I took him to a reception given by native publisher Ariel Melchior for Al Neuharth, CEO of the Gannett newspaper chain, which had just purchased the *Virgin Islands Daily News*. All of the Islands' notables were in attendance. Liquor was flowing freely, and as usual Brother was charming and outgoing, especially with the older women, who responded to his gallantry. I caught sight of him dancing with the governor's wife just as they both fell over a drum near the bandstand. I got to his side only a step behind the governor's bodyguards. I took Brother by the arm and told him it was time to leave. The next day, I had calls from various guests. They had no idea, they said, I had such a charming, brilliant, handsome brother, who was such a successful brain surgeon, trial lawyer, businessman, mortician, minister, professor. I put him on the next flight out.

For a few years, I deliberately exorcised Brother from my life. It was my own maturing parenthood that brought us together again. Watching my daughters together and observing how much they were becoming part of each other's psyches, I realized I could not bury the part of my brother I kept in my heart as well as in my memory. I felt comfortable with my life and knew that it was intact, no matter what he might do. I understood that his behavior could not diminish me, so I ceased to be embarrassed by it. In terms of that issue, I had finally grown up.

I helped him do research for his college courses. He received his undergraduate degree at forty-seven while out on bail, awaiting trial for arson in which he and several others were implicated. He maintained that he was a fall guy for a group of criminals who made insurance money by burning down buildings. One of them was convicted of masterminding the crime, but Brother, too, was sent to jail. He was completing his prison sentence and looking forward to returning to civilian life when he contracted lung cancer. Prison authorities transferred him to Hartford Hospital, where, although he was too weak to get out of bed, he was sometimes shackled to his cot. The shackles became a focus of rage for me as they seemed to be a metaphor for my brother's life.

The last time I saw him was in the hospital two days before he died. Gaunt to the point of emaciation, his once chubby face revealed a truer profile. When I left the room, I cried, not because he looked bad, but because I was able to see for the first time how much he resembled my father. At that moment I understood that my brother's pale skin had been a barrier to recognition, even to me. I said, "You know, I never realized how much you look like Daddy until now." My admission seemed to please him and he flashed his familiar grin, which now took up most of his face.

He was forty-eight years old when he died. Four of his five wives came to the funeral, each assigned to ride in a different car.

As a family, we never talked about my brother, although my sisters and I would discuss him with each other and our mother. My father was reluctant to join in, as if he could not bear the anguish, possibly the guilt, the discussion would arouse. As I worked my way through my parents' lives, I wondered how Brother had been affected by the lack of family role models who looked like him. All of our male heroes had been dark. Mother's father and all of her male siblings had been light, not to their credit. She clearly preferred dark men, as did my sisters and I. In addition for my brother there was the pressure of his sisters' success and of being a prominent minister's only son.

When my father first took my brother to a psychiatrist, the doctor advised that Brother be called by his real name, Julian, rather than his impersonal nickname. That advice was never passed on to the rest of us, but I happened upon a note in one of my father's diaries that read, "Take Julian—*not Brother*—for a new pair of shoes."

Looking back, I find it a pity that my brother's talent for con-
fabulation never found the right channel. I think about him often,
with an equal mixture of fondness and sadness and sometimes with
glee. Someone once wrote that in death, a man or woman is free
of the weight of his past. I hope for my brother that this is true.

I still dream about Frankenstein. My brother is also part of the
dream. It is always the same dream: It is night and we are on the
bridge. My terror is so great that I cannot speak or scream. My
throat is closed with fear. Brother is trying to distract Frankenstein's
attention from me. As he works frantically to divert the monster,
a tall figure comes up behind him. It is the Silver Man.

Chapter Seven

But always the violence was distant, the words vague and terrible, for we were protected children.

—LILLIAN SMITH
Killers of the Dream

Every August, my father would take the whole family on a vacation by car. The itinerary mandated a stop in Washington so that my parents could visit their relatives. The night before we were to leave, we had to go to bed at seven because we were going to get up at three. My father liked to get on the road before the sun came up, so that he could make the eight-hour drive to Washington before dark. Lingering powerfully in the bouquet of my memories are the fragrant smells of those cool, dark Connecticut mornings as I stood outside and waited for my father to finish, in his precise way, packing the car. It was not until I was thirteen that I understood the real reason for the early departure. It was not safe for a Negro to drive below New York after dark. It was especially unsafe for a Negro driving a shiny, expensive car with a wife and children who looked white.

Mother packed a lunch of fried chicken, sandwiches, boiled eggs, bananas, peaches, grapes, cupcakes and cookies, because we could not be served at restaurants once we crossed the Hudson River into New Jersey. My parents would not let us use rest rooms marked "Colored," and I disliked the feel of the coarse roadside grass on my bare legs as I squatted to relieve myself beside the car. It was one of the small reasons that made part of me hate the South.

In Washington, we usually stayed with my father's oldest brother,

Bill, the dentist. He had a large house filled with satin, brocade and velvet, and we thought my cousin Joyce lived like a princess. Her room was full of ruffles and white furniture and she even had her own nanny.

Bill had a successful practice and a flourishing private mortgage lending service. Much taller and wider than my father, he was an imposing, gregarious man with wide jowls and an aggressive manner that made me wary. With a cigarette dangling from the corner of his mouth, he sat sideways thumping his right foot as he played the piano. In his presence, my father became a little brother. Although Bill gave my father unsolicited advice, they got on well and seemed to enjoy each other's company. Bill told us stories of doing the town with his friend Paul Robeson when the singer lived at the Theresa Hotel in Harlem. Bill's second wife, a beautiful, lively woman named Kathryn, had been a movie actress of some notoriety—she appeared in a race film, *Children of Circumstance*—and was now an elementary school principal. The two of them were expert bridge players who followed the bridge circuit around the country.

From Bill's we would pop over to the beautiful house next door belonging to Uncle Waddell and Aunt Irene. They had no children of their own, and we loved the way they spoiled and pampered us. Irene would give us clothes and jewelry and perfume. Waddell would give us money, in reward, he said, for our good grades. With her large eyes, long auburn hair and chesty laugh, Irene was as alluring to me as any of the reigning movie queens.

My father's relationship with his ex-wife, whom we called Aunt Viola, was warm, and we visited with her and her daughters when we went to Washington. The information my parents shared with us concerning my father's first marriage and divorce was hazy, and I did not understand at first what Viola's relationship to my father was. For the longest time I thought she was just a close family friend. Like my mother, Viola was a beautiful woman. Her skin was translucently pale and her hair was light brown, long and straight. She had a long, sharp nose, a strong chin and lidded eyes that languidly orchestrated her expression. I was fascinated by the fact that she smoked cigarettes. Slowly and with what I thought was great drama, she would move the elegant hand that held the cigarette to her lips, take a long, slow puff, and lift her chin as, almost imperceptibly, she blew out the smoke.

I sensed in that room many things I could not understand, but whatever tension existed between the two wives was carefully masked. Only once when I was a teenager did I overhear a brief quarrel between my parents about a visit my father made to Viola when he was in Washington alone. After my half sister Doris married, we sometimes stayed with her and her husband, DeWhit, in their two-bedroom apartment in northeast Washington. I watched Doris become a little girl again in my father's presence and sensed he was trying to make up to her for something.

It was in Washington at the black theaters that I saw for the first time black newsreels and films, such as *Cabin in the Sky*, *Green Pastures* and *Stormy Weather*. Back in Connecticut I wanted to see more of Fredi Washington, Nina Mae McKinney, Lena Horne and later Dorothy Dandridge, but Hollywood had few roles for them. I could not understand why there were not more colored women up there on those screens, when I knew so many true black beauties. If only the directors who made the movies would go to Washington, I thought, they would have their eyes opened. I had no idea that the moviemakers thought black stars, no matter how attractive and talented, would turn audiences away.

My father conscientiously took us around to visit his family, my mother's few available relatives and our godmothers. Next on the schedule would be a visit to Uncle Bob, managing editor of the Washington edition of the colored newspaper *The Pittsburgh Courier*. Like his brother Bill, Bob was large. Unlike Bill, he was soft-spoken and gentle, his expression often in the middle distance, as if he were rewriting a story in his head. My father savored the chance to catch up on politics with him, and my mother enjoyed talking with his wife, Violet, who raised chow dogs and horses and worked for the first home for unwed black mothers in Washington. Bob had been an army officer in World War II, and my image of him is romantically entwined with his photograph in uniform, astride a gigantic horse. His thumping, stumping, aggressive piano-playing style was at odds with his quiet personality, although his notes came out softly. My cousin Billy Taylor, the jazz pianist, said that Bob's style most influenced his own.

No trip to Washington was complete without a visit to my two godmothers. One was Gregoria Goins, a college-educated piano teacher who was also my father's godmother. She still lived next door to the Taylor family home on 13th Street. Her mother had graduated from Howard University Medical School, then the only medical school that admitted women, to become one of the first Negro female physicians in America.

Gregoria was red-brown in color, tall, stately, self-possessed and well-to-do. She had the look of old money: wide, high cheekbones, a serene, direct gray-eyed gaze, and long, straight silver hair that she wore in an aristocratic pompadour. Dressed in floor-length, turn-of-the-century gowns sprinkled with long chains and dangling lorgnettes, she glided quietly through her house, a brownstone opulently furnished with antiques and souvenirs from her world travels.

Gregoria was unlike anyone else that I knew in real life. She reminded me of Ethel Barrymore of the silver screen, but grander, I thought. A member of the Rosicrucians, a sect with roots in ancient Egypt who believe in reincarnation, she would speak of people's auras and essences and tell me fantastic stories. Quietly and without drama she told me she had lived many previous lives. I sat enthralled as she related how she had seen a picture of herself on the mantel of a cottage in India, owned by people she had just met. In the cool of her shaded solarium filled with overgrown potted ferns on tall ornately carved stands and crammed with books and objects, this elegant woman in her seventies talked to me as if I were a peer. When I became engaged years later, she gave me the heart-shaped emerald ring that had been her father's engagement gift to her mother in 1868. "In paintings of faith, hope and love, love was always dressed in green," she wrote.

My godmother Rosa, who had been engaged to my mother's uncle, Eddie Scott, still worked for the Glover family. We visited her at Westover, the family's enormous Georgian estate on Massachusetts Avenue, and at her brownstone in LeDroit Park. The Glovers themselves would be in Maine for the summer, leaving Rosa in charge of the reduced staff at the mansion. I remember being ushered through enormously tall, quiet, lavishly furnished rooms whose eggshell-colored shades were partially drawn against the August heat. We would pass through a massive white butler's pantry with sparkling glass cabinets filled with beautiful dishes. The sun glared against the white walls of the cavernous kitchen. A unique hush hung over the house. It was probably there that I realized my family was not rich.

I would swing and play in the formal gardens while Miss Rosa fixed us a white folks meal: pink lamb or rare roast beef, barely cooked string beans and Yorkshire pudding. Her service for us was as correct as it was for her employers. She brought out their fine china soup bowls, finger bowls and individual silver nut dishes, along with gleaming silver and crystal, and handsomely embossed linens.

In her own home, it was clear how much Miss Rosa's taste was influenced by the people for whom she had worked all of her adult life. Her brownstone was furnished with tapestries, small statuary, Chinese vases and antique furniture. Freshly laundered linen hand towels hung on heated racks in her bathrooms. In her own dining room, she served us as if we were eating at the mansion, Westover. She put doilies under soup bowls and provided delicately carved fruit scissors for each place setting.

Under five feet tall Rosa seemed dwarfed by the high ceilings of her home. Everything about her was tiny, including the bun of thin hair at the nape of her fragile-looking neck. Her small face and quick movements reminded me of a squirrel. Her manners were those of an upper-class lady.

She always wore simple, well-fitting cotton pastels, usually buttoned from the white Peter Pan collar to the hem. I thought it eccentric that her dresses were all the same style. I later realized that they were in fact part of the uniform she completed at work with a white ruffled apron and matching cap.

Rosa shared her brownstone with her equally small, gnomelike sister, Miss Betty. Betty was odd-looking. Thick cotton stockings rolled to the hem of her dress covered her spindly, bowed legs. Round wire-rim eyeglasses framed her heavy lidded, widely spaced eyes. Several long gray hairs extruded stiffly from a mole on her chin, reminding me of a cat's whiskers. A noticeable mustache extended above her wide, thin lips. She had a deep raspy voice, drank several bottles of beer every day, and told me she had not slept in months. With a pursing of her lips and a shake of her head, the teetotaling Miss Rosa made it clear this was nonsense. Year after year the dialogue was unchanged.

Manners were of grave concern to Miss Rosa. She believed that ladylike behavior was key to getting ahead. When I stayed with her as a teenager, she insisted that I have enough white gloves for each day of my visit. My clothing must be wrinkle-free and never have the slightest smudge or streak. Whenever possible, I should wear a small hat. I should sit up straight with my knees together and my legs crossed at the ankles. My fragrance should never be heavy, and I should speak in soft, well-modulated tones. When I was engaged, she gave me her diamonds, which had come from Uncle Eddie, and some of the fine old china, crystal and linens she had used to entertain us when I was a little girl. Her dream to enjoy them in her own marriage had never materialized.

Until I was a teenager, each summer I was also taken to see my mother's Aunt Mamie in Washington, the only one of my mother's family who had not folded herself like meringue into the white world. I remember her best from a visit when I was ten years old. She was an older, pleasant-faced white-looking woman with intensely blue eyes. She was caring for her bedridden mother, Margaret Maher Morris.

My mother took me upstairs to see the old woman. It was my mother's first visit with her grandmother in more than twenty years, since their confrontation at Michael's funeral. I had never met her, nor had I heard much about her. Just before we entered the room, my mother told me that the invalid behind the door was my great-grandmother and that she was Irish. This was a puzzle to me because the woman in the bed looked like all the other women in my mother's family. She had blue eyes and a halo of white hair. Her filmy eyes loked at my mother for a long time. Then she said, "You're Will Morris's girl." My mother said, "Yes, and this is my daughter Shirley." My mother repeated the same ritual with Jewelle and Brother. That was the only time we saw her. All I recall is how wan she was.

Mamie lived on Girard Street in the Howard University section of northwest Washington. Hers was a house of deep secrets and partly told tales. As the grown-ups sat drinking ice tea or ginger ale, I could feel how we were on the perimeter of my aunt's family, compared with how we blended into the center of my father's relatives. I did not understand or like the unarticulated unease I sensed.

During our visits at Mamie's, there was a preoccupation with hair texture and color, our own and everyone else's. Many of my mother's cousins had long, straight, sandy hair that they wore unbound. I wore my lightly pressed, darker brown hair in three braids. Their eyes were blue, gray, green or hazel, and their skin was almost without color. My eyes were dark brown and I was tan. My father was much darker than their fathers. Some of them referred to us as "very distant cousins." Much was made of my New England accent and proper manners, as if these were compensation for skin that was less than white enough, and hair that was less than straight enough.

Those visits with Mamie seemed formal and reserved. She addressed my father as Reverend Taylor, never as Julian, although when she talked about him to other people, she would call him "that Julian." She had never forgiven my mother "for running off with that Julian." He usually did not stay. He would come in, greet everyone, then say he would pick us up later. The meetings were a duty dance for my mother, a dance whose rigid choreography never altered. When Mamie died in 1969, her obituary listed my mother as Mamie's niece and one of her survivors. The obituary did not list either her niece Grace or her nephew Bill Morris, both living in Cleveland at the time. Even from beyond the grave, Mamie managed to protect the "white" relatives.

My father had a standing invitation to speak at his father's church while we were in Washington, and his visits always occasioned a note in the local Negro press. As the most illustrious son of the church and a favored child of its founding pastor, he turned his guest appearances into high drama. He wore his whitest suit, his newest shirt and his shiniest shoes. He made sure that his family sat in the center of the third row.

Compared to Macedonia, Florida Avenue seemed like a cathedral to me. It seated one thousand people and had a massive pipe organ taking up most of the wall behind the pulpit. The chancel could accommodate three large choirs. In the center of the pulpit behind the rostrum was a large, carved mahogany chair. I knew it was the same chair where my grandfather had sat, waiting to preside or preach. My father's appearances in his father's pulpit were grander, more effusive, more intellectual than in Ansonia. Sometimes he delivered one of his father's sermons. These would draw yeses and amens from the oldest members. When he completed his message, he invariably sang, "His Eye Is on the Sparrow," reducing the old ladies to tears.

Often, as part of our Washington visit, we spent time with some of my relatives at Highland Beach on Chesapeake Bay in Maryland. An uncle, two cousins and a godmother owned cottages there. In the family scrapbook there are pictures of my formally attired grandfather, immaculate straw hat in hand, escorting his family for a weekend at the beach.

Highland Beach was originally farmland when Frederick Douglass's family purchased it a century ago. In 1892, the story goes, Charles Douglass, a Civil War veteran and the son of the great abolitionist, had taken his wife to a café in Bay Ridge Resort, a fashionable recreation spot just southeast of Annapolis. The couple were refused service. They walked to nearby Black Walnut Creek, where they saw a forty-four-acre tract of waterfront land for sale. Within a few days they bought the property and shortly thereafter began selling lots to their friends.

For decades, Highland was a snug, exclusive and homogeneous community for privileged Negroes. Langston Hughes, Paul Laurence Dunbar, Booker T. Washington and E. Franklin Frazier all enjoyed the bay breezes there. There were eighty or so cottages and three main streets, crossed by narrow, leafy lanes. People arrived in elegant, open touring cars. Well-kept tennis courts were in constant use, and there were gatherings for games in the pavilion. Residents with special talents such as music or oratory regularly performed. Two small hotels had been built, much to the disdain of the residents, who thought they might attract "the wrong element." One burned down mysteriously on Christmas day. Many believed it was arson.

The idea of being in a colony made up of Negroes who could spend the entire summer in their second homes reaffirmed my sense of specialness. Yet I felt the place was not a true fit. It was filled with people who looked too white, East Indian or Native American. There were not enough brown faces for my comfort. There was too much talk of color, hair texture and family connections. In Connecticut, there seemed to be less emphasis on those things. Of course in Connecticut there was no Highland Beach.

My clearest memory of Highland is not of color or class, but illness. One summer when polio was raging, I became sick with fever, head and body aches and weakness, the symptoms of polio every parent dreaded. I remember leaving Highland in an ambulance with my frightened mother, for what turned out to be a diagnosis of the flu. It was one of my last visits to the beach.

For many successive years, colleagues from the Carolinas invited my father to conduct revival services during August. We'd stop in Washington and Bluefield, West Virginia, with my father doing all of the driving. A white-looking woman at the wheel was too risky. One day when I was thirteen, we were driving through a small town in Virginia just after lunchtime. I remember it seemed as if we were going much too slow following a long line of cars. Just as my father said, "There must be an accident ahead," a dusty black and white police car with two officers in it pulled alongside our car. One of the officers told my father to follow them. My father pulled out of the line and obliged. My mother's face suddenly went red and she seemed to be biting her bottom lip.

We drove behind the police car to what seemed to be the center of town. The policeman told my father to get out of the car and follow him. My father seemed very small between the two officers as they climbed some stairs and disappeared into a red-brick building. He was gone a long time. The midday air was full of flying things. We sat in the hot afternoon sun with the car windows open, but we were unusually quiet. From time to time Brother tried to catch the dragonflies or moths that fluttered through the windows. My mother stroked Pattee's hair and hummed over and over again a ditty I could not recognize.

After a while, my father came out. An expression new to me was on his face. He told my mother he had had to pay a fifty-dollar fine for speeding. He also told her that the officers wanted to know if she was his wife, and whether she was white. My father said maybe my mother should get in the back with the children. She acted as if she had not heard, and did not move. For the next leg of the trip to West Virginia, we did not make a sound.

Later I would hear stories of how some of my father's minister friends would put on chauffeur's caps when they drove their light wives through the South. I knew we would eventually shrug off the incident, because things like that did not happen back home, at least not that I was aware of then.

Sometimes we stopped in Greensboro to visit my father's brother Clint, who was teaching art at North Carolina Agricultural and Technical College. Clint usually took me to tour his classrooms and studios. He had an Asian aspect about his face, looking more like his Indian forebears than any of his brothers. But like his brother Bob he had a calm expression that suggested a contemplative life. For Clint, the piano was an ivory and ebony canvas. As if creating a painting, he played with delicate grace and precision, lightly coloring his notes and varying his tones in intricate shadings.

On one of those trips to North Carolina, my father married Clint to his bride, Lelia Sharpe, a tall, big-boned, pretty woman who looked whiter than my mother. All of Lelia's family looked white but they were of modest means. As some in the family told it, Lelia was preoccupied with color and status. She grew dissatisfied living on a teacher's salary and wanted her husband to "move up North with his brothers." Often she threatened to leave. Clint would retreat upstairs to his study and invariably lose his dinner. But we did not know about their problems then.

Clint and Lelia had a daughter, Blanche, who I thought looked like me with her grave expression, three braids and white bows. She was the only cousin near my age, a quiet, mannerly child who seemed to enjoy the boisterous invasion by her New England cousins. She had inherited the family's musical gifts and played the piano brilliantly from an early age. Later, she would go on tour as a member of the Fisk Jubilee Singers. Blanche married a white anthropologist and now lives in a log cabin in upstate New York.

We continued south, my father driving cautiously from dawn to dusk with brief rests at the side of the road. Until I was older and could read and understand serious matters, I mostly loved those trips south. I felt as if I were going into a different world. I knew there were restaurants, movies and stores where I could not go, but I was young enough that those things were not foremost in my mind, and my parents shielded me from the deeper evils.

For me, the South was long, slow hot days when you looked for excitement and absolutely nothing happened. It was friends who thought my accent was as funny as I thought theirs. It was women in starched summer housedresses and aprons, busy in kitchens that produced an endless supply of biscuits, rolls, grits and lemonade. It was my father sitting on the front porch with his friend, fanning himself and drinking ice tea. It was my mother, looking pretty and cool in a summer dress, setting the table for her hostess.

In Hartsville, South Carolina, we stayed with the Spanns, a Baptist minister and his wife whose four children's ages mirrored our own. The family treated us like visiting royalty, giving up their beds, preparing all the foods we liked, and advising the entire Negro population of that small town that the Connecticut visitors had arrived.

The road in front of the Spanns' home was unpaved, and there were no sidewalks. Spanish moss hung from the trees in the front yard. I loved swinging on the dusty gate of the slatted fence that surrounded the house. My daily adventure included walking up the sandy road, looking for frogs, snakes and other children. There seemed to be more fireflies to catch and bigger trees to hide behind in the evening than there were back in Connecticut. Sometimes we huddled together on the porch as one adult after another told tales of local "hants."

The revival lasted a week, and we usually went with my father on the first and last days. Located in neighboring Darlington, Reverend Spann's church was a modest white structure in a clearing at the end of some piney woods. The unforgiving wooden pews were barely more than upright benches. Over the week, attendance grew, and on the last two days, there were capacity crowds.

At revivals, my father preached without restraint, his performance a sharp contrast to his New England and Washington styles. He'd wear a white linen or gabardine suit, a white shirt, black tie, white shoes and socks. He jumped, hopped, chicken-strutted and duck-walked. He held a white linen handkerchief in his hand as he hummed, moaned and sometimes dropped to the floor, preaching until he was hoarse. When he had concluded his sermon, he collapsed into himself and resumed his dignified, reserved demeanor.

My siblings and I nudged and eyed one another, waiting for the responses we knew my father would evoke. Sitting among us, with Pattee on her lap, my mother would reach out and pinch us if our inattentiveness was too obvious. Among many of the other congregants, there was much thrashing about, swaying from side to side, jumping up, hand-waving, amens and falling-outs. A revivalist's effectiveness was gauged by how many joined the church at his invitation. My father brought in droves of new members.

On Homecoming, the last night of the revival, everyone put on their newest and best-since-Easter outfits and hats and loaded down their cars and trucks with food. Each year I was surprised afresh at the mountains of fried chicken, pies, potato salad, greens, lima beans, ham, roast beef, cakes, yams, rice, potatoes, chitterlings, neck bones, salads, fish, pork chops, string beans, squash, peas, dumplings, corn on the cob, jellied salads, Jell-O, rice pudding, corn bread, rolls and biscuits. A carpet of food seemed to fill the entire clearing behind the church.

One year in Darlington my father took us to visit Joe McFarland, a tobacco farmer who owned six hundred acres of planted land. At dusk, before the biting things came out, my father insisted that I walk among the rows of tobacco with McFarland. My father wanted me to see and remember that a Negro owned and profited from this extensive piece of property. In my patent leather shoes, I tramped through symmetrical rows of plants that were as tall as I while the farmer explained what happened to the tobacco after it was picked. Much later I wrote an essay about that walk for my high school English class in Ansonia. The essay generated a lively discussion among my working-class white schoolmates, who could not envision a Negro owning so much land.

Still later I thought about McFarland when I read the true story of a little slave girl who was put out to work in the tobacco fields. She was only five when her master decided it was time. He took her to the fields and explained that it was her job to walk through each row of plants and pull "suckers"—long green worms—from the plants. Behind her was another girl, six years old, who had done the same work for a year.

"Make sure you get 'em all off," the veteran child kept urging. But when the overseer came by, he could tell the new recruit had not done her work to his specifications; there were not enough worms on the ground near her feet. On the leaves she had passed by, he saw a cluster of offenders. Without a word, he reached down to the ground, scooped up a handful of worms, and forced them into the girl's mouth. "I bet you won't leave no more worms," he said as he walked away.

The writer John Weir once said, "There are two essential American journeys. One is a discovery, the other an escape." I equated McFarland's journey to ownership and prosperity as an escape from the little girl's condition of servitude and exploitation.

When I was thirteen, I found on my father's shelves Lillian Smith's *Strange Fruit*, about lynchings in the South. Right next to it was *Scottsboro Boy*, the story of the boys who had been falsely accused of raping a white girl in Alabama in 1931. The fact that some of the young men were not set free until 1937, the year I was born, horrified me. I demanded to know why my father and others did not work harder to get the boys out of jail sooner. His explanations about the difficulties of fighting Southern justice did not appease me.

It was not until Emmett Till, a boy visiting from Chicago, was lynched in Mississippi that my feelings about the South changed dramatically. His crime: whistling at a white woman. I was a senior in high school when I saw the pictures of his mutilated corpse in the black press. The photographs did not hide the gaping wounds, the bloated body and the pathetically thin, young arms.

Every black person carries around a reservoir of rage. For some it is always full, sloshing around and overflowing at the slightest provocation. For others, like me, its level tends to stay low. But it is always there. When I saw Emmett Till's pictures my chest was full of water. I could never really love the South again.

But as I grew up, I realized it was not just the South. No matter how powerful we become, no matter how many presidents or queens we meet, whether we go to Ivy League schools or buy mansions in New Haven or on Long Island Sound, we know that, still, black people can be lynched. Will the day ever come that the noose is no longer a threat, that the gasoline will never be poured, that the shotgun will not be fired? I was certain in my lifetime things would be different. The boring litany of Howard Beach, Rodney King and the black tourist torched in Florida screams: not so.

☙

One year, my father drove us to Montreal, where we stayed at an elegant old hotel. We took a sightseeing tour in a horse-drawn carriage and ate most of our meals in the hotel's turn-of-the-century dining room. I was eight at the time, and it was in that French city that I first became conscious of white people looking at us with curiosity and puzzlement. Wherever we went, stares followed us. My mother was self-conscious, but my proud father was unfazed by the scrutiny. I think he enjoyed it. His step was more sprightly, his diction more precise. He was conscious of being on a kind of stage.

Even in the States, we unfailingly elicited interest ranging from sidelong glances to outright gawking. In the words of black film-maker Isaac Julian, we became "objects of a certain gaze that is, in the end, ethnographic." Once we trooped into the dining room of the largest hotel in Ames, Iowa. Just after we sat down, a white diner came to the table, told my parents they had a beautiful family, and asked what country we were from. We thought this was hysterically funny, especially when my father said, in his most punctilious manner, "The country of Connecticut."

Sometimes my father took us to his conventions as part of our vacation trip. The National Baptist Convention, eight million strong, is the largest organized group of black people in the United States. Its founders and leaders were friends and colleagues of my grandfather and my father and included some of the greatest black preachers in the world: its president, J. H. Jackson of Chicago; his predecessor, D. V. Jemison; Gardner Taylor of New York; C. L. Franklin (Aretha Franklin's father) and A. G. Wright of Detroit; and M. L. King, Martin Luther King's father. My father was a vice president of the group.

Later the National Baptist Convention would split, and a group called the Progressive Baptist Convention would be formed. My father's loyalty remained with the original group, of which he and his own father had been longtime members. Like many of his generation, he thought the young Martin Luther King was an upstart. Eventually my father would come to admire the tactics of civil disobedience and speak with awe of the students who risked their lives in demonstrations and marches. But he would never be a fan of Dr. King, Jr., because of what he saw as King's betrayal of J. H. Jackson.

At an early age I absorbed the dramatic cadence and colorful similes that these men invoked to make their sermons ignite the thousands in the audience. Each successive speaker would wax just a little more histrionic until on the last night, reserved for the most powerful preachers, the crowd would respond to each pause, each swipe of the handkerchief, each ecstatic moan. The ministers' pacing, their picture painting and their supreme certitude laid the foundation of my own presentation techniques. The music was glorious, too, with visiting gospel choirs competing like the ministers to see who could move the audiences the most and who could match Mahalia Jackson's performance as the convention's official soloist.

The crowd was more than one hundred times the size of Ansonia's tiny black population. I was enchanted with the women's hats, their summer dresses of silk, chiffon, linen, brocade. The season did not dictate the fashion. In spite of the August heat, many women wore velvet, wool jersey, shedding feathered boas and fur capelets matted in spots from storage.

When the convention hall got too hot, or there was a break in the program, I played outside on the steps with my sisters and brother and other beautifully dressed brown children whose hair, elbows, knees and patent leather shoes shone with Vaseline. They had come from churches in small towns, big cities and rural places. Their parents were ministers, auto mechanics, hairdressers, bus drivers, merchants, barbers, maids, cooks, chauffeurs, teachers, die cutters and practical nurses. They afforded me my sense of black life outside of Ansonia and Washington.

Among the missionaries, the choir members, the deacons, the trustees and the workers bustling about, it was easy to spot the clusters of ministers, dark and dazzling in their immaculate summer whites and straws. My father mingled with his colleagues, more animated and engaged than at home. The ministers' camaraderie was an outlet for men who had to be leaders, paragons and pillars in their home communities. At their meeting, they could talk about ways of getting rid of troublesome deacons or dodging needy matrons. With great good humor and familiarity, they called each other "Doc," "Rev," "E.W." and "Taylor." Many were men of hyperbole, culture, education and often flamboyance. Others were unlettered but charismatic. All were part of my large security blanket of powerful dark supermen.

My parents rounded out my summer experiences by sending me to a coeducational Negro camp for two weeks of several successive summers. Camp Atwater, founded in the 1920s for children of Negro professionals who were not allowed to go to camps built for whites, was located just outside of West Brookfield, Massachusetts. It had a large lake and acres of rolling woods dotted with cabins and pavilions. Its campers came mainly from the Eastern Seaboard, many of them the same children I had met in Washington and Highland Beach. When I was in college, I discovered that the camp was a common denominator for most of the Negro students I met.

At first, I could not understand why my parents would pay a lot of money to send me to a camp whose program did not seem as full as my Girl Scout day camp in Ansonia. After a few days, I saw that they wanted me to know more children whose lives were similar to my own. They were only partially correct in their reasoning. The children of most black professionals tended to live in a single-class cocoon. Working diligently at disassociating themselves from the poverty and perceived ignorance of the masses, their parents banded together with other professionals. Many of them joined Jack and Jill, the national organization whose mission was to bring middle-class black children together and expose them to black history and positive experiences. The children had little experiential knowledge of working-class black or white life. Few of them knew poor colored people, and many of them disdained anything out of the rural South, equating it with ignorance, poverty and slavery.

Back home, I took the college-bound academic course and continued to bring home all A's. My teachers took a special interest in me, and I knew I was a favorite. I eagerly consumed Latin for four years. Learning the origins of the words I used every day made me feel powerful and all-knowing. Race, though, was not talked about much by whites, and mentioning it in "mixed" company was considered bad manners. I continued to win essay and oratorical contests. Once I wrote an essay about Negro soldiers in the Korean War and the segregation they would face when they returned home. My English teacher praised the piece and asked me to read it aloud. It was greeted with silence, as if I had committed a faux pas.

Being enthusiastic, athletic and well coordinated, I made cheerleader my junior and senior years, the cheerleading ranks having only recently been integrated. Editor of the senior yearbook, vice president of the senior class and voted most popular, I graduated third of 125 students. There were eight other Negro students in my class; all but three were from my father's church. Sheer numbers and academic interest ensured that most of my friends would be white, but I dated only Negro boys. There was little dating between the races, and I was never attracted to men with white faces anyway.

The only Jewish boy in my class, a good friend and academic buddy, often invited me to play tennis with him. I sensed he wanted to see me after the game but he never did. I also sensed that he felt he was an outsider. In Ansonia, where there were not many Jewish families, anti-Semitism was also in the closet. When we drove to New Haven, I remember my parents pointing out the new Jewish country club in Woodbridge, which they said was built because the old WASP club in New Haven would not admit Jews. One Jewish couple who owned the liquor store was especially friendly with my parents, and the wife brought my mother into the College Club. My hunch is that having my mother there made her feel less alone.

The boys I dated from Ansonia and New Haven had certain similarities: they were smart, fashionable and dark. Although I would repeat their names, my father called all of my dates "young man." He said it was his way of not getting them mixed up. I believe it was his way of letting them know they were not central to my life. All the boys were intimidated by my father. When they came to visit, he sat in the living room, reading his paper or listening to the radio. Beyond acknowledging their presence, he offered no openings for small talk, and few tried to engage him in conversation. Their awe of this man who was my father was amusing and incomprehensible to me.

While in high school I had two marriage proposals, one from a much older boy on the rebound from a college sweetheart who had broken off their engagement. The second was from a handsome air force man who had been a classmate of my sister Jewelle's. During halftime at a high school basketball game where I was cheerleading, he gave me a diamond engagement ring. Flattered and surprised, I took it into the girls' room and put it on in one of the stalls. I stayed for as long as I could, examining the solitaire from every angle. When the halftime bell rang, I took the ring off, put it back in the box, came out of the stall and returned it to my disappointed beau. I told him I could not accept it because I was too young and planned to go to college. I also told him I did not want to marry a minister, which is what he planned to be. If he changed his mind about his profession and went to college, I suggested, I might feel differently.

Every day after school for twelve years, I would pass Abel Prince as he went to work in the foundry. Prince was a tiny, wiry blue-black man who came from Nevis, a British island in the Caribbean. He was one of a few West Indians in our town. No matter the season, he wore the same battered, stained panama straw with a wide black band. He never appeared without a crumpled linen sports jacket, and more often than not, he wore a narrow black tie. Those few teeth he had left were mostly gold. He had neither wife nor family in Ansonia. Every day he'd call to me in his heavy West Indian accent, "Hello, Miss Lady, keep getton dem A's and tings," to which I'd respond without fail, "I will, Mr. Prince, I will." By the time I reached my senior year, I towered over him. But we still continued the exchange.

While I was in college, my parents told me that Mr. Prince inquired about me several times each week. After my engagement was announced and my picture had appeared in the local paper, Mr. Prince handed my father a grease-stained envelope for me. Inside was a torn piece of yellow lined paper, no more than two inches wide, and on it, written in a shaky hand, was: "This is for all dem A's and to help get your wedon dress." He had enclosed five one-hundred-dollar bills.

When I was sixteen my parents gave me a formal birthday party for one hundred guests, essentially a private coming-out party. I felt like a princess in a strapless, ruffled tulle dress of robin's egg blue. Taking a fashion cue from Rita Hayworth, Susan Hayward and Elizabeth Taylor, I wore a matching blue net stole as a long scarf, with its panels thrown back dramatically over my shoulders.

The next year, I did in fact "come out," along with twenty-five other Negro girls, in a cotillion in the ballroom of New Haven's historic Taft Hotel. The event was sponsored by the Girlfriends, a national black women's organization founded in the late 1920s by four college friends determined to preserve their college relationships. For several months before the evening we rehearsed the intricate steps of a nineteenth-century cotillion quadrille and were feted at teas, luncheons and concerts. For me, the experience had little social significance. Even at sixteen I felt I had been "out." I had traveled extensively and met people all over the country. I had relatives and friends who had come out in Bridgeport, Hartford, Washington and cities throughout the South. And I knew that in Washington all but a few of the girls would have been lighter than I.

For all the experiences my father allowed me, he would not permit me to take a part-time job or baby-sit. He said he did not want me to take time from my studies. But more important, he felt that baby-sitting was too much like being a maid for white people's children. He did not want it to appear that his daughters had to work, much less work for white people. It was not until I was a sophomore in college that he relented somewhat. We had moved to New Haven by then and he agreed that I could baby-sit for the Jewish next-door neighbors with whom he and my mother were friends. He rationalized that my sitting for them was a favor for friends rather than a service for strangers.

When Jewelle was in high school, she was recruited for a role in a summer stock production at the Southbury Playhouse in Connecticut. The company was a group of professional actors from New York. Jewelle was to play the role of an eccentric maid for the

eccentric family in *You Can't Take It with You*. When he heard she
would play a maid's role, my father balked. He insisted on reading
the script. After determining that the role was indeed humorous
and to his mind in no way demeaning, he relented.

❧

The summer after my high school graduation in 1955, I took a
real job for the Southern New England Telephone Company in
New Haven. Getting dressed for work in summer suits, linen
dresses and the white gloves my family required made me feel
grown-up and sophisticated. Every morning I walked across the
bridge to catch the seven o'clock bus for the half hour ride to New
Haven. I waved to Miss Hattie and Nornie and the church members
I passed on their way to the factory.

At one point on the bridge, you could look right into the foundry.
Overhead was a vat on a moving crane that poured molten metal
into another large vat on the floor. Showers of hot metal would fly
about like miniature fireworks displays each time the vat was filled.
Men handling long forklike instruments gingerly moved red-hot
rods of different lengths. It was profoundly dangerous work and I
felt fortunate and sometimes guilty that my father did not have to
do it.

The telephone company's headquarters was a stately bronze and
reddish art deco building on Church Street near the New Haven
Green. I was assigned to an office of white people who all seemed
old to me. Most of them were lifetime employees in their mid-
fifties. They were called pole engineers because they knew the
location, age and condition of every telephone pole in Connecticut.
In that office I learned the real geography of my home state. There
were so many towns whose names I had never heard. My father
said that was because they were all white.

My job was to collect all of my officemates' daily output, organize
it and file it away. Telephone pole geography was not the most
stimulating subject for a seventeen-year-old, so I concentrated on
interpersonal relationships. I was one of the first blacks to be hired
by the company, and none of my colleagues knew anything about
Negroes. Their curiosity about me was not subtle. They were
openly admiring of my manners, my clothes, my intelligence and

my industriousness. They asked me where I learned to speak so clearly. They wanted to know why my skin was so light, and who selected my wardrobe. I gave all the credit to my family. They were astounded I was planning to go to a Seven Sisters college. How, they asked, could I afford to go to such an expensive school? They saw my father pick me up in his Cadillac on several occasions and concluded my family must be rich.

Because I was the "baby" of the office, they became protective of me and made sure I understood how the informal network operated. They advised me not to work too hard or too quickly, or they would look bad. When I left for college, the supervisor assured me I would have a job there the next summer. At my farewell, my officemates presented me with a cake, one hundred dollars and a pair of white kid gloves. Such was my introduction to the world of work.

With a teenager's confident naïveté, I took for granted that I would get accepted to the college of my choice. Being an A student all through school, an extracurricular activities "junkie," and continually the "first and only Negro" this or that had to count for something, I figured. I focused on Wellesley, Smith, Mount Holyoke, Vassar and Goucher.

The only Ansonian I knew who had attended Wellesley was my French teacher. But Jewelle was attending Radcliffe and I had a cousin from Washington who had graduated from Mount Holyoke. In my larger family circle, there were many who had attended the Seven Sisters or the Ivy League schools. We knew they were tokens. That knowledge did not deter or intimidate me. My history as a token was grounded in years of experience.

My parents drove me to each of the schools for interviews and the obligatory campus tours. My mother took great care in how she dressed for those occasions as if she too were being judged. My father looked forward to the portion of the interview reserved for parents, when he could wax eloquent about the history, tradition and importance of education in our family. By then we had all perfected the routine of being "exemplary Negroes." I thought it was a role I would have to play for the rest of my life.

The first time I saw Wellesley College was through a screen of swirling whiteness. My parents had driven me from Ansonia to

Massachusetts for my admissions interview, negotiating a December snowstorm. Scenes from the Saturday movie matinees I loved came to mind. I could not believe that such a place truly existed. It was too beautiful to be real. Although I had been around Yale all of my life, its beauty was compact, urban and familiar. Passing through Wellesley's main gate, I saw myself sledding on the rolling hills, sailing on the hidden lake and walking under the Gothic arches. At last I would be one of those college coeds in a plaid pleated skirt, sweater set, bobby socks and saddle shoes, carrying my books beneath the eighteenth-century lamplights. I had found the campus of my dreams. I had no doubt that I would get in and fit in.

All of the colleges I'd applied to accepted me, offering a range of financial aid. My father hoped I would accept the Goucher, Smith or Holyoke offers, but he did not seem disappointed when I chose Wellesley, even though it had made only a token grant.

A few months before, Dorothy Dandridge had been nominated for an Academy Award as best actress for playing the stereotype of the sensuous, free black woman in *Carmen Jones*. A few months later, Emmett Till was lynched. I saw them both as victims of a society I believed I could help change, and evidently that was how my high school classmates saw me. Under my yearbook picture, my coeditor had written, "Shirlee is going to go out like Napoleon and change the world."

Chapter Eight

Until lions have their historians, tales of hunting will always glorify the hunter.

—AFRICAN PROVERB

Royal blue is the official color of Wellesley College. It is a handsome foil for the pale skin it nurtures from late adolescence to early adulthood. In 1955, I was one of three Negro students entering my class. Only one of us was obviously black. By the end of my freshman year, two of us remained. The other light-skinned freshman, the daughter of the publisher of a Negro newspaper, chose to return to her home in the Midwest.

Wellesley's blue had been accommodating darker shades for generations. Like most of the other Seven Sisters and the Ivy League, the college had been accepting one or two ladies of color into each class since the late 1800s. I extended the long tradition of Negroes who passed the college's muster with good manners, good families, pleasant faces and bright minds.

I was assigned to Homestead, a small dormitory that housed twenty-six first-year girls. I thought it was luck to be given a single room in the homey, white wooden building that had been one of the original eighteenth-century houses on Wellesley's four hundred acres. I learned several years later that Wellesley did not assign roommates to entering Negro students. At an opening week reception, the dean of freshmen greeted by name each of the more than four hundred of us. She knew our faces because she had studied our pictures for weeks before the start of the term. I fantasized that one of my white cousins might be in my class. But there was no way for me to know, because Morris might not be her last name.

While waiting in orientation and registration lines and eating in the dining room and at the president's reception, during my first few days at the college, I was surprised when several girls asked me politely my country of origin. They were much too genteel to ask me the bolder question of what race I claimed to be. As matter-of-factly as I could, and with equal gentility, I let the girls know that I was a Negro, in my father's words, "from the country of Connecticut."

During the succeeding weeks, I learned from the girl next door, who in subsequent years became my roommate, that a number of our dorm mates had also asked her about my nationality. It baffled me that people could not immediately "see" what I was. Then it dawned on me that I had left my brown community behind and had become part of a totally different context. I could be a different race, if I chose. For the first time I began to understand how my mother's family had become white.

Once it was generally known that I was a Negro, many thought I must be a good singer. I was elected class song leader. My primary responsibility was to lead the class in "step singing" on the stairs of the college chapel and at ceremonial occasions. Actually, I enjoyed the office and ignored the stereotype. I liked to sing. I liked to lead. I saw it as an extension of my high school cheerleading.

Once I entered college I no longer went to church. The closest Negro churches were in Boston. It was an effort to get up in time to catch the bus for the forty-five-minute drive into town. After going once or twice, I gave up on the Sunday chapel service at Wellesley, too. The sermons were delivered by visiting white ministers in dry lecture style. Their content and delivery had little to do with what I knew and loved about church, and the ministers were not men who could connect me to my inner self. I missed the music and the comfort of the brown faces. I asked the college to invite my father to speak, providing them with his résumé, which I thought was impressive. They said the calendar was full for the next two years. I did not request another date. During my four years at Wellesley, I don't recall a Negro minister in the college chapel.

The other immediate problem college presented me was getting my hair done. I had still not gotten the knack of doing it, because my mother had taken care of it until I was old enough to go to the hairdresser. There were no Negro hairdressers in the town of Wellesley. Through a friend of my parents, I finally found a hairdresser in Cambridge.

During those years, a revolutionary way of doing black hair was devised: the chemical straightener. My hairdresser called and asked if I wanted to get a free hairdo by being a demonstration model for the new process. Having heard about the new wonder treatment and knowing that my allowance could not cover the cost, I eagerly accepted. I was told you could get rained on or go swimming and your hair would not crimp up and get nappy. I thought the millennium had come.

On a stage in a Cambridge auditorium, the demonstrator prepared my hair. She coated my scalp with a protective Vaseline-like substance, then applied a white cream. Before she had finished, my scalp had turned bright red in reaction to the chemical. I didn't feel a thing, but the technician was afraid that all my hair would fall out. She scurried me off the stage and washed the chemical from my scalp. In a room behind the stage, my nervous hairdresser completed my hair in the traditional press-and-curl fashion. On stage, the show's directors were turning the calamity into an opportunity to advise the audience of hairdressers that they should first test a small patch of skin to avoid what happened to me. Eventually my hairdresser found the right straightener for my hair, and I knew I'd make it through the next four years.

The first two years I was in college, there were eight Negro women on campus, two in each class. We kept polite distances from one another, wanting to demonstrate our blendability. I continued looking for some connection, but sensed it would come only with numbers. In the meantime, I made a host of new friends and explored all the treats that a place like Wellesley has to offer. Most of the time I felt like an insider. Once I was startled to see a large group of black tourists alighting from a bus in the main parking lot. "What are *they* doing here?" I thought, and then recognized my lapse—I had identified with the majority.

At the time, I had no idea how fortunate I was to spend four years among rolling hills, memorable vistas, a wooded lake, beautiful buildings and ample green space. I had no idea what a luxury it was to study the classic and the obscure, to have unlimited access to great libraries, diverse ideas and often brilliant teachers and students. I had no idea what it really meant to worry about money or the future.

But Wellesley did not entirely isolate itself from the rest of the world. In 1957, my junior year, eight Negro freshmen came onto campus, doubling the number of black souls walking across the green lawns. I was deliriously happy and curious. No longer reticent about making contact, I invited all the Negro students for a get-together in my room. Not being sophisticated enough to have an agenda and not knowing what the agenda should be, I told the other girls that just being together was important. The conversation was mostly about our off-campus social life and our lives at home. We kept our feelings about the college environment to ourselves.

Long after graduation I learned that a number of the girls in that room had been unhappy and ill at ease at Wellesley. The college, they believed, did not recognize or accept their differentness. In listening to them, it came to me that I had maintained a special place for my colored self that did not need Wellesley for its validation, a place back home with my family and my church community.

Despite the lack of a significant number of black students, my years at Wellesley were happy, productive ones. Each fall its physical beauty seduced me anew. Its most important gift was the expansion of my mind. There was nothing Wellesley could not teach me. I became a sociology major but studied Russian literature, biblical history, organic chemistry and music. There was no such thing as Black Studies then, and no black professors. Affirmative action had not yet been born. Unlike some of the black students who came to the Ivy League in the 1960s, those of us who entered before the civil rights movement had great confidence that we were there because we were smart, not because we were needed to salve consciences or fill quotas. With a quota of only one or two, we knew we were the best and the brightest.

Exotic sports became old hat. I learned to ski on rubber hills. I conformed my body to the postures and thrusts of fencing. My loud voice gained me the position of coxswain for the class crew. As much as I wanted to, I did not join the swimming club, which

performed intricate water ballets. I was not sure how much chlor-
inated water my newly straightened hair could tolerate. And to the
music of Aaron Copeland's *Rodeo*, I danced as a cowgirl on the great
lawn for Wellesley's traditional springtime fete, Tree Day. I was
unable to escape typecasting as a native maiden in the junior show,
chanting away on some mythical yellow island.

Although for me Wellesley was a good place to make the transition
from girl to woman, it was there that I encountered for the first
time a way of behaving that I call the *politesse* of deceit. No matter
how angry or vindictive some of the truly upper-class white Wellesley women became, they never let it show. They were not prone
to argue or to defend a point of view with spirit or passion. Everything controversial was handled behind closed doors or with
clenched smiles and soft words. It galled me to realize I would
never know what many of my classmates thought about important
issues. I could never know what their anger would cause them to
do, because they never appeared angry. I did not think this was
one of the mannerly strategies that my father admired. Even the
queen let on when she was not amused.

When I was a sophomore, I was a maid of honor at Jewelle's
wedding, along with Pattee. Then Jewelle and her husband, Jim,
went to Africa to stay in a village outside of Monrovia, Liberia,
where he would do research on native law. They lived in a mud
hut with a thatched straw roof for almost a year. It was the first
time a member of the immediate family had been so far away. For
Christmas, Jewelle sent us necklaces of colorful African trading
beads that she had strung herself.

My parents also moved, but not to a mud hut. My father had
found a large white colonial on West Park Avenue in New Haven's
west side, facing Edgewood Park. There was a central staircase,
several living rooms, a sun porch, well-kept parquet floors, a room
that my father designated the music room and a pleasant yard. Pattee
was the only one living at home then, and my parents had reserved
a front bedroom with a window seat and fireplace for me. I didn't
miss Ansonia or the river. I was immediately at home in the new
place, and the house became a model of what I would look for in
a residence.

Black sororities and fraternities were the social lifeline for the scant number of Negroes in the Ivy League in the 1950s. The Boston chapters invited membership from the surrounding colleges. Over a period of weeks, I passed the rigorous pledge rituals to become a member of Alpha Kappa Alpha sorority, one of the nation's oldest black groups. A flurry of meetings, teas, and dances gave me a new brown community. Many of the students were alumni of Camp Atwater or Highland Beach. They had belonged to Jack and Jill, or their mothers were members of the Girlfriends or the Links.

It was at one of those sorority functions that I met a tall, handsome student who was majoring in drama at Boston University and unlike any other Negro I had ever encountered. He had grown up in Lexington, Massachusetts, the son of a successful, Harvard-educated businessman. His mother had been born in Canada and looked part Indian. She passed her Indian looks on to her son, who had chiseled features, curly hair and red-brown skin. He had attended private school in Concord, and then on to Putney, an experimental high school in Vermont. Until he met me, he had never dated a Negro or been to a Negro church. He was fascinated by the negritude of my life. I was incredulous at the racial isolation of his. We dated exclusively for several years and thought we might marry.

Then one afternoon a sonorous voice invited me for an afternoon of study. It belonged to Harold Haizlip, a cheerful graduate student studying the classics at Harvard. His fraternity brother from Amherst was engaged to one of my classmates at Wellesley and each thought it would be a splendid idea to bring their "two nice Negro friends" together. As was the custom, we met to study in the recreation building of the college, but we were too interested in each other to open a single book. So began a love story that has not ended.

Harold had planned to be a doctor, but had fallen in love with words and languages. Except for my father and some of his ministerial friends, I had not met anyone who reveled in Latin and Greek. Tall, dark and attractive, Harold carried himself with grace and assurance. A native of Washington, D.C., he had been valedictorian of Dunbar High School.

Federal judge James Dandridge Halyburton, Richmond, Virginia, circa 1860. Great-nephew of Martha Washington and father of Edward Everett Morris.
(Courtesy of Virginia State Archives)

Edward Everett Morris, son of Judge Halyburton and slave Ruth Morris, circa 1889. Born a slave in Richmond in 1849, he died a free man in Washington, D.C., in 1903.

Margaret Maher Morris, circa 1920. Born in Tipperary, Ireland, in 1856, she immigrated into the United States as a child and defied the customs of the times by marrying an ex-slave.

William Morris, Sr., father of
Margaret Morris, circa 1896.

Rosalind (Rose) Scott Morris,
mother of Margaret Morris,
circa 1899.

Mary (Mamie) Morris
Smith, aunt of Margaret
Morris, circa 1904.

Edward T. Morris, uncle of
Margaret Morris, circa 1896.

Ruth Morris Jones, aunt
of Margaret Morris, in a
portrait painted for her
mother, circa 1917.

William C. Morris, Jr., Margaret's brother, with first daughter, Dorothy, in Cleveland, circa 1922.

Edward Morris, one of Margaret's twin brothers, circa 1913. He died in the great influenza epidemic of 1918.

Grace Morris, Margaret's older sister, circa 1921, after she
moved to Cleveland.

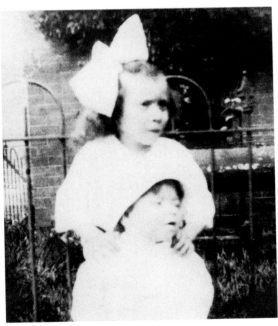

Margaret Morris and her brother Michael,
around the time her family vanished, 1916.

Bessie Everett Clay, Margaret's cousin, godmother and first guardian, circa 1898.

Henry Clay and Bessie Clay on the steps of their Foggy Bottom house, circa 1914.

Rebecca Allen, the neighbor who became surrogate mother to Michael Morris, circa 1895. Margaret became heir to her house and other assets.

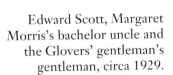

Edward Scott, Margaret Morris's bachelor uncle and the Glovers' gentleman's gentleman, circa 1929.

Thelma Burt, Margaret's "sister," Washington, D.C., circa 1930.

Anna "White Cloud" Fortune, mother of Roberta Fortune, circa 1898.

Roberta Fortune Taylor, wife of William Taylor, Sr., circa 1906.

Rev. William Taylor, Sr., in the pastor's chair of the Florida Avenue Baptist Church, Washington, D.C., circa 1914.

Chanie Robinson Taylor, mother of William Taylor, Sr., with grandsons William and Clinton, circa 1899.

The children of William Taylor, Sr., circa 1912. *Left to right*, Robert, Julian, Blanche, Clinton, and in the chair, Percy. William, Jr., was away at college.

The Taylor men in front of the family brownstone, Washington, D.C., circa 1935. *Left to right, sitting:* Robert, William, Sr., Percy. *Standing:* Julian, Clinton, William, Jr.

My father in his engagement portrait, 1932.

Julian and Margaret's circle of friends,
Stratford, Connecticut, circa 1934.
Margaret is third from left. Jewelle is
the baby sitting in her godmother
Matiel Robinson's lap.

The extended family of William Taylor, Sr., in Washington, D.C., circa 1935. Margaret Morris Taylor is seated on the patriarch's right and holds Julian Taylor, Jr.; to his left is Marjorie Taylor Black and her son, Robert. *Standing from left to right: (front row)* Charles, Rudolf, Doris, Antoinette, Thelma, Mauryne, Jewelle; *(back row)* Billy, William, Robert, Clinton, Julian, Percy.

Julian and Margaret in the parsonage in Ansonia, Connecticut, circa 1943. (*DeWhit Keith, Jr.*)

My wedding to Harold Haizlip, at Dwight Chapel, Yale University, 1959.

My family, in Ansonia, circa 1943. *Left to right on sofa:* my mother, Pattee, my father, my half sister Doris and her son DeWhit Keith III. *On the floor:* me, Julian, Jr., Jewelle. (*DeWhit Keith, Jr.*)

Mauryne Taylor, my half sister, in *Come on Cowboy*, flanked by
Mantan Moreland, *left*, and Flornoy Miller. The movie was filmed
with a cast of real black cowboys in Rahway, New Jersey, 1946.
*(Courtesy Southwest Film/Video Archives, Southern Methodist
University)*

Julian with Attorney General Robert Kennedy and President
Lyndon Johnson, as brother Robert Taylor, *right*, looks on.

A second wedding for Margaret Morris Taylor, *center*, flanked by *(from left to right)* my daughters Deirdre and Melissa, my brother's daughter Julie, Thelma, Jewelle, me, and Pattee. Granddaughter Robin Hancock is the flower girl.

Margaret Morris Taylor and her sister, Grace Morris Cramer, reunited after seventy-six years in Anaheim, California, 1992.

Harold's father, Allen, was one of thirteen children who had grown up on a farm in Belews Creek, North Carolina. Following five of his brothers and a sister, Allen had left for the promise of a better life in Washington. Two of Allen's brothers became undertakers. Allen and three others became railroad porters who worked out of Union Station. Their sister opened a beauty parlor and later became a popular caterer. Allen died at forty-three. His widow, the former Nellie Hill, a mulatto from Kernersville, North Carolina, took a full-time government job to support eight-year-old Harold and his two siblings.

Nellie's father, Robert Hill, was the grandson of white indentured servants. He appeared out of nowhere one day in Kernersville, North Carolina, a little colored enclave no bigger than a road and a few trees. He was wan, with dark hair, a thick dark mustache, sky-blue eyes and a gaunt, unsmiling face. He never talked about his family, and no one knew why he had come to Kernersville. Pale white Hill married coal black Kettie Martin, a former slave who had memories of running away from her owner's plantation at the end of the Civil War. Together, deep in the hills of central North Carolina, they raised Nellie and eight other handsome children, all caramel color with straight hair. When Hill took his children into town, the locals would ask him what he was doing with "them nigger children." "Taking care of 'em," he would reply, and keep walking.

Until he went to Amherst College, Harold had lived a totally segregated life. He finished high school in 1953, the year before the Supreme Court school desegregation ruling. His neighborhoods, his schools, and his social life were contained within Washington's colored world. Like many other black boys growing up in the South, Harold knew he had to be careful where he went and what he did. His mother taught him to avoid encounters with the white world at all cost. He got glimpses of that world, though, from a part-time job delivering dry-cleaning, and occasionally in academic competitions against white schools, when the inequality of their separate facilities did not escape his notice.

Harold was graceful and loved dancing and ice skating. He also enjoyed music, and played the piano with skill. With the callowness of a twenty-year-old, I abruptly broke off with my Boston University beau. A few weeks later I was sporting a fraternity pin from the avid reader of Thucydides.

Harold was not intimidated by my father. Each time my father called him "young man," Harold would remind him of his name. With constant good humor and helpfulness in practical matters, he penetrated my father's reserve. When the time came, Harold asked for my hand in the traditional manner, as my father expected. The two of them spoke for almost two hours, while my mother and I chattered in my bedroom. No matter how much I prodded, Harold has never divulged the contents of that conversation.

❧

I married a few weeks after my graduation from Wellesley, in Yale University's Dwight Chapel, because my father's church could hold only half the invited guests. The day before the event, Harold and I were scheduled to pick up our wedding bands, our last and most important errand before the rehearsal and dinner that night. The downtown traffic was light. As we passed under a yellow traffic light and turned onto Chapel Street, a policeman flashed the amber light on the top of his car and told Harold to pull over.

My father had always told me to speak up if I felt my rights were being violated. As the policeman asked for Harold's license and registration, I advised him we had not committed any traffic violation. Harold told me to stay calm and said nothing to the policeman.

After looking over Harold's papers, the policeman told Harold to follow him because we had gone through a red light. Imperiously, I said we had more important things to do than traipse around after him, especially since he could not tell the difference between a yellow light and a red one. By the time we arrived at the police station, I was at the high end of my rage level. Harold was polite and stoic as a booking sergeant filled out formal arrest papers for him. Another policeman frisked Harold and relieved him of his wallet and valuables. He was led around a corner to a cell containing a number of other detainees. I paced back and forth in front of the sergeant's desk, threatening lawsuits and loss of jobs. It was my first negative encounter with the law, and it reduced the sergeant in my eyes to a redneck, poor-white-trash, cracker lawman. When he said, "Lady, you had better be quiet or we'll lock you up too," without skipping a beat, in my most intimidating and cutting voice I said, "You just try it."

Calling home from the police station, I heard a houseful of noise and guests. Within a few minutes, my father arrived at the station with the family lawyer. In his most diplomatic tones, my father, whom most of the policemen instantly recognized, asked for an explanation.

As the officer began to tell his story, I began yelling that he was a redneck, fascist, Nazi liar. Quietly, my father asked me to get some fresh air. I took my pacing and muttering to the front steps and, shortly, Harold was released on the promise to return to New Haven for a court date. We got to the jewelry store just before it closed, secured our wedding bands and returned home to much good-natured ribbing and high hilarity over our "prison escapade." Some of the men kidded that Harold might want to rethink what the marriage might portend. What went unsaid was the suspicion that Harold had been stopped because he was driving with a woman the policeman thought to be white. And that what had made matters worse was that the "white woman" had defended her black companion.

The next day, before a gathering of five hundred guests, my father and two of his closest ministerial colleagues, who had known me since I was a baby, performed the nuptial rites. My uncle Percy played the organ as if he were in St. Paul's Cathedral. My sisters and brother were in my wedding party, as were three classmates from college and one of my foster sisters. Several of my bridesmaids were white, as were four of my husband's groomsmen. There were almost as many white guests as black. The assemblage looked like a poster for Brotherhood Week.

When a minister's daughter marries, the first several hundred names on the guest list are the church members. They came en masse. It was the social event of the year. Some of our professors and dozens of our friends from our various colleges traveled from Boston for the occasion. My father's political cronies and a host of neighbors also crowded into the chapel. My mother's Washington relatives did not come to the wedding. My father's people made up for their absence. I wondered if the weddings of any of my white cousins had been as grand.

While on our honeymoon in Vermont, we made the decision to pay a fine for our alleged traffic violation, rather than begin our marriage with litigation we knew we would not win. It was one of the few times in our life together that we opted not to struggle.

I had given up my thought of becoming a doctor when I met Harold. Instead, I had taken the legal aptitude tests and had been accepted at Stanford and Boston University law schools. But I did not feel ready to plunge into another round of books, classes and exams. I wanted to get to know the good-humored, brilliant man I had married without the pressure of performing in a high-powered professional school. Harold had graduated with honors and had won a fellowship that allowed him to continue his study of classics at Harvard. I would be free to explore what I thought would be endless opportunities for me in Boston. After a number of turndowns that we suspected were based on race, we found a first-floor apartment in Boston's Back Bay and began our life's journey as a couple on the eve of the country's most tumultuous decade.

In the late 1950s and early 1960s, Boston was still ostensibly an open place, for students at least. Harold and I kept close connections with our college friends. I took a job as an editorial assistant in an immunological research center that published articles about allergies and asthma. My boss was an eccentric English physician who loved me because I shared his passion for the English language. Harold completed an advanced degree and became the first Negro teacher at the prestigious Wellesley High School. The year was 1959. Except for driving through yellow lights in New Haven, I still believed that all things were possible.

That fall, my sister Pattee entered Fisk University in Nashville. She had grown into a beautiful girl, full of zest and bravado. She wrote home about her first sit-in:

A bus took us from the campus to downtown Nashville. A group of us sat at a lunch counter, waiting for service we knew would not come. Everything was fine until a husky Red Neck came up behind me and stood, breathing on my neck. First he called me a nigger lover. Then he honked and spit a mouthful of something down my back. Forgetting everything I learned, I jumped up, ready to scratch eyes, bite cheeks and kick balls.

It wasn't until a fellow demonstrator had taken her to the bus to cool off that she realized the heckler thought she was white. That upset her more than anything.

In 1961 Pattee married Joe Williams, a classmate from Fisk who liked to play the trumpet and wanted to be a lawyer, and they moved to New Haven. That same year, my father asked Harold and me to drive him and my mother to Kansas City for the annual National Baptist Convention. He did not want to drive alone because he needed to marshal all of his strength for the battle he knew was waiting.

The previous year in Philadelphia, as recounted by Taylor Branch in *Parting the Waters*, J. H. Jackson had put down an attempt by an insurgent group led by Martin Luther King, Jr., Benjamin Hooks and Ralph Abernathy to elevate their own candidate, the dynamic and brilliant Gardner Taylor of Brooklyn, to the presidency of the convention. Their goal was to bring the NBC into the forefront of the civil rights movement, which conservative "Old Jack" had essentially eschewed.

I had not been to a convention since I was a teenager, and was happy to see that it had not changed. At any time of the day, there was some type of service or musical activity going on. This year, though, there was a palpable tension in the air. The hotels were full of ministers having private caucuses in their rooms. My father himself was in meetings most of the night. Despite Baptist doctrine, we noticed bottles of liquor on a number of the room service trays being wheeled up the corridors.

My father told us the fireworks would probably begin when Jackson delivered his always dramatic annual president's message. As in the past, there would be an attempt to give Jackson the presidency through simple voice acclamation. Branch describes the insurgents' plan:

> If Taylor did not rise instantly to make his challenge—to demand a head count by the court-appointed monitor—the moment would not come again. Tests of convention security established that the

invasion could not be done by stealth, because there were too many Jackson people at the doors. Therefore, with as much surprise as possible, the Taylorites tucked Gardner Taylor into a "flying wedge" of several hundred preachers and stormed through the largest entrance to the convention floor. Pushing aside the officials who objected to their improper credentials, they shouted the name of their deposed president as they headed for the podium in a thundering mass. King remained outside.

I was about fifteen rows back when the wedge came in. It looked like a team of linebackers moving as one through the crowd, encircling Jackson. My father was sitting with the other faithful on the stage, in one of the inner rings. Because of his small size, we could only catch glimpses of him as the rings swayed and moved.

People began to shout. Some of the women moaned, and others began to pray. Fists flew and colorful, unpreacherly epithets were uttered. A shoving and yelling match turned into a slugfest. I could not get to my father and I could no longer see him in the swirling mass on the stage. Rumors spread that one of the ministers on the stage had had a heart attack. Others said the man had been pushed off. Still others said he had been stabbed. Finally, I saw a large body in a dark suit being passed over the heads of the crowd. His opened suit jacket revealed wide suspenders and a dangling gold watch chain. Those up close identified him as A. G. Wright. An ambulance took him away.

The battle continued, and stairs to the platform collapsed. More ministers were injured. I still had not seen my father and edged closer to the stage. Riot police arrived but could not restore order. H. Roe Bartle, the mayor of Kansas City, was escorted to the podium. His immense presence and call for brotherly love seemed to mollify the crowd. At last my father emerged, apparently unscathed, on the stage. A group of larger ministers had protected him as he huddled close to Jackson. Wright died of injuries related to a fractured skull when he accidentally fell from the stage. There was no truth to reports that he had been deliberately pushed.

Old Jack was still in control and would remain there for another twenty-two years. Eventually, Taylor, King, Abernathy and the others formed their new group.

∽

After two years at the asthma research center, I had a job interview in the lobby of the venerable Parker House Hotel with William Lynch, director of Boys' Clubs of Boston, the city's largest social agency. He was a handsome, aggressive, blustery Irishman who constantly smoked a long cigar. Having asked me about my nationality, he ignored the darker components and became fixated on my Irish ancestry. Unable to resist teasing him, I pointed out that we could be related.

Lynch hired me to be his executive assistant. The organization had its headquarters in Charlestown, a branch in South Boston, and another in Roxbury. At the time, each of those areas was scheduled for urban renewal under the auspices of megaplanner Frank Logue. A decade later they would all be scenes of major civil unrest.

Reflecting the city's housing pattern, the Roxbury branch catered to a Negro clientele, while the other two had an all-white membership. With the exception of one program person in the Roxbury club and me, the leadership and staff were entirely white. I worked at the headquarters on Green Street in Charlestown, just a few feet away from the Bunker Hill monument where Crispus Attucks, the first black to die in the Revolutionary War, is alleged to have fallen. Climbing the narrow streets lined with small wooden houses and Irish faces reminded me of my treks to Willis School in Ansonia.

My job at the Boys' Clubs was to help Lynch with the board of trustees, fund raising and public relations. Lynch joked that my manners, education and behavior were more like the board members' than his. The trustees were representatives of the old Boston society families—white, well-tailored men who looked like the bankers or lawyers they were. How different they were from the scruffy, sallow-faced boys who came to play basketball and shoot pool.

At the Boys' Clubs I learned about the world of big-time charity. True altruism was seldom a motive for service. Rather, the board served as a channel for community recognition and business connections. The trustees viewed the staff members as faithful retainers.

Nevertheless, I got caught up in the energy and possibility of sweeping social change. Here, I thought, was my métier. This would be living, breathing sociology. I enrolled in a Harvard extension course at night, a survey of city planning. Ignited by what I learned, I applied to the graduate program at Harvard's School of Design.

In the meantime, I gave birth to our first daughter, Deirdre, named after the heroine of Irish legend. I liked the sound of the name and did not consciously connect it with my then-submerged Irish roots. Deirdre's arrival coincided with my plans to be a wheelchair participant, because of my advanced pregnancy, in the great civil rights March on Washington. Instead, a few hours after her birth I listened and took hope for my new child from the words of Martin Luther King as he addressed the swelling crowds in front of the Lincoln Memorial. What a great day for a black child to come into the world, I thought, even though Boston was still using the term "colored" on its birth certificates. Just two weeks later my spirits would plummet after four little black girls were blown apart by a bomb in the Sunday school of a black church in Alabama.

I was packing to go to Connecticut for the weekend for Deirdre's christening when I heard that President Kennedy had been shot. I was home alone with the baby. After I heard the news, I could not put anything else in the suitcase. I took my child in my arms and rocked her until Harold came home hours later. He finished the packing for me. The November night was cold and blue-gray as we made the three-hour drive to New Haven. We didn't talk much, just listened to the radio.

We arrived to a houseload of guests. That somber Sunday, a full crowd at Macedonia saw its minister christen his granddaughter. As he welcomed the girl child to his family and his church, he prayed for the children in Washington who had lost their father. I worried about the future of the world Deirdre had entered. Only three months before, the prospects for her had seemed so bright. Then the world began to crack apart. As my father had cried for Roosevelt, I cried for Kennedy.

In the late winter I was offered a semester teaching fellowship in the doctoral program in sociology at Tufts University. Since I was waiting to hear from Harvard about admittance the following fall, I had some time on my hands. I decided to accept the assignment, just in case the Harvard opening did not materialize. My students were freshmen and sophomores enrolled in the introductory sociology course, and I found I loved the possibilities of shaping minds and directing lives. But late in the spring, the letter from the Harvard School of Design came. I had been admitted.

As a student at Wellesley, the sister of a Radcliffe graduate and the wife of a Harvard graduate student, I had been on the Harvard campus many times. But I expected my first day there as a graduate student to bring its own epiphany. As I walked across Harvard Yard on that warm September afternoon, my feelings were unexpectedly flat. Instead of "Fair Harvard," running through my mind was the question "Is that all there is?"

There were fourteen in my Harvard class, eleven white men, one white woman, an Egyptian woman and another exotic, me. From the beginning, the faculty paired us, because most planning work is group-oriented. The courses ranged from soaring to boring, but I was itching to get to the real thing—the people, the streets, the buildings.

The most exciting thing to happen during that year had nothing to do with the School of Design. Malcolm X came to Harvard to give a speech. I had first heard about Malcolm in 1959 when I was at Wellesley. Invariably, it was the most sensational parts of his speeches that were broadcast. His candor and courage gave me a nervous thrill. We listened to such talk at home, at club meetings or in church but I had never heard black men talk publicly about what they believed to be the ills of white people. What manner of man was this, I wondered, what daring manner of man?

But I was primarily taken with the Afrocentric focus of his speech. We did not use that word then, of course—we would have referred to his emphasis on "blackness." It jarred my sensibilities to hear Malcolm say, "We are just as much African today as we were in Africa four hundred years ago, only we are a modern counterpart of it. . . . When you hear a black man playing music, whether it is jazz or Bach, you still hear African music. In everything else we do we still are African in color, feeling, everything. And we will always be that whether we like it or not." I had to think about that a lot. I knew I would always be a black American, but I had to wrap myself around the African part to make it stick.

During that year, I conceived our second child. Melissa arrived two months after Malcolm X was assassinated, just before final exams. We chose a mellifluous name to signify sweetness and serenity. I nicknamed her "Missy." It tickled me that white people would have to call her the name slaves once called their young mistresses.

∽

With some anxiety, we were leaving our much loved Cambridge and Boston. Harold had been recruited by Xerox in New York to help the corporation develop educational programs. He would join a group of eclectic, sandal-footed brain trustees, all white and by our standards bohemian. Good, I thought, maybe we can relax at last.

We began looking for apartments in Manhattan, and found ourselves drawn to the vitality of the Upper West Side, with its faces of many colors. Through an ad in *The New York Times*, we found a sunny, spacious, riverview apartment, in an unpretentious prewar building at West End Avenue and 80th Street. For years, the apartment had been occupied by one of the blacklisted screenwriters of the Hollywood Ten. But when Harold went to complete arrangements for the lease, the rental agent told him we could not have it.

Since we liked the apartment and were not accustomed to being denied anything because of our color, we decided to fight to get it. Our furniture was put in storage and my two baby daughters and I went to stay with my parents in New Haven while Xerox corporate counsels and black judge Constance Baker Motley intervened. After several months we rented the apartment without going to court. We lived there harmoniously for six years and formed close bonds with four white couples who had children the same age as ours. The day Martin Luther King was shot, one of those neighbors rushed to our apartment. She did not know what to say, except "sorry." She looked dreadful as she fixed me tea and answered my phone. All she could hope, she said, was that my feelings about white people would not change. The assumption, of course, was that she knew what my feelings were.

As I watched my children grow from babies to toddlers, I worried about their lack of immediate connection to a larger black entity in which they could feel embraced and secure. They did not have the church as I had, nor the tight-knit black community of a small town. Most days I walked with them to Riverside Park and scanned the sandbox and swings for other black children.

To vary the routine, we often took afternoon and morning strolls on Broadway. On Broadway we sometimes encountered the Screaming Lady, my daughters' only childhood bogeyman. She was a white bag lady who shambled up and down upper Broadway. Short, fat, dirty and dressed in malodorous rags, she was not much taller than the girls. Stringy black hair covered her face. She carried large canvas shopping bags that she swung back and forth, up and down, aiming at whoever was in her way. She was like a small, dark, impenetrable whirlwind, sucking up everything in its path as she screamed obscenities and sometimes racial epithets.

If I saw her coming, I would duck in a doorway, cross a street or make as wide a berth around her as I could because I knew she terrified the girls. Sometimes they would wake up from their naps or during the night crying that the Screaming Lady was after them. Even to me she was a scary sight. She reminded me of the woman I used to visit who lived in dimly lit rooms with shrouded shapes.

In 1967, the board of directors of the New Lincoln School in New York City recruited Harold as its headmaster. New Lincoln was a direct descendant of the Lincoln School that had been founded by John Dewey and the Columbia University proponents of Horace Mann's educational philosophy. It had long been a racially, and to some degree an economically, integrated school. But neither there nor at any of the other elite preparatory schools on the East Coast had there ever been a black head.

I was soon surrounded by the eminent writers, actors, librettists and artists who sent their children to New Lincoln. One of the parents was Jerry Leiber, the songwriter who had collaborated with Mike Stoller on such hits as "Hound Dog" and "Jailhouse Rock." At a party and in what I thought was an offhand way, Jerry said he was looking for someone who looked "creole" like me to be the lead in a musical project he was developing for Broadway. He asked me if I could sing. Naturally, I said yes, with absolutely no idea what a Broadway audition entailed.

I asked a few friends in the theater what to do, and they told me to select some songs and practice, practice, practice. I called my uncle Percy to coach and play for me. My children sat, sang and clapped for their mother during the two weeks of intense rehearsals at home.

On the appointed day, I had my makeup done by a professional. I wore extra-long false eyelashes. I decided to work off my nerves and anxiety by walking to the audition. It was a warm spring afternoon. A few blocks away from my destination, the largest cinder in New York City found its way into my eye. I began to tear copiously. I could feel wide smudges of black kohl running down my freshly foundationed and rouged cheeks. In a contolled panic, I stopped at a gas station and got the key to the ladies' restroom. It took quite some time to repair my now zebralike face, and the attendant, who obviously thought I was sick or shooting drugs, knocked on the door. The eyelashes, which had come mostly unglued, had to go. By the time I had finished, I was certain I bore little resemblance to Broadway material.

Concerned about losing more face than I already had, I continued on to the audition. I went in, signed my name and received a number. It was an invitation-only try-out, and the other actors, all of whom seemed to know one another, chatted about their last or next jobs. None looked creole. In the meantime, from somewhere behind me, glorious trained, professional voices were belting out standards. By now, it took all of my determination and pride to stay until my name was called.

When I entered the auditorium, the countless movie musicals I had seen flashed before my eyes. Jerry Leiber and another production principal were the only two people sitting in the audience. Jerry greeted me warmly and explained to his colleague who I was. He asked what I was going to sing and whether I had music. It was clear he would have to walk me through every step. By this time I was a zombie.

I managed to get through both of my songs. Jerry said it was very nice and that he would call me. Abandoning my show business aspirations, I rushed out of the theater.

❧

The trusteeships of the great cultural institutions in New York were coveted and often passed on like legacies. Having caught the attention of the city's cultural guardians with his New Lincoln stewardship, Harold became the first black appointed to the board of the Museum of Natural History. To enable the museum to develop its upper-class black outreach, Gardner Stout, the museum president, and the women's committee asked me to plan a function that would bring black and white together in a social way.

The guest list was to be divided up equally between the races, and each table was to be strictly integrated. I asked the greater New York chapter of the Links to assist me in developing the list and planning the event. African flowers were centerpieces, and small African sculptures were the favors for each guest. A program featuring African dancers and a slide show of the people and places of Africa followed in Education Hall, decked out as an African cabaret. The event got an unprecedented full page in *The New York Times*, and the museum was delighted with its successful foray into the black world.

Harold and I became charter members of the Interracial Duty Squad, a group that was sure to be invited everywhere. That was fine with me, because I wanted to see and experience more of the riches that the white world had to offer. I wanted to bring that knowledge back to the other side and say, "Look what we've been missing and should have had all these years." That feeling still returns each time I go somewhere blacks have never been.

Art Linkletter invited us to a small soiree at his Central Park West apartment because he said he had never met a Negro who was not an entertainer, a sports figure or a maid. Bob Bernstein, president of Random House, called to invite us to an intimate dinner for Truman Capote in his home. In the short, cherubic figure whose head seemed too big for his body, I saw intimations of the truncated white boy of my Waterbury past, Little Man. Flirting quite openly with Harold, Truman kept referring to Harold's wonderful "Gauguinish" floral tie. I was disappointed that he was not so attentive to me.

A protest letter from me to Mayor John Lindsay brought about a small change in how the city welcomed its visiting dignitaries, for a while at least. In the accounts I read of the welcoming functions, I never came across any black people's names. I told the mayor that to welcome guests to the city by having all-white parties did not reflect New York's unique heterogeneity and did a disservice to the interesting blacks who called New York home.

A prompt response from the mayor invited me to volunteer for the Office of Special Events that planned such functions. It was suggested that I might provide them with lists of names, because other than politicians and celebrities, they had little to draw on. I jumped at the chance and soon many of the black people I found interesting were participating in Lindsay's dinners, luncheons and teas. Nor was I left out. Harold and I were among a very small group invited to dine with the queen's cousin, Princess Alexandra, at Gracie Mansion. The princess told me what "smashing earrings" I was wearing. Her husband said he liked my dress. Why yes, this *was* the same royal small talk my father had taught me.

Everywhere, people wanted to meet "nice and interesting Negroes." I realized we were being used, but at the same time I thought we could accomplish our own agenda—that is, personally affirm that Negroes were indeed terrific people who could infuse much into the American mainstream. I envisioned not so much a trickle-down effect as a healing flooding by the biblical "mighty stream of righteousness." I thought that we could help lay the groundwork for the day when large numbers of brown faces would be commonplace at every level. The rich and famous would open doors that everyone could walk through. I was wrong. Thirty years later, social groupings have not changed. In all too many places we are still tokens.

There was a burgeoning black avant-garde in New York in the late 1950s and early 1960s, clearly a second Harlem Renaissance. Ellis Haizlip, Harold's cousin, was one of its leaders. We became part of his inner circle of intellectuals, poets, writers and performers. In late-night sessions at the fashionable club Aux Puces, or the Pink Teacup, we discussed the merits of those he was considering inviting to be on his nationally aired television program, *Soul!* Any given night we might be eating fried chicken with Leroi Jones, Alvin Ailey, Nikki Giovanni, Maya Angelou, James Baldwin or Betty Shabazz, widow of Malcolm X. This was a wonderful new world of people of color who were changing the way we were thinking about ourselves. Under Ellis's tutelage, we left "Negro" and "colored" behind and became "black."

Making the change in labels was not so easy for my parents. My father resisted it longer than my mother. He had struggled too hard for the right to be called Negro, with an emphasis on the "o." As a Washingtonian, black to him was usually coupled with "dumb" or "ugly." It took him another ten years before he referred to people as blacks, and then with some difficulty. My mother's approach was more casual. I think she saw the labels as meaningless anyway.

Just as I was determined to be black, I also wanted to be in black groups that were progressive. I joined Liaison, a group of young black college-educated women who planned to do things differently from the way their mothers had. Among our members were Eleanor Holmes Norton, who later became a congresswoman, and Alma Brown, later wife of the secretary of commerce, Ron Brown. We focused on integration and social change. We introduced a group of young black designers to one of New York's fanciest stores, Bergdorf Goodman, and served chitterlings and grits at their fashion show, which we called "Basic Black at Bergdorf's." Reviewing political issues as they affected the black community, we honestly believed we could change things. But we were also our mothers' daughters, and as such could stray only so far from their paths. We were still considered a "bougie" group.

I had transferred from the Boston chapter of the Links, and tried to bring activism to that group as well. As program chair, I introduced young black poets, musicians, writers and other creative artists to the rather conservative club. There was a steel band from East Harlem, followed by author Verta Mae Grosvenor, talking about *Vibration Cooking*. The Links hadn't vibrated in years.

❧

I decided to join a massive anti–Vietnam War demonstration scheduled to march down Broadway in my neighborhood. I put my daughters in a large English pram my parents had given me when Deirdre was born. At that time, most of the demonstrations were peaceful, so that I was not unduly concerned about the children's safety. I joined a line of at least twenty abreast, all seemingly white.

As we moved slowly down Broadway, chanting slogans and sing-ing "Give Peace a Chance," an older white woman, a stranger, turned to me and said, "What is it like being married to a black man?" I was so taken aback by the woman's impertinence that I could not think of a snappy response. I simply said, "You have made a mistake, I am not white." I could not shake off the as-sumption. In different formats and different situations, the question would be raised again and again. Running with the ultrablack crowd in New York had only given me spiritual camouflage.

We never knew when or how color would spill over into our lives, but we were seldom surprised when it did. In May 1969, we invited about seventy of our friends to a "barely there" celebration of Har-old's birthday, challenging them to come as bare as they dared. Our inspiration for the theme was the musical *Hair* and the trans-parent clothes that were then in fashion. Betty Shabazz, Malcolm X's widow, made a concession to bareness by wearing a sleeveless dress. The director of a film festival wrapped himself in a bear rug. Ellis wore a leather jumpsuit, bared to the waist. Ann Rockefeller Pierson (now Ann Roberts), one of Nelson's children and a friend from Wellesley, wore filmy, floral print evening pajamas.

Vivian Jackson, a longtime friend and colleague of my husband's, had called and asked if she could bring a guest to the party. Vivian and the woman, a visitor to New York, had been working late together on a New York City Poverty Program project. A well-dressed woman whose Southern manners could have matched Me-lanie Wilkes's in *Gone With the Wind*, Vivian described her guest as a white woman who had been a freedom rider and spent a great deal of time working with the Congress of Racial Equality through-out the South. We told Vivian there would be plenty of room and plenty of food for extra mouths.

From the moment I opened the door, I knew there was something strange about the woman. She wore her dark hair deep over one eye, in the 1940s style of Veronica Lake and Lauren Bacall. Despite Vivian's pointedly correct introductions, the stranger did not speak or acknowledge me as she curled herself around the doorjamb and slithered into the room. Mildly puzzled, I left Vivian and the odd newcomer and went back into the swirling, writhing living room.

Less than half an hour later, someone tapped me on the shoulder and asked me to come into the dining room where "Ellis was having a problem." Moving in that direction, I saw Ellis lightly but firmly trying to disengage himself from the arms of Vivian's guest. He was having no success. Her hands were clasped tightly together at the back of his neck. As people tried to pull her away, she became more frantic, swearing at them and clawing Ellis's bare chest.

I asked someone to get Harold, then quietly interrupted the spirited dancing of Dr. Hugh Butts, noted black psychiatrist, and his wife, June, a psychologist specializing in black sexuality. I watched as Hugh oversaw a group of men who forcibly disengaged the stranger from Ellis. The intensity of her hysteria increased, and her cursing rose to a more colorful level. Hugh suggested moving her into the bedroom where he could talk to her and try to calm her down. Betty Shabazz was quick to advise the group holding the woman that its composition should be of both races and sexes. She was prescient in her counsel. As they lifted the woman toward the bedroom, she began yelling, "These black motherfuckers want to rape me. Every black man at this party wants my white body."

Ann Rockefeller was sitting on the bed, sedately hemming her pants, which she had stepped on while dancing. Without missing a beat, she finished her task, put the needle and thread on a pin cushion on the dresser, and left the room. My father would have been proud of her manners. Butts calmed the other woman down somewhat, but as she was still dazed and incoherent, he and his wife took her to be admitted to a hospital for observation. None of us really know what set her off. My own theory is that seeing integration practiced in so intimate and casual a manner was too much for a closet racist posing as a professional liberal.

I continued my personal crusade to integrate New York City. I cochaired a benefit with Mary Lindsay, the mayor's wife. For entertainment we got the New York City Ballet, with a program featuring then rising black dancer Arthur Mitchell. With Adele Auchincloss, the shy sweet wife of author Louis, I screened a short film about race relations that featured Deirdre for a combined group of our friends. I was excited about the events that I was helping to bring about. Surely, I thought, the leak in the dam would become a steady stream. Surely the world would turn faster, bringing great change. Surely people could learn to get along.

My efforts did not go unnoticed. *The New York Times* called to say they wanted to profile a young black woman doing good works around town. I was pleased with what I saw as an opportunity for advocacy. I remembered that when my engagement picture appeared in the *Times* in 1959, the photograph did not suggest that I was black. This time I wanted to make a visual as well as verbal statement.

At that time, few black middle-class women were wearing Afros, which were associated with the daring radicalism of Angela Davis. I purchased the biggest Afro wig I could find for the *Times* photograph. It seemed even larger than Davis's halo. The feature, which took up most of a page, appeared in the Sunday society section. Everyone told me it was a flattering article, but none of my friends mentioned the hair.

A few years later, when I was attending a black convention in Washington, a fair-skinned girl with a small, neat Afro came up to me and said she recognized me from my picture in the *Times*. She told me that picture had changed her physical appearance. She had wanted to wear an Afro, but her parents, both of whom were physicians, told her that only radicals wore them. When she showed them the picture of a "society lady" in the *Times* wearing an Afro, they relented.

Icons, images and symbols were important in the 1960s. I adapted whichever of them seemed to fit my needs. I gave myself long dark brown hair with a fall to be photographed for *Ebony*'s "Best Dressed" roster. I selected a black sequined jumpsuit for my fashion and the hot discotheque Studio 54 for my setting. My getup made quite a contrast with the satin gowns, silk dresses and "good little suits" my sister honorees wore. How I longed to bring them into my world, a place I thought was more real, more comforting, more in harmony with their black psyches. More and more, I was shedding the need to be conventionally middle-class, to be like respectable white folks. My friends liked the hair but thought the suit was "a bit theatrical."

တော

In New York, something happened to my husband that for a long time I had hoped would happen to me. In 1969, as president of the greater New York chapter of the Links, I was a delegate to their national convention. That year the meeting was to be held in Cleveland. I had put some time aside to study the phone books and city directories, looking for my relatives. My mother had told me she could not find their last address. I sensed she was afraid for me to look.

Harold joined me for the trip. We were delayed on the way to the airport by traffic and arrived late at the departure gate. It was the era before universal computerization, and we were to be checked in right at the plane's door. When we got there, the stewardess looked at the roster and told us there must be some mistake. There was already a Dr. Haizlip on the plane. Harold told her we were traveling first-class and asked her to check the passenger list again. She did, found our name, and apologized for the error. There were in fact two Dr. Haizlips on the roster.

We were greatly intrigued. At that time in the Manhattan phone directory, there were only two Haizlips, Harold and his cousin Ellis. We had never met another Haizlip who was not a relative. My husband asked the stewardess if she would identify the other Haizlip for him once the plane was in the air.

When we were en route, Harold got up and went back to the coach compartment. This is the story he told me when he came back: The stewardess had pointed out the other Haizlips, a white, prosperous-looking couple in their early sixties. My husband, who is unfailingly charming and polite, said to the older man, "Excuse me, but I understand your name is Dr. Haizlip. So is mine, and I have never met a Haizlip who is not related to me." The wife stiffened and stared. The man replied in a courtly Southern accent, "Son, it's nice to meet you. My name is James O. Haizlip."

Hearing the accent and sensing from his manner that the man was receptive, Harold asked him where he was from. The man replied, "A small place I'm sure you've never heard of: Belews Creek, North Carolina." Harold said, "Well, isn't this something.

That's where my family is from." The other Mrs. Haizlip turned red, squirmed sideways and looked out the window.

Still friendly but obviously surprised, the elder Dr. Haizlip bowed his head, rubbed his forehead and said, "It must have been Great-Uncle Henry C." Harold queried, "What did the C. stand for?" "Cornelius," said James. "Cornelius is my middle name," volunteered Harold, clearly enjoying the turn in the conversation. The perspiration on Mrs. Haizlip's forehead seemed to be uncurling her halo of tightly curled gray hair.

"Uncle Henry liked to get out at night, you know," said James. Harold knew exactly what he meant. They exchanged addresses and promised to send each other copies of entries in family Bibles. James said they were traveling to Cleveland to see a new grandchild. When we got off the plane, there was a boisterous group waiting to welcome the white Haizlips. They held up a large sign that read, "Congratulations, it's another Haizlip." As we walked past them, we said to each other, "If you only knew."

I have told this story many times to suggest how interconnected black and white Americans are. Years later, when we were living back in New Haven, a reporter heard me relate the anecdote at a party and asked if he could write it up. I gave permission, and it was sent out on the Associated Press wires as a human interest item. Bart Giamatti, the late former president of Yale, read it. The piece appeared in the paper on the day the citizens of New Haven were honoring Giamatti's departure from the university. Although Bart and Harold met just about every Saturday morning for coffee and a chat at Clark's Dairy, a local luncheonette, they had not gotten around to that particular story.

At the testimonial that night, we went to greet Bart at the head table in a room of hundreds where there seemed to be no other black people. In a booming laugh Giamatti said, "How many other Haizlips are out there?" The smiles around him seemed thin.

∽

From the time we first married, my husband and I spent vacations in Vermont, Maine and, less frequently, New Hampshire. We rented or borrowed friends' homes. Our preferences were for places that were beautiful, green, quiet and secluded. Essential also was access to second-hand stores and junk shops where we browsed and purchased unusual tapestries, ink wells, Rookwood pottery and old picture frames.

In Maine, we stayed at Herrick's, a turn-of-the-century resort close to the picturesque town of Blue Hill near Penobscot Bay. We were not far from posh Bar Harbor, where my great-uncle Eddie Scott had spent most of his adult summers as a valet. In addition to attracting painters and novelists, Herrick's turned out to be a favored recuperative spot for writers from *Harper's*, *The New Yorker* and *The Saturday Review*. It was a civilized, restful environment. For several successive years we added color to its guest list, and later brought our children there. At the time, we thought little about being among the minuscule numbers of blacks in an ultra-white environment.

Not far from Herrick's, on a small wooded island in the bay known as Little Deer Isle, Ted Foote, one of Harold's Harvard classmates, summered in a house that belonged to his family for three generations. The first time Ted invited us for lunch and a sail, we stopped beforehand to browse, do laundry and buy groceries and postage in Stonington, the last tiny town before the bridge to the island. We did not notice that our presence made a deep impression on Stonington's citizens. When we reached Ted's house, he told us that at least four people had kindly advised him of our itinerary and our progress.

❧

Resting beside our bicycles on a shaded dirt road in Vermont in the summer of 1971, we came to an important decision. For a year, Melvin Evans, the governor of the United States Virgin Islands, had been urging Harold to visit St. Thomas. The purpose: to consider becoming part of the governor's cabinet as commissioner of education for St. Thomas, St. Croix and St. John.

We made an exploratory trip and were bewitched by the weather, the turquoise sea and the black faces wherever we went. We loved the green and hilly beauty of our vacation retreats in New England, but we were becoming distanced from its virtually unrelieved whiteness. The physical beauty of the Islands rivaled that of Vermont, and the Islands had something Vermont lacked: black people. Our daughters were in the early years of their schooling and we thought that an environment where the government, the schools, the newspaper and many businesses were black-owned and black-run would be the most self-affirming gift we could give them. We decided to make the move.

Chapter Nine

Memory remains, master, sovereign, working the materials of the past, naming subjects and objects of desire.

—U. Y. MUDIMBE
"Letters of Reference"

It piques the natives that most Americans know little about the Virgin Islands. U.S. citizens frequently think that the Islands' residents speak a foreign tongue and that they are a homogeneous people.

On his second voyage beyond Spain in 1493, Columbus encountered dozens of land masses that he named the Virgin Islands. He sent a boatload of men ashore at St. Croix to search for fresh water. They were not met by friendly folk. Records indicate that the Carib Indians put up a fierce resistance to the people of no color.

After the Spanish, the Islands had a stormy history and were ruled by a succession of seven European nations, Denmark being the last. Slavery ended in the Islands in 1848, fifteen years before its abolition in the States. In 1917, the United States bought the Islands from Denmark for $25 million. Congress approved the purchase because it was thought the Islands would be valuable as a buffer against German submarine operations, and as a naval base. Many Virgin Islanders were opposed to the sale. To them, pristine, white Denmark was the preferred mother country.

By the time we moved to the Islands in 1971, the mostly black population was nearing a hundred thousand. The open-armed acceptance we expected did not come right away. The Islanders regarded us as intrusive Continentals first and distant black cousins second. We quickly learned that because of their history and what they perceived as beneficent treatment by the Danes, European whites (especially Danes) were the favored visitors.

The notion of race was the direct opposite of that in the States. In the Islands, if you asked if someone was black or white, a native would answer according to skin color, not race. But if one had any white blood in his heritage, he could claim to be white. We learned to our dismay that even in the Islands white was the race of choice. Many dark-skinned people had "Caucasian" on their birth certificates. We heard numerous tales of children of wealthy natives who were sent to private schools in the States and experienced devastating culture shock when people lumped them in with "ordinary American Negroes." One, we were told, had a nervous breakdown when he was called a "nigger."

∽

We acquired our house in the Virgin Islands through a set of circumstances I can only describe as mystical. The governor had put us up in a beautiful government guest house, high on the north side of St. Thomas overlooking the Atlantic. Each time we came just a bit down the mountain, we passed a house gated in bluebit stone, the handsome native slate. The house was built into the side of the hill. From the front all we could see were two impressive gateposts and stairs leading to a black marble entryway. Large glass doors bordered expansive white marble floors extending out to a balcony that overlooked the harbor and the Caribbean.

Although we saw a gardener each time we passed, the house seemed unoccupied. One day Harold stopped and asked the gardener the name of the family who owned the house. The gardener, Albery Brin, was a white native "Frenchy," the island designation for descendants of immigrants from St. Barthélemy, one of the few white islands in the Caribbean. In the Virgin Islands, the Frenchies were as disdainfully stereotyped as poor Southern whites are. They had no presence in government, business or the arts. They usually held one of two types of jobs, fisherman or gardener.

Albery reported that the house had been empty since its owner had died six months earlier. The estate was in probate, which in the Virgin Islands might take several years to resolve. He gave Harold the number of the lawyer handling the affairs. That same afternoon, Harold called the lawyer, asking if the house was available and whether we might see it. The lawyer told him the owner's sister, who lived in Caracas, was now in charge. The house could not be sold for a while, and she doubted the sister would rent it. Persisting, Harold asked if he might call the sister in Venezuela. The lawyer relented, and the sister said she would indeed be interested in renting the house and advised the lawyer to show it.

As soon as we went beyond the glass doors into the empty house, I knew that it had been waiting for us. It was as if I were familiar with everything about the place, as if I had been there many times before. We entered a library that might have come from a Georgetown mansion. Five or six books with French titles remained on the bottom shelf. I took one from the shelf and opened it. A small photograph fell out onto the marble floor. Retrieving it, I was stunned. The photograph of the dark-haired woman with the prominent nose looked like my mother when she was twenty-three. I did not need to see any more.

We lived in that house for eight years. Its owner had been a glamorous French perfume heiress who owned several homes in different countries. On this island of simple beauty, she had built a monument to luxury. In a place with a chronic water shortage she had put a bidet in every one of the five bathrooms. She had painted murals of clouds and water lilies in the entryway, palm trees and tropical blossoms in the living room, clusters of orchids on her closet doors. In her cantilevered backyard, she had created hanging gardens with specimens of flowers from around the world.

Something of the owner was still in the house; her spirit, her aura, her ghost? We experienced it one Saturday afternoon on our return from a day of browsing in town. Only the dog was at home. As we drove up the hill in front of the house, Harold stopped the car suddenly. He told the girls and me to stay in the car. I said I was coming with him.

We went to the front door. It was locked as we had left it. Hannibal, our terrier, was sitting in the foyer, wagging his tail in welcome. We went around to the garage door. Closed tight. Down past the garage to the back door; locked. We came back to the front and I said to Harold, "Be careful and look in the closets." Cautiously, quietly and slowly we opened the door and examined each space. There was no one there, but the house was filled with the fragrance of a perfume I did not recognize.

For the first time since we had stopped the car I asked Harold what he had seen. "Legs in gray slacks and navy blue shoes," he said. The top was cut off by the slanting line of vision down into the house. I had seen the same thing, but the legs and the shoes were nowhere to be found.

We asked the two young French women who occupied the guest house of the estate if they could come up to the main house. They had known the owner. As they came in the door, one said, "Ah, you are wearing the perfume Madame always wore." I asked what it was. "Bal à Versailles," she said. I had none in my supply of fragrances. We asked the tenants how Madame had dressed. They both replied, "Always in a white shirt, gray slacks and navy blue loafers."

A year later, when Madame Eveque, the owner's sister, came to meet us, she cried when she came into the living room. We thought it was because it was the first time she had been in the house since her sister's death. "No," she said, "you have made this room just like Hélène did." Our tastes, it seemed, were identical.

Madame Eveque wanted us to know how Hélène had acquired the house, because she too thought we were destined to have it. In the late 1800s, a French gentleman of means came to the island of St. Barthélemy from Alsace-Lorraine. It seemed he had tired of his family's business and wanted a more adventurous life. He found St. Bart's too small, and decided to move to the bustling, commercial port of St. Thomas. He took his manservant, a black native named Joseph Sibilly, with him.

The French adventurer purchased a pie-shaped wedge of land from the harbor to the top of the mountain. In time, he lost touch with his family. He remained unmarried and died intestate. Officials in St. Thomas had no idea where to find his heirs, and the land remained unclaimed. After some years, with his savings, Sibilly paid the back taxes and his master's land became his. Eventually, real estate in the Virgin Islands soared in value. Sibilly sold some of the land, gave some to his children, and kept a few of the most desirable parcels near the top of the mountain for himself.

In the 1950s, two French sisters from Caracas were making their way through the Caribbean islands looking for a site suitable for a vacation home. They were driven around St. Thomas, and were drawn to a site on the north side of the harbor, overlooking the Caribbean. The realtor told them it was unlikely that the owner, a Mr. Sibilly, would sell this particular piece. They asked to meet him so that they could at least make an offer.

At the meeting, in a modest white house near the top of the hill, they spoke in French to Joseph Sibilly, the little black man who had himself come from a French island. They told him their name was Dieudonné, and Sibilly asked where they were from. Their family, they said, was from Alsace-Lorraine. They had had an uncle who lived on St. Bart, but they did not know what had happened to him. Overcome, Sibilly told them he had worked for their uncle and the land they so wanted had been his. That is how it came to be that one of the richest land owners in St. Thomas sold two white Frenchwomen the most desirable piece of the land that had belonged to their uncle, at a reasonable price. At its crest is where Hélène Dieudonné built her house, the house that became our home for eight years.

೧೪

As we had hoped, we were buoyed by the black sea we found in the Islands. What a change it was to be in the majority. But there were many anomalies. By custom, social and club life were segregated. At major island events given by each group, one would find a few tokens from the other side. White Continentals sent their children to mostly white private schools. The public schools for the black natives were staffed primarily by young white teachers from the States, in St. Thomas to enjoy the sun and the beach. We enrolled our daughters in the Joseph Sibilly School, the only integrated public school on St. Thomas, not far from our home.

Politics were controlled by the blacks; Main Street commerce by the whites. The whites leased the stores from a few black families that owned most of the property on the main streets. The black Islanders working in the stores were not natives. They came from the British Virgin Islands. The native Virgin Islanders felt it was demeaning to serve white people, even though they knew their tourist economy depended on it. The natives would not work the earth either, because it was too close to slavery. On the other hand, they would keep beautiful gardens, mostly maintained by their French gardeners.

A small number of mainland whites invited us to travel in their circles. We did not make it a frequent practice. For the most part, we put our membership in the Interracial Duty Squad on hold. Our interest turned in a darker direction.

St. Thomas's warm weather and our frequent trips to the beach was a combination that my hair could not defeat. I resorted to Diana Ross–type wigs in varying lengths and styles. One day I decided I was tired of hiding my hair under hot hairpieces. Off came the wigs and after some coaxing with a three-pronged comb, out came my own Afro, small this time. Afros were not popular among the professional set in St. Thomas then, but I was comfortable in mine. I wore it for the remainder of our tenure.

I went to work at the CBS television station in St. Thomas, which was owned by a white man who had been an engineer at NBC in New York. Most of his small staff was white, including the newscasters. The station's signal was received in Puerto Rico, St. John, St. Croix, Tortola and some of the other British Virgin Islands.

In front of a bare curtain and with just two chairs, a native woman, Leona Bryant, produced a daily five-minute segment on local people, community events and visiting celebrities. All other programming was canned American products, soap operas and prime-time fare, taped in Orlando, Florida, and sent by daily plane to St. Thomas. Except for Leona's segment, the Islanders saw no other images of themselves.

I had a new mission: to bring more island presence and color to the station. I started out by sprucing up Leona's program. With her enthusiastic support, we installed a new tropical patio set, arranged for the loan of an upscale wardrobe from one of the elegant tourist-oriented stores that lined the palm passageways, and added realistic-looking island scenes by rear screen projection. When I swam at local beaches or walked down Main Street, the natives voiced their approval of the results.

The station was sold to a group of black investors from Washington, D.C., a first in the United States. We began to do documentaries on local issues: the chronic water shortage and the need for a new airport. This was well before the crash of a commercial jetliner into a mountain at the end of the runway with the loss of more than thirty lives. We profiled a local artist and the successful members of the first graduating class from the local high school. We hired native newscasters and added other black faces on the air. Along the way, I became the general manager, prepared editorials and produced my own program on women's issues.

The Virgin Islands was a good place to raise a family. In many ways it reminded me of life in Ansonia. Crime was not pervasive; the culture stressed the importance of family and respect for elders. With few outside distractions, the four of us spent most of our free time together. Aside from water sports and the weather, entertainment sources were few. Intergenerational mixing was the norm, and most parties and other social events included children of all ages. We spent Saturdays at the local market and browsing in town. Sunday was beach day.

Carnival was the one event that brought the island's residents together. Anyone could take part, although as many shunned the two weeks of revelry as participated. We were invited to join the Gypsy Troupe, one of the oldest and most prestigious of the island's associations, whose sole purpose was to develop a group theme and then create its float and costumes for Carnival. For nine months out of the year, young, old, black, white, native and Continental, we met at the troupe's open-air clubhouse. Against a background of neighing goats or noisy chickens, we cut and sewed costumes, glued glitter and sequins, gathered ruffles, wired frames and braided wigs. Architects, draftsmen and engineers designed and built the large float that would be the centerpiece of our theme and serve as our moving bar and restaurant.

Carnival morning started before daylight with Jouvert, a march of thousands in their pajamas and bathrobes dancing down the Waterfront and Main Street behind several champion steel bands from Trinidad, Jamaica, Tortola and the Virgin Islands. Sunrise was the signal to go home for an hour's sleep before changing into your costume for the parade. One could be whatever the imagination of the troupe allowed, within the bounds of island taste. One year we were Spanish bullfighters and señoritas, the next a deck of cards.

Still another year we calypsoed down Main Street as storm clouds, silver linings, lightning shafts and raindrops. We didn't march or walk, we danced the entire route. Even the children danced in their own parade the day before, usually as Indians.

While we were in the Islands, Boston erupted in racial wars. It was disturbing and infuriating to us to read the accounts of race hatred in a city we had loved. Where had all that racism been, we wondered, when we were there? Or had we been too blind to see it? We knew we could not go back to Boston when we left the Islands. We would not feel emotionally or physically safe.

On that beautiful island, ours was a privileged life. The government provided a car, a driver and a secluded vacation retreat on St. John. By virtue of our positions we were invited to meet everyone of interest who came to Charlotte Amalie, the capital city. Our social calendar included evenings with heads of state and soap opera personalities. Sometimes it was hard to tell the difference.

For visiting dignitaries, the governor would host lavish receptions at the two-storied colonial-style Government House. Lush tropical flower arrangements loomed over the guests. The food was mostly American. In a crush of people, Margarethe, the queen of Denmark, almost lost her tiara as she danced a stately calypso played by a group of elegant, silver-haired natives who had made music together since they were boys.

∞

More friends came to see us in the Virgin Islands than anywhere else we had lived. A good deal of our time was spent entertaining or acting as tour guides. The visits provided welcome interruptions to the soft sameness of island living. The most peculiar attempt at a visit was from the manager of the building on West End Avenue in Manhattan who had been chief in the effort to bar our tenancy. He called us as soon as his cruise boat had docked. We accepted the call and wished him well. Our personal code of ethics would not allow us to give him a tour of the island or extend the usual hospitality. We could not practice the *politesse* of deceit.

Aside from the informal pattern of self-segregation, there was little overt racism directed at blacks by whites. If anything, it went the other way. But one day, my secretary knocked on my door and told me my daughter Melissa was at the office, sobbing and terribly upset. I called her in and closed the door. She said she had been barred from a local department store nearby, but her friends had been let in. She did not know why. Instantly, and in a mother's fury, I left my office, walked down to the store, entered and asked to see the owner.

On seeing me, the white owner was oleaginous, because I was now something of a local celebrity. She seemed puzzled as to why I was holding the tear-streaked Melissa's hand. She did not immediately realize we were mother and daughter. She had no comprehensible explanation for denying entrance to Melissa. Making as much of a scene as I could, I demanded an apology and assurance of future unharried access for my daughter and any other child who happened to be her color. I received both. The incident was a confirmation that majority status does not guarantee protection.

&

During our stay in the Virgin Islands, some young black men on St. Croix attacked white tourists with machine guns on a resort golf course. A number of the whites were killed. Shock waves hit the Islands like tsunami, and there was an immediate drop in tourism. Some whites thought the incident signaled the beginning of an all-out racial war. Rumors spread that other attacks were imminent. The incident occurred several weeks before a national lieutenant governors' conference was slated to be held on St. Croix. I was the executive in charge of planning the conference. We feared it would be canceled. But an effective campaign of reassurance by Governor Evans and the lieutenant governor kept the conference plans intact.

&

I read somewhere that the most significant and dangerous problem most people face is how to get through a lifetime of ordinary days. Our lives in the Virgin Islands were never ordinary. There was an assassination threat against Harold after he temporarily closed down a particularly troublesome school. That brought a twenty-four-hour guard for all of us for several weeks at home and at the office. There was a flight in a navy helicopter to the U.S.

carrier *Nimitz* and tea with Rear Admiral William Warwick as we brought the ship to safe anchor in Charlotte Amalie. I was the only woman on board with five thousand men. There was tea with the queen of England, who was visiting nearby Tortola, part of the British Virgin Islands, on board the *Britannia*, the royal yacht. I wore a lemon yellow silk dress. As I approached the queen in the receiving line, I was chagrined to discover she, too, wore a lemon yellow silk dress. Then I recalled the words of a royal social secretary—"The queen never notices what other people wear"—which I'd read somewhere. She didn't.

But no matter how deeply we became enmeshed in the life of the Islands, for Harold and me it was not home. The experience had altered my perspective on race, majority and color, though. In the future I would find it hard to put people into carefully delineated categories. For my daughters it was a different matter. We had brought them to a larger black community than they would have had in New York City. For eight years it did become home for them. St. Thomas was their Macedonia, their National Baptist Convention, their trips south. I was glad of that.

❧

We returned to the States in 1980 to enter our daughters in high school. New Haven became our city of choice. My family lived there and we liked its proximity to Boston, New York and Washington. But much had changed in New Haven since I was a little girl. Now it was labeled the seventh-poorest city in the United States.

My parents had moved again, to a larger home in one of New Haven's most prestigious residential communities. Their new neighbors were primarily high-ranking professors associated with Yale, bankers, lawyers and other sundry professionals. My mother called their new home, "Julian's dream house." It was a small Tudor-style mansion built in the 1920s. My father loved the grandeur of the circular driveway, the pillars at the entrance and the acre of land it occupied. My mother hung his oil portrait over the fireplace in the main living room.

Even in the 1970s, my parents were the first blacks to own a home on their street. Ironically, in the 1980s the producers of a public television program about interracial marriage and identity problems asked to use the house as a location. It was supposed to represent the residence of a successful black Ivy League professor who had married a white woman and whose child was having problems negotiating between the white and black worlds. The producers were pleased they could leave the family pictures on the wall.

Taking a risk, we had come back to the States without jobs. I thought I would have little trouble landing a new spot, because my position as the only black and female general manager of a CBS affiliate had given me much press and a high degree of visibility. Harold's portfolio had also grown impressively, and we thought he too would be in great demand. What we faced was a different reality from the one we had left behind. The country was in an economic recession and hiring black people had gone out of fashion. For almost six months, we stayed with my parents in their baronial home.

I thought our children fortunate to be able to live in the home of their grandparents, and I secretly liked being my parents' daughter again. But the time was not without stress. My father was ailing and depressed. He had been voted out of his church because of his age and fragile health and awarded a pension that barely surpassed the salary of his first few years in the Ansonia pulpit. We ate late, my parents ate early. Harold and my mother competed for time in the kitchen, and the girls liked to race up and down the central staircase.

Pattee had divorced but had remained in New Haven, with her son, Dale. She would marry twice more and have two more sons, Taylor and Max. The little girl who hated to go to school would earn a graduate degree and become a school administrator. Jim and Jewelle had first settled in Minneapolis upon returning from Africa, and now had two sons of their own, Geoffrey and Lowell. In the seventies they moved again, to Stanford, California.

One evening after we had been back in the States for about nine months, a man whose name I did not recognize called me. He had a remarkable way of expressing himself, brilliantly circuitous and maddeningly elliptical. From the conversation I gathered he was with WNET, the public television station in New York. He invited me to come see him for a chat. I took that to mean a talk about a job. I called Harold's cousin Ellis, who had been a producer at the station for many years. Ellis told me that my caller was the president of the station.

The station's president could trace both sides of his heritage directly to this country's ruling social class. He went to the right schools, Exeter and Harvard; belonged to the right clubs, the Fly and Century, and knew the right people, George Plimpton, and Brooke Astor. But his brilliance and intense curiosity enabled him to escape some of the stultifying parameters of his class.

Although he had finished law school, he never practiced law. A former editor of a popular national news magazine, he brought a highly literate perspective to the sometimes down-and-dirty world of television. By sheer force of mind and an uncanny ability to raise money through one-on-one conversations, he gave form and shape to WNET. The station became the major producing entity in the public broadcasting network. It also had the network's largest budget, a cause for much professional resentment and backbiting throughout the network.

He was a small, slight man standing no taller than five foot three. His elfin size and long dark hair parted on the side gave him a perennial boyish look. He had a wide smile and mobile features that gave his face the quality of a Dr. Seuss character. Except to scribble off flattering one-line notes to colleagues, board members or staffers, he rarely remained still. One of his hands was always at his mouth, the nails bitten to the quick. He talked on the phone nonstop for hours and was invariably late for all of his meetings, where he would stare into the middle distance and write notes.

After a series of lengthy chats, we agreed that I would come to the station as his special assistant. The idea was that I would get an overview of all of the station's workings and then select an area to oversee. For me it was the best of all possible worlds. *Brideshead Revisited* was in production, as were *The Brain, Civilization and the Jews,* and black filmmaker Bill Miles's *I Remember Harlem. MacNeil/ Lehrer* was moving toward its revolutionary hour format, Bill Moyers was assembling his *Creativity* series, *Nature* was offering the most dramatic footage of natural phenomena that had ever been seen, and *Great Performances, Dance in America, Live from Lincoln Center* and *American Playhouse* filled the cultural cup. I became one of the lesser gatekeepers who reviewed cassettes, scripts and story ideas.

I was also the person to whom the president would refer countless children of friends looking for jobs, generic complaints, unique requests and trustee needs. I had become a professional passe-partout. A year later I became secretary of the board, with additional responsibilities that included the creative services area that looked after music, art and public relations, and the editorial board that reviewed all the station's programming projects. Like school, it was something I loved going to every day.

❧

In the meantime, Harold had been appointed vice president of the Borough of Manhattan Community College, one of the largest units of the City University of New York. Together we commuted to New York by train. One morning, as we were leaving the train at Grand Central Station, Harold got caught up in the surge and was moved ahead. Amid the sea of bobbing white faces, I looked for his dark head. The moment is a freeze frame in my mind, my personal metaphor of how difficult the journey a black man has in America. How fast he must walk and how strong he must be to keep from being trampled by the white crowd! I had never before isolated Harold in my mind like that. He had always been grouped with my platoon of strong dark heroes. When I caught up to him, I kissed his cheek and squeezed his hand. I never told him why.

❧

The WNET board was like most of the boards of great New York cultural institutions: membership was greatly valued and a mark of prestige. During my tenure its members included Elsa Ives, the General Motors heiress; Gay Vance, wife of statesman Cyrus; Casey Ribicoff, wife of the senator; Tony Marshall, son of Brooke Astor; Frances Schumann, wife of former director of Lincoln Center William Schumann; Jock Elliott, chairman of Ogilvy & Mather; Bill Ellinghaus, chairman of AT&T, and philanthropist Al Stern. Author Ralph Ellison was literally an invisible man at board meetings, but Lucius Gregg, a former board member of the Corporation for Public Broadcasting, and George Brooker, a Harlem real estate mogul, provided the requisite minority presence.

My father believed that rich white people were less prejudiced than their poorer brethren, reasoning that they were more secure. It was at WNET that I learned he was wrong.

Adding new board members was a ritualistic process, most of it hidden. Nominations were suggested by sitting board members and the station's president. As the corporate secretary, I managed the nominating process, saw the names, went to the meetings and heard the conversations.

During my tenure, no additional black names were submitted, but there was a major drive to add more Jews to the board. Endless lists of names were suggested. Many were the leverage-and-buyout kings of the 1980s. One was subsequently sent to prison. Two others were forced to resign as leaders of their Wall Street firms. Holding one such list in his hand, the president stood at his secretary's desk outside his office and studied it as if it were the Rosetta Stone. "There are definitely no sleazeballs on this list. That's what the nominating committee is worried about, sleazeballs." At least three from the proposed list were eventually recruited to the board. It was said their membership cost them $1 million, far more than the contributions of their WASP counterparts.

Another time, I was riding with the president to New Haven in a rented limousine so that he could speak to students at the Yale School of Management, where he sat on the board of advisors. As we began our drive, he said, "The damnedest thing happened to me last night." That morning, he had already told the tale several times to friends and to the press, and he was relishing this further telling.

He proceeded to relate how the preceding evening he had found a handsome young shirtless black man talking to his wife in his kitchen. As soon as I heard the word "black," I felt as if I were having an out-of-body experience there on the Merritt Parkway. It was as if I were looking down on a black limousine carrying a white man telling a black woman about some weird experience his family had had with a man of color—without once acknowledging her own.

The young man told the president he was a friend of his son at

Harvard. He correctly identified the son's name, college residence and close friends. The young man said he had come into town to meet his father and had been mugged at Grand Central Station. Having no money, he looked in his address book and found the president's home phone number. He called, and the president's wife invited him over.

He asked to spend the night and said he would meet his father, Sidney Poitier, in the morning. At that point I told my boss that anyone who knew anything about Sidney knew that the actor had six daughters and no sons. The president, who believed he knew a great deal about a lot of things, seemed embarrassed to have missed that vital statistic.

He continued his story. During the night, he heard noises in the house. He got up and encountered the young man in the downstairs hall. The front door had just closed. The visitor claimed he had just chased an intruder from the house. By this time suspicious, the host returned to his room and spent the rest of the night anxious and sleepless. He wondered if he and his wife were going to come to bodily harm. Would the visitor steal something of value from the house? Rising at his customary early hour, he awakened "Sidney's son," gave him a small sum of money and told him he had to leave.

A few hours later, the former dean of the Columbia School of Journalism called my boss to tell him of an unusual encounter with a young black man. It was the same person. His name was David Hampton. Several years later his adventure became the core of John Guare's successful play, *Six Degrees of Separation*. Hampton threatened to bring suit against Guare, claiming he should receive some of the royalties from the play, since it was about him. Some would say he had a valid claim.

The president concluded his story and scratched the side of his head. I wondered if he had colored the tale any differently from the way he had related it to his white friends. At the end of our ride, we arrived in New Haven to share conventional secrets of success with conventional young white men. Afterward I walked the two blocks home, thinking about the strange moxie of a shirtless black man whose skills might be better honed at the Yale School of Management.

After I had been at WNET for about five months, I was selecting flowers for my daughter Melissa's sixteenth birthday party at a florist on Elm Street one day when Harold came to find me. My father had been taken to St. Raphael's Hospital. He had been ailing with emphysema and had unexpectedly worsened that morning while all of the family were getting ready for Melissa's event. As if trying to postpone whatever awaited me, I told Harold I must finish selecting the flowers before I could go. Sympathetically, the florist told me she would complete the task.

At the hospital, I waited with my mother and Pattee as my father struggled to live. He died while undergoing shock treatment to his weakened heart. An attendant told us we could see him. Taking a deep breath, I forced my legs to move. He looked as if he were sleeping. I thought how noble his long nose made him look in death. My mother held his hand and patted his cheek. We all cried.

Planning a minister's funeral involves endless protocol. The service was set for New Haven's Community Baptist Church, the church of Adam Clayton Powell, Sr. Although we had decided that the funeral would be as short as dignity would allow, my father's colleagues had other plans in mind. There were almost one thousand mourners at his funeral and at least three dozen Baptist ministers. They all had to say a word, several words in fact. The competition among the ministers surfaced and brought some levity to the event. And as one of them said:

> After all, this is all we have. When a white man dies, they name a bridge, a street, or a building after him. Now you all know, it will be a long time coming before they name anything after Taylor. This service is his span, his boulevard, his edifice. And we'll take all day to build it if we have to.

I imagined that this was what his own father's funeral had been like. Afterward, the guests attended Melissa's party, a strangely happy affair.

The same week that my father died, Ellis was fired along with a number of other WNET employees. Being relatively new on the job, I had not been privy to the station's budgetary plan, but I was experienced enough to know that retrenchment choices are political. Ellis had been the premier black producer at the station since the 1960s. But blackness on the air had gone out of fashion. The station would continue to favor its more Eurocentric fare under the direction of its creative white leadership.

A third-level financial analyst had also been laid off. It happened that this particular analyst was a neighbor and friend of Laurance Rockefeller. In a brief letter of supreme politeness, Rockefeller pointed out to the president that, set adrift in his late middle years, the faithful retainer would have difficulty finding another job and building a retirement nest egg. Within a week of the receipt of the letter, the analyst was back at his desk at the station. No such patron rescued Ellis. The subject was so painful to both of us that Ellis and I never discussed it.

After Ellis, three more black men would leave their mark at WNET. The first of these was Carl McCall, who became for a time vice president of the station's metropolitan division. It was he who gave me the opportunity to represent the station at a meeting of producers in Senegal.

I walked the streets of Dakar exhilarated. No one had told me it was such a vital, cosmopolitan city. A poet was president, and tall black guards dressed in crisp white uniforms stood sentinel before his blinding white mansion, where noisy white peacocks walked the lawns. A royal blue similar to Wellesley's was a favored color for the boubous that wrapped the tall, dark women. Men wore brightly colored damask suits and robes. Lepers sat in front of Charles Jourdan shoe stores. Muslims chanted throughout the city. Discotheques showcased beautifully coiffed African aristocrats.

And there were the Mauritanians, light-complected people with loose, curly hair and prominent noses. Their eyes were hazel or dark brown. They held the most menial jobs and were members of the lowest class in Senegal. Some of the Senegalese we were with called the Mauritanians the "niggers of Senegal." For centuries there had been bad periods between the Senegalese and the Mauritanians. Each had taken the other's people as slaves. In Senegal, the slave-holders' mentality persisted.

Out of that African trip came the controversial PBS series *The*

Africans, produced by WETA in Washington. WNET had the opportunity to be the coproducer but passed it up in favor of more Eurocentric offerings.

～

In New Haven, my daughters Deirdre and Melissa went to Wilbur Cross High School, then a large, mostly black city school with a corps of white Yale professors' children. While still in high school, both took courses for credit at Yale. And it was Yale both of them chose as a college home. On campus, they lived a world away from Prospect Street.

Each of my daughters had at least one hundred black students in her class. They found it hard to understand how their father and I had navigated the scarcity of students of color at our alma maters. Looking back, we wondered too. Once Deirdre had a party and invited all the black students at Yale. Four hundred of them came to Prospect Street for soul music and soul food. Harold and I marveled at their new world.

That next fall, Jewelle, Jim, Harold and I went to a Yale-Harvard football game at Yale Bowl. Deirdre was a varsity cheerleader for the squad that year. The number of black spectators had increased dramatically since my college years. During halftime, we passed a group of tailgaters that included one of the organizers of the Friends of Thirteen, a group of volunteer fund raisers for WNET. "Well, I am surprised to see *you* here," she said, then asked: "How do you feel being at *this* game?" as if I were a stranger in a strange land. My sister was not amused, but I brushed the query off with an airy, "Oh I've been coming since I was a little girl" and walked away.

～

Hard times persisted at the station and pressures were being put on the top executives to find remedies. There was talk in the air of the need for an executive vice president. Such talk had floated around for years, but now it had become a conversation that would not go away. A search was initiated. The president's executive secretary, a beautiful black woman whom I had brought into the station, came bustling down the hall one day to tell me she was sure that the finalist was a black man. I could not contain myself. I looked at his search portfolio, which I had not examined closely. One sentence stood out. "He is not a Shakespearean scholar, but he will not let you steamroller him." There was no mention of his race in the report.

It was necessary for the board to ratify the new appointment. The candidate came to the meeting and was asked to wait outside while his candidacy was being discussed. Of course it had already been decided in a series of phone calls and smaller meetings. The various executive committee members who had met with him presented flattering summaries about the candidate. Race was never mentioned. One board member merely said it was clear that "this man will never be president." Another said, "Yes, he will never be president." The candidate was invited into the room and welcomed to the staff. He was indeed black.

The few villains in my life have all been white men—except one. The new executive was a tall, broad dark man with a big forehead, flaring nostrils and an engaging wide smile. He was one of the few black men who really do look like Paul Robeson. Genuinely affable but plainspoken, he could be an intimidating presence. His voice was loud and he was not above yelling when he got excited.

He never liked me. This in itself was unusual, because I worked hard at having people like me. No one had ever openly disliked me. I never had anyone say, as the new man did, that he had "a low level of comfort with me." He told me that black people like me could never understand black people like him. I believe he saw me as one of those black people who automatically looked down on him, rejected him, held him back because of his color or his background. He had grown up in a housing project, a member of a poor but respectable family. He made a point of how far he had come without losing touch with his roots. Now he lived in an expensive home in a suburb outside of New York and had a vacation house in the islands off South Carolina.

He blocked the president's plan to promote me and told me he would strip me of all my other titles. He would make good on his word. The president called me to his office less and less. I was excluded from a fevered series of meetings to plan yet another version of the station's future. The tipoff came when a board member stopped by my office to thank me for all the things I had done for him and the board. He thought I had already been told that I had been, as they say in England, "made redundant."

One Thursday afternoon in May, the executive vice president asked to see me. Clearly ill at ease, he told me what I already knew: the station was being reorganized. In the new structure, he said, there was no place for me. Although I had expected the blow, I felt drained, betrayed. In all my life's experiences, I had never had such a setback. I had never been made a victim. I had never been treated unfairly.

One of my jobs at the station was to plan parties for departing senior executives. No one planned one for me. With my files and my plants, I left quietly late one Friday afternoon. I put my emotions in check because I had my mother's wedding to plan. It gave me something to focus on as I began one of the most trying times of my life.

Several months later the president's resignation was announced on the front page of *The New York Times*. The search for his successor was on. Both the executive vice president and the black vice president of national programming were passed over. WNET was not ready for a black gatekeeper, no matter his credentials.

∞

On the third Saturday of June in 1986, on a shaded triangle of a large Connecticut lawn, a mostly white woman married a man the color of walnut shells. It was the seventy-fifth summer for both the bride and groom. The bride, who was ending her widowhood, was my mother, Margaret Morris Taylor. The man, Graham Hancock, was a widower and native of Virginia who had lived in New Haven since the end of his military service in World War II.

Still beautiful, warm and generous at seventy-five, my mother had attracted the attention of the handsome deacon by whom she sat every Sunday at New Haven's Dixwell United Church. When she told her children she wanted to marry again and hoped we would approve, we proposed the major public celebration she had never had.

I was in my mother's wedding. So were my two sisters, our husbands, our children, my brother's children and Thelma, the woman my mother calls her sister. Including the bride and groom, the wedding party numbered sixteen. The setting was the back and side lawn of the Caribbean blue Victorian home my husband and I lived in on Prospect Street.

The bride wore lavender chiffon. It was a challenge to find a dress that would suit and flatter the bridesmaids, who ranged in age from fourteen to fifty-something. We chose a flapper-style chemise made of soft lawn, with a sailor collar and dropped sleeves trimmed in lace, reminiscent of the dresses my mother wore in the 1920s. We selected two of her favorite colors, pink and lavender. An uncommonly handsome brigade of sons-in-law and grandsons wore snappy blue blazers over crisp white pants.

Our skin tones ranged from alabaster to dark chocolate. But my mother's wedding differed in one significant feature from her daughters': there were no "real" white people in it.

There are some times when one is more acutely aware of time and place, motion and color, scents and textures. This was one of those days for me. Nothing had prepared me for the jumbled feelings I would experience being in my mother's wedding. I do not remember actually walking in the procession. I felt as if I floated across the blue-green lawn on a cushion of June-soft air, touching just the top of the grass. Under century-old trees, I waited with those I love most for my mother. In her wedding album, there is a picture of the women in the wedding party at that moment of waiting. Our heads are bowed and garlanded. We pause, with arms curved around our blossoms, like dancers after a pirouette. A small wind blows our translucent dresses around our knees. We are each still and absorbed in the moment. No one else exists for us but the woman we await. Our mother and grandmother, our source and our beginning. At the end of the ceremony, unbidden, we would send a secret signal and admit the groom to our circle. Our family would be whole once again.

Chapter Ten

When we searched our hearts and found
The quilted patches of their lives
We knew they were ours to piece together. . . .

—NAGUEYALTI WARREN
"Quilt Pieces"

In his book *The Black West*, William Katz tells us that Los Angeles was founded by forty-four persons, of whom twenty-six had African ancestry. One of those black families owned Beverly Hills, and another, all of the San Fernando Valley. Things have changed.

I live in Los Angeles now, in a faux manor house that Mary Pickford built in 1928, after she returned from a European grand tour with Douglas Fairbanks. In designing her house, she said she wanted a place that looked like the castles and buildings she saw in Europe. With the help of architects she imported from France, she succeeded in building a structure with turrets, round rooms, balconies and fifty-foot ceilings. She and Fairbanks stayed there until they completed Pickfair.

Sometimes at night, as I walk her halls, I imagine I feel her glamorous presence. I think that the glamorous women in my family—my mother, my aunts, my sisters, my daughters—would also be very much at home here. I wonder how America's Sweetheart and the number-one image of white American manhood would feel about a colored couple living in their intimate spaces.

In the neighboring apartment building lives Helen Bennett, an actress of a certain age, a former contract player for Universal Studios who was the leading lady in numerous B films of the 1940s. Before she came to Los Angeles, Helen had entered a national

beauty contest as Miss Missouri. Her roommate and fellow con-
testant, Miss New Orleans, was Dorothy Lamour. "Dorothy was
darker than you, you know," Helen told me, "and among the Hollywood insiders there was a rumor that would not go away that she
was black. They said that because of her dark coloring and her
Louisiana connection. Course in those days, if you had just one bit
of black blood, that was it." I wondered if Dorothy's "secret" was
what had drawn me to her.

I moved to Los Angeles because of a job, but a more important
reason was that I thought the city was growing toward becoming
the ideal heterogeneous urban place of the future. My new neighborhood is peopled by skin colors that copy the colors of the black
man in America. There are Armenians, Egyptians, Salvadorans,
Colombians, Jews and thirty-seven other ethnic groups. There are
not many blacks.

I came to California as director of the National Center for Film
and Video Preservation at the American Film Institute. An Asian
and four white males had preceded me in the job in the space of
five years. I should have examined the swinging door of leadership
more closely. The preservationists were also all white, mostly male,
in spite of the fact that most preservation is state or federally funded.
A black female leader was an oxymoron to them.

Until I joined the community, Hollywood's whiteness was something I read about once a year in articles in the arts-and-leisure
section of *The New York Times.* I thought black Hollywood would
be revealed to me the first time I attended the Oscars and the
Emmys. But mine was one of the few black faces in the audience.
And as the evening's programs proceeded, I understood why—they
were irrelevant to actors of color.

Hollywood is not alone in its color blackout. It is part of the
larger Los Angeles disease. Most events are segregated. At one
dinner, a benefit for a college, Harold and I were the only black
couple. Seated on my right was a wealthy WASP industrialist who
told me about his daughter working for a Jewish law firm and how
in spite of "their excitability" she was learning a lot from "them."
On my left the talk was of an upcoming Pavarotti concert and "boy
could those wops really sing." I lost my appetite. I supposed I
would have to leave the table before the talk about blacks began.

What to do in this tawdry situation? Everyone at the table was elderly. Should I, we, make a scene? Whose views would we change? We left early. In race and ethnic matters, Los Angeles had not progressed any further than New York in thirty years.

I began to take a good hard look at my job. In the clear, cold light, I admitted to myself that my life's work now centered on preserving a key part of white cultural America, much of which never had the interests of black people at heart, and most of which deliberately and consciously excluded the black presence. I had dedicated myself to preserving the dreams, stereotypes and unreal images of a white America that never existed, an America as seen through the eyes of immigrants who wanted it to live up to the expectations of their soft-focus dreams.

When I fired a white male employee who had been grossly insubordinate to me, his mentor, the former director of the center, began an open campaign against me. I decided the skirmish was not worth fighting. I resigned. The preservationists could breathe easy, everything would be white again. A national preservation board could go on to vote *Birth of a Nation* "one of America's greatest film treasures." There would be no black voice in a position of power to question the purity of their motives or the depth of their understanding.

A journalist acquaintance asked me recently if I had ever wanted to pass for white. I told him that I had no need to, but that I certainly could not control the perceptions or assumptions other people might have. My color, I said, had allowed me to sit on top of and look over both sides of the high wall that separates the black and white experiences. And yes, that has been an advantage in the revelation of the dark secrets people have in their white souls.

My father, though deeply and vocally proud of his race, was nonetheless a staunch integrationist. He passed that mantle on to me. In the 1950s I wore it tightly secured at the neck like a cape; by the 1960s, it had slipped to the waist, coming open sometimes like a wraparound skirt. The 1970s found it riding low on my hips, loosely encircling each leg like chaps. It hobbled my knees in the 1980s. Now, in the decade before the year 2000, it frequently trips me, and I can feel myself step out of it from time to time. It gets harder and harder for me to honor my father's dream and the reality of my mother's life. But I know my parents will not let me leave that mantle behind, even if I drag it for a while. My father's words and the measure of my mother's life will assure that I pick it up and try again.

༄

In the early part of 1992 my daughter Deirdre was spending several weeks in Cleveland doing research for her law firm. She gleaned the telephone books of Cleveland and all its bordering suburbs and sent me all the listings for William Morris. There were sixteen, including Willys, Bills and Billys. Through something called a legal locator, she was able to match six of those listed with the age range of my uncle. Public records listed their age, Social Security number, homeownership, political party, home tax paying status. I called each one, but none seemed to fit the bill.

Thelma's granddaughter, a judge in Cleveland, suggested that I employ a private investigation service. I got a recommendation from someone at one of the city's top law firms and turned over the scant information I had, a letter listing my uncle Bill and my aunt Grace's last address in Cleveland in 1936. I gave the agency their ages, their place of birth, their last known address from the "rejection letter" sent by the Cleveland chief of police, the approximate age of Grace's daughter, Patricia, and her college affiliation. They asked why I wanted to find the Morrises. I told them the siblings had been separated when they were young children, and I wanted to reunite them for my mother's birthday. I did not mention race or color.

༄

In April I went east to see Melissa open on Broadway in *Jelly's Last Jam*, a dramatic musical about Jelly Roll Morton that became a smash. How ironic, I thought, that my daughter, a product of a family that had divided over issues of color and race, should be in a play about a man who refused to accept his black heritage and denied its influence on his work.

I went back to see the show several times, on one occasion taking my uncle Percy with me. The next day, he suffered a massive heart attack at a butcher shop just around the corner from his apartment in Harlem. A few weeks later he died without regaining consciousness. I followed his instructions and had him cremated, and we decided to have a memorial service within the month. I would have to return to New York to clear out his apartment and his life.

I had never been inside Percy's brownstone on the gentle slope of West 141st Street. A foyer with dark oak window seats and a mirrored Victorian fireplace leading to a rickety carved banister bespoke the former elegance of the place. But the pale yellow walls of his rooms were grimy, and over the windows were hung blankets and tablecloths. Percy's pull-out bed was rumpled as he had left it. In the small apartment there were seven radios, two television sets, two turntables and two tape players. A red plastic milk carton contained dozens of cassettes featuring Percy's voice and piano playing.

How do you sift through eighty years of a life? In Percy's case, it was an archaeological expedition. He had saved an improbable number of items from his eight decades. Cards and letters, snapshots, newspaper clippings, graduation announcements, wedding invitations, funeral programs, birth and death notices crammed albums and spilled out of drawers, shelves and cardboard boxes. One entire room was devoted to clothes. There must have been a hundred hats and caps. Boxes full of colorful beads, necklaces and men's bracelets lay about.

Isaac Bashevis Singer liked to say that "secrets struggle to reveal themselves." I did not know my uncle Percy was gay until I was forty years old. The subject had never been mentioned, at least around me. I knew he had been married briefly, and that he was an outrageous flirt. I had attributed his flamboyance and histrionic personality to the theatrical strain that seemed to run in the Taylor family.

We were living in New Haven and Percy was staying with us for a few days. Whenever he was visiting, he would take our dogs Ginger and Hannibal for long walks, all the way downtown and back. Routinely, after he took the dogs on his rounds, he would go back downtown. Compared to New York City, nothing much happens in downtown New Haven, and I could never understand what fascination New Haven's Green could hold for such a sophisticated man. It was a warm spring day, and Percy had just left the house. Suddenly the thought came to me: Percy was cruising.

When my husband came home, I said to him, "Is Percy gay?" He said, "Yes, I thought you knew." The revelation confounded me. I called my mother, who had been Percy's classmate in high school in Washington and his good friend throughout her marriage to my father. She said she had known Percy was gay since high school, but it was not something the family discussed, nor did it matter to her or my father. It had mattered greatly to other members of the family, however, which was why Percy had relocated to New York. Two of his brothers had told him explicitly not to bring any of his male companions to Washington because it would be a disgrace to the Taylor name and to the Florida Avenue church.

So Percy had carefully choreographed his encounters with his family. Among his gay friends, he had chosen to be known by another name, "Teddy." I thought how sad it was that his personal life had created an invisible barrier between him and some of his family, and I marveled at the energy he put into maintaining the facade. Throughout his life he had carried a secret identity as great as the one my mother's family harbored.

Had I not known about Percy's homosexuality, I would have been stunned by the homoerotic magazines, books, photographs, postcards and knickknacks that crammed the apartment, most of it under his bed. There were also several scientific tracts about homosexuality. We packed the library in plastic bags and set it beside the curb. Within an hour, a woman with a close-shaven head came up the stairs. She identified herself as a lesbian and said she knew where the material could be put to good use. We were pleased to pass this part of Percy's legacy to someone who would welcome it.

Word of Percy's death as a "son of the church" was broadcast to thousands in Washington on the weekly Sunday radio service of Florida Avenue Baptist Church. We held his memorial service on Lenox Avenue at one of the many senior citizen centers that he called his "hangouts." On a dark cloth we laid out six of his most distinctive hats. He opened his own service, singing and playing on tape "You'll Never Walk Alone." We knew he would have loved that touch.

೧೨

I was in Washington at Jewelle's when the detective agency I had hired to trace the family called from Cleveland. "We found your mother's sister." She was eighty-eight years old and living near me, in Anaheim. How appropriate, I thought, that she should be located near Disneyland, the world of make-believe.

The detective who had located Grace told me he'd called all the Morrises and Cramers in the Cleveland phone book, with no luck. His first break came with the Cleveland city directories, where he found both William Morris and an Earl Cramer listed as the husband of Grace Cramer. The paper trail traveled from the 1930s to the 1960s, through various neighborhoods and jobs. Then the families seemed to vanish. He got a Western Reserve alumni listing for Grace's daughter, Patricia, in southern California, but she was classified as deceased. This was the same Patricia Cramer that Deirdre had found months before and I had discounted. I could not believe that the first cousin I had been looking for since I was a girl had died without my meeting her.

Knowing that when some parents retire they want to be close to their children, the detective searched the southern California telephone directories for Grace and Earl Cramer. He found a Grace Cramer in Anaheim and called her. She confirmed that she was indeed Grace Morris Cramer and had a brother named William Morris. She confirmed that her brother, her husband and her only daughter, Patricia, had died. All she had left, she said, were her son-in-law and three grandchildren.

The detective told her he had good news for her. Her sister had been looking for her. At first she seemed bewildered and said that she didn't remember having a sister. But first thing the next morning, she called him back. She did have a sister, but that was a long time ago. She said she would accept a telephone call from me, but she was not sure she wanted to go any further with it. "I don't want my family dragged into this," she said.

Jewelle and I immediately began to plan how to get to see Grace, and more important, whether and how to get Grace and my mother together. My sisters thought I should not even tell my mother Grace had been found until after I had made contact with her. They feared my mother would suffer still another rejection at the hands of her family. But I was beginning to think differently. I thought the prospect of a living sister might be one of the most life-affirming experiences my mother could ever have.

At my mother's eightieth birthday party, I presented her with the two pictures, in filigreed silver frames, of her grandparents that Jewelle had retrieved from our aunt Mamie's family. She showed little emotion or interest. Then I reminded her that I had promised to find her sister by her eightieth birthday. I said, "Today I can honor that promise. I have found your sister, Grace, and she is alive and well." Without skipping a beat my mother said sweetly, "Where is the hussy?"

❧

When I returned to California, I decided to pay Grace a surprise visit. I fretted for days over the little questions. What should I say, how should I look, when should I go, should I take my husband with me? My mother's fears of rejection resurfaced in me. The big questions were no longer academic. What did I owe to others—my mother, my family, my aunt—and what was rightfully mine? How should I act when I knew that to be true to myself might be a betrayal of my aunt? Where should my deepest loyalty lie? To myself, my mother, my husband, my children? To my race, and if so which one? To my history or to my future?

I must have been thinking about the 1950s television series *The Millionaire* as I made my plans. I hired a limousine and bought an oversized bouquet of flowers. In a tote bag I put a camera, pictures of my mother and grandparents, and a list of questions. I asked my husband to ride with me for moral support, but I knew the visit itself was mine alone to make. I also knew that if Grace caught sight of my husband's brown skin, there was a good chance she might not let us in the door. I would play another round of the game my relatives had played so well for so long.

The drive to Anaheim took less than forty-five minutes, but when we got to the street we could not locate the address. We stopped in a gas station and the driver unfurled himself from the car to ask directions. No wonder we had missed it. We hadn't known we were looking for a trailer park. A few minutes later, we drove up to a well-maintained, walled entrance with a sign that said "Friendly Village." The lots were small but clean and neat. They did not fit my negative stereotype.

Grace had a double-wide yellow mobile home with dark brown trim, the next to the last in the final row of homes. Faded teal indoor-outdoor carpeting led up three steps and covered an empty side porch. The trailer looked closed up, as if no one was at home. Harold wished me luck and said he would be back for me in an hour. Trying to look graceful and confident, I stepped out of the car and walked up to the door. The name under a brass bell gone black with age was Cramer.

Behind a screen door, the inside of the house looked dark and cool. I rang the bell. In a few moments, a tiny woman who looked like my mother came to the door. She was barely five feet tall, and her delicate figure seemed sizes too small for the blouse and slacks she wore. She was a shade darker than my mother but her face was covered in a white powder. Her smile was warm as she opened the door.

"I have flowers for Mrs. Cramer," I said, my throat almost closed.

"Well, that's me," she said in a soft, Midwestern accent, smiling as I handed her the bouquet. "Who are they from?"

Again I could barely get the words out. "They're from your sister, Margaret, and me, your niece Shirlee."

A look I could not read registered instantly on her face. It was as if a cloud passed between us. Then, in the same quiet tone, she said, "Well, come in."

A teal blue shag rug carpeted all the floors. The living room was small and tidy. Beyond it I could see a dining room and sitting room. The interior very much fit my image of the typical working-class white American family home. But I was struck by the absence of family photographs. There was not one to be seen.

Grace motioned me to sit on the sofa while she went in search of a vase. A long-haired orange and white Persian cat sat in one of the easy chairs, licking his paws and eyeing me lazily. To put Grace at ease, I asked her about the cat, an animal I happen to love. I described my gray Persian and told her that cats were my mother's favorite pets. She said, "I figure people who love cats can't be all bad. I've loved them since I was a girl. I never had a doll, but there were always cats around." We had established a bond.

I told her I had not come to upset her life or make trouble for her, and my visit would not be long. All I wanted to do, I assured her, was to meet her and ask her some questions about the family. She seemed to relax. As she talked, I saw my mother in her face and gestures. Both sisters had inherited their mother's oval face, round eyes and well-proportioned mouth. Grace had my mother's quick, unstudied movements, and there were moments when I glimpsed in her my mother's eagerness to please. But my mother's hair is silver, while Grace had colored hers a chestnut brown, leaving a gray streak in front. "I hate gray hair," she said. "It may look good on some people, but it does not do a thing for me. I don't want to look old."

Much of what Grace told me I had already learned from the detective's dossier. I knew of the death of her brother Bill, her husband and her daughter. I asked if I might see pictures of her surviving son-in-law and his three children. She disappeared into her bedroom and returned with a handful of photographs. Most were of her daughter, Patricia, at different ages, some were of her and Pat together, a few were of her son-in-law and her grandchildren, and one or two showed her husband.

Earl Cramer, Grace's husband, had brown hair and a brown mustache. She said he was English and German and had grown up on a farm in Wisconsin. He came from a large family headed by a woman Grace described as a stiff English dowager who sat on her hands whenever she came to visit. Grace's daughter, Pat, had been a pretty girl, with curly black hair, blue eyes and a pleasing oval face. As if following her stream of consciousness, Grace told me how her handsome, dark-haired Italian son-in-law had changed his ethnic sounding, three-syllable family name to Scott at the suggestion of a boss who thought he "would not get too far" otherwise. How ironic that he selected the maiden name of his wife's mulatto grandmother.

His family, Grace said, was not too pleased that he had chosen to marry "a girl with an Irish background." She explained that the three grandchildren took their dark coloring from the Italian side of the family. All three had dark hair, and one girl had the naturally bushy, crimpy texture that children of mixed race often have and fashionable white salons work hours to achieve. Only one granddaughter was married. To Grace's displeasure, the other sister preferred Hispanic men. "I asked her, 'Isn't a white man good enough for you?'" she recounted to me, seemingly oblivious to what I might think or feel about such concerns. I let her talk. Several times during her conversation she stopped and told me how pretty I was.

Seventy-five years of a life cannot be captured in twenty minutes. I spoke in outlines. I told Grace that once my mother had married, she had lived mostly a comfortable life. I sketched a picture of Julian as a good husband and father. I showed her the photographs of my mother taken over the years. She looked with a flat, distant curiosity. She was more interested in the pictures of her grandmother and grandfather Morris, which I had borrowed from my mother. Of her grandfather, whom she had never seen, she said, "Wasn't he a doll? My grandmother always said, 'He was the best man there ever was.' " She made no comment about his curly hair and broad nose.

She went into the bedroom again and brought out a number of snapshots of Margaret Maher Morris. "All that I am today, I owe to my little Irish grandmother," she allowed. "She was a cute, fine little lady who taught me so much. She especially told me to be truthful. But sometimes you have to lie to save people. I'm very honest, you know, and I get that from my grandmother. She hated liars. I had no mother, you know, and my father was an alcoholic. My brother hated him until the day he died, because he didn't do right by us.

"We were very poor, you know, and my brother Bill kept us alive. He would sell fried oysters on the street for a dime and deliver groceries for a few nickels. He would spend that money on food for us. I had no warm clothes and I hated to be dirty. My grandmother said it was all right to be poor, but there was no excuse for being dirty.

"When I was seven I tried to wash the one dress I had to wear to school. I did not give it enough time to dry, and I can still feel its wet collar around my neck and its damp cuffs around my wrists. What does a seven-year-old know about washing a dress? I hated the way I looked. The other girls had nicer clothes. I never had a warm coat. I was always cold. I never had a doll, and I said if ever I had a daughter, she would have dolls and all the things I never had. And she did. My young life was terrible, and it was a miracle we survived."

Grace seemed to take comfort from what she was telling me. I guessed it was an unburdening of sorts. We had not yet talked of race or color, and my time was getting short. I said I had a difficult question to ask, but it was something my mother especially wanted to know. Did Grace know why her father had left my mother behind? She shook her head. "I was a little girl too when our mother died. I don't know."

I sensed it was time to go. I also sensed that to bring up the matter of race at that moment would cause Grace tremendous pain. Was it my responsibility to remind Grace who she was, to dredge up a past she had buried? Despite all the years of longing and conjecture, despite the fact that race was the central issue, I could not bring myself to broach it yet. Instead, I asked her if I might take her picture and take a picture of her daughter's photograph as well. Without hesitation she agreed.

I had one more favor to ask. If I dialed the number and paid for the call, would she speak to my mother and wish her a happy birthday?

Again without hesitation, she said, "Sure, let's do it."

I needed to sit down to make the call. "Mother," I said, "I am at your sister's house."

"Is she being nice to you?" she countered.

"Yes, quite. And, Mother, she looks like you, acts like you and loves cats like you. She would like to speak to you."

After seventy-six years of separation, the white sister held the telephone to her ear and said to her black sister, "Hello, Margaret, how are you?"

The conversation was brief and probably awkward for both of them. When it was over, I said I had to go. But as I walked toward the door, Grace reached up on tiptoes, put her thin arms around my neck, and gave me a long hug. I did not expect it, and it was difficult for me to react. She thanked me for coming and said she hoped I would visit again. The next time, she said, she would show me some more family pictures. I pushed the screen door and saw the waiting limousine. The chauffeur was standing by the open car door. Grace watched me as I walked down the steps. She waved as the car door closed after me. That afternoon, I wrote to her, thanking her for spending time with me and enclosing a picture of my mother and me. As an afterthought, I included my mother's address and telephone number.

That night again, I could not sleep. I kept replaying the conversation in my mind's eye. My aunt had painted a portrait of a marginal familiy, broken and poor, all of them victims of an alcoholic, unreliable father. For the first time, I began to feel sorry for Grace. But most of my questions about the family remained unasked.

∽

The second time I visited Grace I called ahead. I said that I would like to take her to lunch and reminded her of the family pictures she said she would show me. Her smile was wide as she greeted me at the door with a big hug. "I have something for you," she said. "It was mine and it is quite old." From the bedroom she brought a small box, wrapped in plain white paper. On it she had written, "To Shirlee, Love Grace." Again surprised, I opened the package. It was a pillbox adorned with rhinestones and jet. She brought out another small box and a card and said, "This is for your mother."

We sat in the living room and talked of her early life. The faces I had wondered about since I was a child, the images of my grandfather, my aunts, my uncles and my first cousins were laid out on the walnut coffee table. My family had many features in common with these relatives from the other side. And yet as I looked at them I thought to myself, But they are different from me, they are white—whatever that is.

We walked to a nearby shopping mall and had lunch. She told me about her current life, which seemed solitary and lonely to me. "I like jazz," she said, "and I was a good dancer. So was my brother Bill." She heard from one of her brother's daughters at Christmas and on special occasions saw her grandchildren. On the way back to her trailer, which she referred to as a "cracker box," her next-door neighbor came out the gateway. He nodded at me, and asked Grace where she had been. She grabbed my arm, pulled me close to her side and said we had been to lunch. She did not introduce me, and we continued walking.

I told her my mother was coming out to visit. She said she hoped she would get down to Anaheim. Once again we parted with a promise of future visits and phone calls.

In the last week of September, two sisters who had not seen each other in seventy-six years were reunited. Both were short, soft-spoken and widowed, and despite their advanced age, of sound mind and in good health. Traces of great beauty in their youth remained in both their fair-skinned faces.

We had laid out birthday gifts for Grace—Godiva chocolates, fancy soaps, a cat calendar and cat notepaper—the night before. The plan was for Harold to drop us at Grace's, then return in the afternoon to take us for a weekend with a friend in Palm Springs. In the morning, my mother was up and dressed to go by eight. Was it tentativeness or anxiety I sensed in her mood? "I have all kinds of feelings," she said. "I'm nervous, hopeful, a little angry, curious and happy. I think about all those years, empty and wasted, when we could have known each other. I never dreamed this day would come. I thought she was dead. I had put all my relatives out of my mind and made them all dead. And there is nothing that can take away all the pain and hurt of those years." She smiled her beautiful, sad smile.

On the lapel of her suit she had pinned an antique sterling brooch of roses twinned and entwined, the gift Grace had sent her. "I hope she notices I am wearing it." I watched her drink her coffee, anticipating that the meeting would be all she wanted it to be, and that at last she would be made welcome. I, who had been surrounded by real family all my life, felt for the first time the enormity of what was about to happen. My mother was making the last leg of her journey to locate herself within her family.

The door to Grace's trailer was closed tight. Mother rang the bell. I got out my camera. The door opened and Mother began to cry. In the end it was she who opened her arms wide and hugged the frail old woman who leaned into her visitor with equal parts stiffness and willingness. At a loss for what to do next, Grace picked up the cat. "This is my sister, Margaret," she said to it, as if practicing a new word. Again I noticed how she covered her entire face in white powder.

I told the two sisters I would sit in the next room and read so they could have a private visit. At first, Grace paced back and forth nervously between her bedroom and the living room. As she passed me, she would stop to say something. I urged her to spend the time with her visitor from Connecticut. I heard my mother telling her the oft-told story of how she'd cut pictures out of magazines and wondered if Grace resembled them. "Did you ever think of me?" she asked. Years of fear and withdrawal constricted Grace's responses. She explained how hard her early life had been. "Much of it I don't remember," she said. "I guess I don't want to remember."

Mother asked Grace if she remembered Cousin Bessie, who nursed their mother, or Miss Rebecca, the neighbor who'd taken care of their youngest brother, Michael. Grace could not recall them. Nor could she remember Uncle Eddie Scott, who'd left her an inheritance, or his brown-skinned mother, Margaret Scott, who lived in the house with her. She had no conscious memories of her colored years. In fact she had no colored memories at all.

Of those she could remember, Grace was forthcoming. She told my mother how kind and sweet Uncle Edward in Buffalo had been, how he had been so much his Irish mother's favorite that his wife, Minette, had been jealous. My mother restrained her feelings as Grace spoke glowingly of their grandmother. She even had good words for their father, whom she claimed was a gentleman when he was sober. She seemed surprised when my mother said she had seen their grandmother only twice in her life. She was also surprised that my mother knew about the death of their father on the Eastern Shore. Grace obviously did not realize how much information their Aunt Mamie had passed along.

They talked of cats and grandchildren. They demonstrated an innate sibling rivalry as they bragged about their children and their children's children. But going to lunch, I noticed how the older sister automatically took the younger sister's arm to guide her.

On the way to Palm Springs, we replayed the conversation. My mother talked of loss and recovery. We acknowledged that there were things we would never know about the transactions within her family. "I guess I did have a better life, didn't I?" she mused.

That night, I had a dream about Grace. I was on my way to meet her to take her somewhere, perhaps to lunch. She met me in a doorway, exquisitely well groomed in a pale blue and white paisley dress. Perched high on the top of her head was a hairpiece in the shape of a loose topknot. Her face seemed to have been profession ally made up, including false eyelashes. Suddenly, my sister Jewelle appeared. She stood by Grace, waiting for an introduction to her newfound aunt. Grace put her arm beside Jewelle's as if comparing the two, then quickly withdrew it. Grace covered her face with a small white polka-dotted veil, which she attached to her topknot with a large hat pin that was ornamented with a tear drop–shaped pearl.

Then we were in the vestibule of my father's church in Ansonia. Grace and I went in and sat in the last row. My mother took her customary seat in the center of the third row. Sometime during the service, Grace simply vanished. I remained sitting until the service was over, then went outside to look for Grace. She was nowhere to be seen. All I could find was her hairpiece and the white polka-dotted veil, perched on the floor like a doll's starched tutu. At the front of the church, the minister, who was not my father, kept saying, "Is there a Grace Cramer here?" My mother came to the vestibule in tears, repeating, "Grace is gone. Grace is gone."

∽

Twelve days later, we returned to Anaheim for a second visit. This time, Grace was eager in her greeting. She spoke again of her father, grandmother and other relatives, but the stories were much the same. And she recounted the loss of her husband and daughter, and spoke of the grandchildren who survived. "My granddaughter is a Spanish interpreter, you know," she told my mother. "She likes to date those men, Mexicans, but they call them Hispanics now. I asked her, 'What's wrong with a good white man?' This one is dark, you know."

"How dark?" my mother asked.

"Like a black man," said Grace. My mother's face reddened, but her lips did not open. I leaned over and touched her on the shoulder. The moment passed. It was the only time race or color was mentioned.

I asked Grace if she had ever heard the name Halyburton mentioned in connection with the family. She said she had heard it often as a child, but could not remember the details. I told her a bit about the judge and reminded her that he was the father of Edward Everett Morris. She did not ask why the surnames were different, but she was eager to know more about the prestigious jurist. We did not press the issue.

The phone rang. Grace went to the bedroom to pick it up. The sound of her voice carried as she told the caller she had "some friends visiting right now." She did not say "family." In the lobby of the restaurant, we passed an interracial couple. Mother and I exchanged a glance, wondering whether Grace would react. She was impassive, and I wondered whether she steeled herself to avoid mirrors of her own history. Or perhaps our presence simply inhibited her.

Watching the sisters sit side by side in the restaurant booth, I sensed a budding comfort. But I also thought it was just as well that after this visit they would be three thousand miles apart. Race still separated them. I understood now in ways I had not that Grace was indeed white. She could not give up being white, nor could she tear down the alabaster walls she had built around her life. She would be content to see us as often as we might like to visit, as long as no one in her circle knew who or what we were. In other words, she would be satisfied to continue the pattern of the past.

I wonder if I can continue to visit Grace. I do not wish to exclude my husband and most other aspects of my life. Not to see her again, I suppose, would be cowardly. But I do not want to feel, in James Baldwin's words, "an increasing chill, as if the rest of my life would have to be lived in silence." I do not understand how those who cloaked their lives carried on for so long, even if they did become the Other. I cannot imagine what it must have been like to hide behind a hundred veils for a lifetime. For me, the toll is far too great.

How do I feel about Grace? Mostly sorry. Sorry that American life and circumstances forced her to make the choices she did. Sorry that she ran and hid, ran and hid again, living in constant dread and anxiety. Sorry that she could not tell her husband and child about a family who could have embraced them. Sorry that she and my mother could not comfort each other when their husbands and children died. Sorry that she is now alone, old and most of the time lonely.

∾

My mother went home to Connecticut a somewhat happier person. Before she left, she told Grace she would call her once a week and write when she could. Through her sister she had found the rest of her family. She could see herself in their faces. She could understand if not forgive their choices. Pity for her father began to dilute the anger she had carried so long. Like the rest of us, she would never know the whole story, but at least she had hold of most of the chapters.

With a few clues from Grace—a married name and a city where she might live—I located my first cousin Dorothy, my Uncle William Morris's daughter by his first marriage to the German woman from Cleveland. She was the one I thought looked like Dorothy Lamour. When I asked the information operator whether she had a listing under the name of Dorothy, she said she had the last name I was looking for but with only the initial "D." I called the number and a recorded message said, "Hello, this is Dotty." I knew I had found her.

Later that night, I called again and Dotty answered. I told her I was doing some research on my family and thought she might be related to me. I asked her if her father was William Morris and if Grace Morris Cramer was her aunt. She said yes to both questions. I told her I was the daughter of her father's sister Margaret. "This is weird," Dotty said. "I didn't know my father had another sister. Then what are you to me?" "Your first cousin," I replied. She said she knew her father had been born in Washington, but she did not know he had any family remaining there, or anywhere else. She explained that when her mother and father divorced it was a "sad affair" and she did not see her father after that. She did not know anything about his second marriage, his other daughter or when or where he died.

I gave her a sketchy outline of my mother's family, laying the separation of the family at the door of bad fortune. Dorothy told me she was seventy-one and had lived in the Minneapolis area since

1952. I told her my sister Jewelle had lived there for a number of years from 1959 on, and who knows, they might have passed each other in the aisles of Dayton's department store or at the Walker Arts Center. Dorothy asked me to send her some material on the family story and pictures of my mother and the rest of the family. I assured her that she and her family would be welcome in my home in Los Angeles, and I was certain my mother and sister would receive her in Connecticut as well. She asked me to stop in to see her if ever I was in Minneapolis.

In the week commemorating the twenty-fifth anniversary of the death of Martin Luther King, Jr., I found another of my first cousins, Bill's second daughter, Carol. I had seen her last name on a picture that Grace had showed me, and on a hunch, I called the alumni office of Case Western Reserve in Cleveland. The alumni office confirmed her matriculation there, but they could not give out any information about her.

I called a friend of Deirdre's who had also attended the school and asked her to see if Carol Morris's name was in the alumni books. She confirmed the name, class year and an address outside of Cleveland. Less nervous this time, I dialed the number. A boy answered, and I asked for Carol by her married name. He put me on hold, cut short another conversation he had been having and called his mother to the phone.

"Hello," I said. "My name is Shirlee Morris Taylor Haizlip and I am working on a history of the Morris family. I am looking for a Carol Morris who is the daughter of William Morris from Cleveland."

"That's me," said a curious voice.

"Do you also have an aunt named Grace Cramer?" I asked.

"Yes," Carol said.

"Then we are related. In fact, we are first cousins. I am the daughter of your father's youngest sister, Margaret."

"I didn't know my father had another sister. I only knew about one other brother who died," she told me. She hadn't even known she had a half sister until a year after her father died.

I gave her Dorothy's address and telephone number, and the information I had gleaned about her life in our one telephone call. I asked Carol what she looked like. "People say I am the spitting image of my aunt Grace. I even have the same silver streak down the center of my hair."

"Then you must look something like my mother, too," I said.

Carol told me she is an assistant professor at a community college and a candidate for her Ph.D. She and her husband live on a farm east of Cleveland, where they raise Christmas trees and produce maple syrup. She has a daughter named Margaret, who lives in San Francisco, and two sons at home as well. I asked her what she knew about her father's early life and family history. She knew only that it was hard, she said. She understood he had left Washington and had gone first to Buffalo, then to Cleveland. She had no idea that her father had left behind a younger sister and brother in Washington, or an aunt Mamie and her three children. She said she was excited to have the information, and asked me if I would send the family history to her.

In retelling the story, I mentioned to Carol that the family's roots included African-American, Irish, English, Italian and Scottish strains. I asked her if she would tell me something about her father as a father. She promised to write, to send pictures, and to come to see me in the summer when she and her husband would be making a trip to see their daughter in San Francisco. I told her I would look forward to her visit. The next day I mailed her a picture of my mother and Grace, and one of Jewelle, Pattee and me.

☙

Back on the East Coast, I got up early on the morning of the verdict in the second Rodney King trial. I wanted to hear the decision first-hand. My mother and I were together, staying in the New York penthouse apartment of a longtime friend from Wellesley days. We sat in the breakfast room, waiting. To my surprise, I felt my face flush and my temples tighten. Having discussed the incident for so long and from every angle, I had no idea I would be so viscerally affected. When the two "guilty" verdicts were read, I exhaled a "Thank God." From somewhere deep within my head, or maybe from that reservoir of rage in my chest, tears forced themselves out of my eyes. But my mother and I agreed that justice had met its obligation only halfway; weighed down by the two "not guilty" verdicts, one of the scales was dragging on the ground.

❧

Carol wrote to my mother, and she and I exchanged letters and pictures. She did her best to describe her father, whom she remembered with affection. But unlike him, she wrote to me, "I've been telling everyone about my newfound family. The reactions I get from people who have always known me as white are not always what I expected. We ought to write a book!"

As if on cue, the day after I wrote my first letter to Carol, someone who identified herself as my "long lost cousin from Minnesota" telephoned and asked to speak to me. It was Dorothy, who had gotten my letter and pictures. "I have already called my children to tell them, and they are as thrilled as I am," she said. "I'm going to show it to my whole family when they come to dinner on Easter Sunday. What more can you tell me?"

Here was an opening I thought I must go through. "What did you know about your father's family?"

"Not very much," she said.

"Do you know what his nationality was?"

"Irish, I guess."

"Your father's grandmother was Irish, from Tipperary, and then she came to Washington, D.C.," I said. "Do you know the story of how she met Edward Everett Morris, your father's grandfather?"

"No, I never even heard that name," she said.

I told her the story, starting with Judge Halyburton, mentioning Martha Washington and ending with the lovers' first meeting in the great open air market in Washington. My coda was that Morris had been a mulatto slave.

On hearing the words "mulatto slave," Dorothy exhaled a long, drawn-out *"Nooooooooooreally?"* Then, "Well, that doesn't surprise me! I used to look at my father and Aunt Grace and wonder. Sometimes I would see black men on television and think that if they were just a little lighter, they would look like my father. But I never asked him about it. Did Pat know?"

"I don't think so," I said. "It was a secret Grace carefully guarded. Even now we have not discussed it." I could tell Dorothy was still stunned by the news. It was a lot to take in. "Are you going to tell your family?" I asked.

"I don't know. I wish you were here to tell them the story."

"I'll be glad to tell them and show them the pictures when they come to visit," I said, and added, "There's nothing wrong with being multiracial these days, you know."

A year after I learned that Grace was alive and living in Anaheim, I spoke with her grandson, Jeff Scott. I had left a message on his answering machine when I learned from Grace that he had gone east and wanted to do some research on his family. I said I was a relative and had some information about the Morris family. I wondered whether he would choose to respond, and was unprepared when he returned the call the very next morning. I blurted out the story in a much less polished fashion than I had intended. He said he was "mind-boggled" but not upset by all the information and asked if he could call me again.

༄

He called again that evening, and we talked for three hours. He wanted to know names, dates, places of birth, descendants, ancestors and, most of all, reasons. Why had the family dissolved, why did most choose to be white, why did they not stay in touch with my mother? I could give him the vital statistics, but stressed that the reasons I offered were informed hypotheses, at best. I supplied him with the names and addresses of my daughters, my mother and Pattee. He said he would at least call them while he was on the East Coast. I telephoned my daughters and my mother to prepare them. I urged them to tell Jeff the truth as they understood it and to show him pictures of the family.

He met Melissa first, in her fifth-floor Chelsea walk-up. As Jeff trudged up the stairs, she felt a mixture of anticipation and apprehension. What would he be like, this cousin who was meeting part of his family for the first time?

Not knowing his taste in music, Melissa had put on James Taylor, thinking it was comfortable crossover fare. Jeff had brought a bouquet of Sweet William. As soon as he crossed the threshold, he seemed at ease. He admired Melissa's African-inspired decor, her Nigerian talking drum, and her collection of black literature, most of which he said he had read. He did not like James Taylor and suggested she put on some World Music instead.

They sat on the sofa exchanging biographies and looking at photographs, stopping every once in a while to look at each other, laughing and saying, "Isn't this fantastic? Isn't this weird? Isn't this great?" They shared a meal, then Melissa had to prepare for an audition. They parted with a promise to meet again before he went back west.

After he left Melissa, Jeff went to see Deirdre at the rap music company where she works. Deirdre showed him around and described all the latest releases, and although, as Deirdre put it, he didn't fit the demographics of the typical rap aficionado, Jeff was familiar with most of the artists the company produced. They left the office and Deirdre took him to a party in a penthouse that she thought would be well-integrated but turned out to be mostly white. "I'm the only other black person here," she joked. They compared notes on family, race and racism. Jeff said that the concept of race had always made him uncomfortable and that he considered himself racially unprejudiced. Just a few weeks before he had told a friend how he wished he had mixed roots. She took him to a new nightclub she had passes for, and he proved to be a good dancer. They, too, agreed to meet again before he left the East Coast.

My mother was apprehensive about speaking with Jeff, even after hearing about my daughters' meetings with him. Her old fears resurfaced. "Do you think he'll accept me?" she asked.

Jeff called and made a date to go to Connecticut. It was raining heavily when he reached Pattee's home in North Haven. He greeted my mother and asked, "What should I call you?" "Well, I am your aunt, so you can call me Aunt Margaret," my mother replied. "I am thrilled to have an Aunt Margaret," he responded. He asked her to tell him about her life, from as early as she could recall. With Pattee sitting quietly to the side, they sat at the table in the dining room, whose picture windows overlooked tall pine trees and a deep green yard sodden with the early summer downpour.

For the next three hours my mother told Jeff her story as she had told it to us all her life. Every once in a while he would stop and ask her questions. Jeff told my mother that he believed that his mother never knew about Grace's background. But he had always wondered, he said, why there was so little family on his mother's side. From time to time he said to my mother, "How sad for you, and how sad for my grandmother." When they both had run out of words, they went downstairs to watch a basketball game with Pattee's husband, Jim.

Jeff spent the night in my sister's home. They gave him a tour of New Haven, showing him Yale University and the Tudor house where my parents had lived. He told my mother that he would stay in touch with his new family. He took pictures with her and told her he would send her copies. He invited her to stay in his home. When he returned to California, he planned to come see me. He had to think about how to tell his grandmother, his father and his sisters what he had found back east. He said he would go slowly with his grandmother, because of the unpredictable effects of unraveling her secret after seventy-six years.

My mother was excited and pleased about Jeff's visit. He had claimed her. He had acknowledged her. He wanted to be her family. And so a young white man from Orange County, California, became the first in his family to come back across the bridge that had long divided it. Maybe others will make the journey.

The evening Jeff returned to California he went to see Grace. He took with him the census records he had copied and the photographs he had taken. With care and deliberation he laid out the Morris family story for Grace, including the African heritage of her grandfather, Edward Everett Morris, and the mixed racial backgrounds of her parents, Will Morris and Rose Scott Morris. Grace said she did not know or remember any of what Jeff revealed to her. She told him that perhaps she had blocked most of it out.

A week after Jeff's visit to Grace, I took the train down to see her. With me I carried pictures of my parents, my husband, Jewelle's husband and Pattee's husband. Grace greeted me with the news that Jeff had a wonderful time back east and enjoyed meeting my relatives. He had told her he could not have chosen a nicer family. She showed me a picture that Jeff had taken with my mother. To my eye, the tall, handsome man with dark brown hair, a cleft in his chin, laughing blue eyes and his arm around my mother looked like her father, her uncles and her brothers. Through him, they had finally come back. The picture gave me the cue I needed. Without fanfare, I showed her the pictures. For each of the men she had special compliments. My father was "handsome"; Harold looked as if he were "full of the dickens"; Jim Gibbs was "distinguished"; and Jim Brown was "jolly." That was all she had to say about the dark-skinned men in the pictures. When I left, she said she hoped she would meet my husband soon.

Epilogue

In the private chambers of the soul, the guilty party is identified, and the accusing finger there is not legend, but consequence; not fantasy, but the truth. People pay for what they have allowed themselves to become. And they pay for it simply: by the lives they lead.

—JAMES BALDWIN
The Price of the Ticket

Abraham Lincoln called those delicate strands that connect us all, one to another, the mystic chords of memory. But among my chords, there were still the unfamiliar notes of unknown tunes.

In the summer of 1993 I made two journeys toward my family's past. Within the course of the same month, I traveled to my father's place of birth, Hertford, North Carolina, and my white cousins' place of life, Orange County, California, and the two journeys remain linked in my mind.

It had been more than thirty years since I had been in North Carolina, or anywhere else in the rural South, for that matter. I went with mixed feelings, curiosity and apprehension. My husband and I wondered where we could stay in the little coastal town of Hertford. At one time in its history the village, whose main streets were named for London thoroughfares, had boasted two hotels. With a current population of only twenty-five hundred, half black and half white, the hotels were now just a memory of a more prosperous and segregated past.

We called the minister of First Baptist, the Taylor family church in Hertford, to ask his advice. He suggested a bed-and-breakfast on the edge of town where he "thought blacks had stayed." A telephone call gave us confirmed reservations.

The proprietor's directions led us to a sprawling, white-columned mansion, a restored Southern plantation house. It sat facing hundreds of acres of soy bean fields. The summer suffered a long season of drought, and in the afternoon sun, the crops looked parched and sickly. At the edge of the fields, a stand of tall old trees marked the border of the land and edged the mouth of the Perquimans River. The wide river gave the county its Native American name, which means "land of beautiful women."

We were sitting in the car, discussing whether we should go in—after all, this was a private home—when the appearance of a tall white figure waving to us from a wide veranda ended our debate. A smiling woman with blond hair wearing a raspberry-colored linen shirtwaist dress strode quickly toward the car and introduced herself as Nancy Rascoe, the hostess of the inn and owner of the property. She reminded me of Blythe Danner playing Blanche Dubois in *A Streetcar Named Desire*.

"Y'all must be the Haizlips," she said, her accent as broad as the river. She offered to help us with our luggage and invited us in to meet the other guests and have some iced tea. "Mind the musqeetas, now," she said. "Don't let 'em in the parlah." She explained that this was her family's home and land. "Yes, we had slaves," she went on, "but some of my people were Quakas. There were a lotta Quakas in this area, you know. They didn't believe in slavery. So we freed our slaves or sent 'em back to Liberia. Did y'all have a nas drive?" All this was said before we got to the spacious entrance hall of the beautifully restored antebellum residence.

It was difficult for me to sleep that night in the carved mahogany four-poster bed. Some of our hostess's unsmiling ancestors were staring down at me from oval portraits in gilt frames. We were in one of the front rooms upstairs, and several times I got up during the night to look out at the fields. I hoped I would see the ghosts of some of the slaves who had labored there. Perhaps some of them were related to me. But all I saw was a cold, bright moon in a cloudless sky, shining over the trees, the river and the drooping soybean plants.

The next morning, Nancy served us and four other guests fried green tomatoes, fried fish from the river, spoon bread, cheese grits, eggs, bacon, biscuits, fresh orange juice and coffee. I was sure my father and grandfather were invisible witnesses as the great-granddaughter of a slave holder waited on the great-granddaughter of a slave. For me, it was a life-changing experience.

In her battered but comfortable station wagon, Nancy took us on a quick tour of five old mansions which belonged to her family. It seemed that her family had been among the privileged few, including my ancestors in Virginia, who had received thousands of acres in land grants from the king of England. As a member of the local preservation society, Nancy extolled the detail of this cornice or that dormer. I asked sweetly, "All these homes were built by slaves, weren't they?" "Why yes, of course, dahlin, of course." The hidden anger surfaced in me again as we passed by blacks in shanties seemingly unchanged since slavery days. I remained quiet for the rest of the tour.

Just before we left, the one black domestic worker Nancy employed pulled me aside, out of sight of the others. Her name was Ruby Lowe, the same last name that one of the Taylors in Hertford had acquired by marriage. "Ah been waitin' to see if she was goin' to rent some of them rooms to black people. Y'all the first, you know," she said. "I'm sure glad to see you. Hope y'all come again."

As we drove toward the airport in Winston-Salem, I kept trying to digest the experience. It was not easy. How do you let go of old demons that you really want to keep close? For the first time I noticed what beautiful country I was traveling through. In all the years of my youth, I had never seen it that way. I was too busy looking for lynchers behind every tree and bad old boys in dusty cars. I did not remember seeing the insistent kudzu which climbed the trees and suggested hidden glades, the quiet lakes and slow-moving rivers that might signify more than bloated black bodies. The small towns seemed welcoming and absent of the evils of urban life. This trip had removed some of my blinders—not all.

When I returned from North Carolina, my cousin Jeff called to invite Harold and me to join him at his home in Orange County and to go over to his father's house for dinner. He reported that his father, on learning of his wife's African-American heritage, joked, "then I guess I'm the only white one in the family." Jeff's sisters, his brother-in-law and his grandmother, my aunt Grace, had also been invited. The group would ultimately include my sister Jewelle, her husband, Jim, and my mother.

Jeff and his father live in a small city behind the foothills of northern Orange County. Few blacks live in the town. The quiet streets are rimmed with row upon row of well-maintained houses and perfect lawns. By the time we reached Jeff's house, Jewelle and Jim had been there for an hour with Aunt Grace. (Grace had finally met Harold a few days before when he brought my mother and me to spend an afternoon in Anaheim.) Jeff was playing African music from his extensive and eclectic collection of compact discs. Grace sat quietly, hugging herself with both arms, as if holding herself together. She looked even paler than usual. Jim, who is an Africanist, discussed tribal music with Jeff. Jewelle demonstrated a few steps from the High Life, a national dance of Liberia. Grace smiled and gripped my mother's hand tightly as she watched her past become her present.

It took us a little more than ten minutes to drive to Jeff's father's house. The exterior of his pale blue and white ranch-style home reflected quiet prosperity and restrained good taste. Jeff's father, Ken, was a tall, handsome, heavy-set man with wavy silver hair. Jeff held my mother's arm and said, "Aunt Margaret, I'd like you to meet my father." "Well, let me give you a great big hug," Ken beamed, setting the tone for the afternoon, and he proceeded to embrace each of us in turn. Beyond the doorway were Ken's two daughters, Laura and Lisa, who shook our hands in greeting. The sisters looked much like their pictures. Their hair was black, their skin fair, and their eyes grey-green.

Paintings of Caribbean scenes dominated the living room. In an adjoining den, a series of black-and-white portraits of Native Americans caught my eye. We sat in the living room around a coffee table filled with hors d'oeuvres. It was a scene that I had thought about all of my life, but one that I had doubted would ever occur. It was like a play within a play, all the actors playing double roles, none of our lines scripted. My mother's face was flushed. She looked excited and pleased.

We all chatted as if we were on a communal first date. Questions echoed around the room. "Where did you go to school?" "What do you do?" "How long have you been married?" With the finesse of a skilled conductor, Ken orchestrated the conversation. Tentatively and with great politeness, we learned the essentials of each other's lives. The deeper questions remained unasked. It was clear that everyone was tacitly concerned about Grace's feelings. She sat on the piano stool by Ken, still hugging herself. Then she moved and sat by my mother. Once again they held hands. She had little to say. Jeff's sisters commented on the resemblance between Grace and Margaret. Mostly they watched and listened. Ken ushered us to the backyard for a family portrait. "Since I'm the outsider here, I'll take the picture," he said good naturedly. Grace moved toward the center of the lawn, holding Margaret's hand. Dutifully, we lined up behind the two matriarchs of the Morris family while Ken took our picture with each of four cameras, so that each of us would have a record of our meeting.

Dinner was an Italian meal laid out in the dining room as if for a holiday. Ken sat at the head of the table, facing Grace, and proposed a toast. I raised my glass and looked across the table at the faces of my mother, Lisa and Laura—my cousins—as Ken said, "Welcome home." Then he turned to me and posed the most pointed question of the afternoon: "Why did you start looking and how did you find Grace?"

And that is the tale I have told.

❧

In the end, or is it a beginning, what have I found? The answers to questions I have asked in my dreams? The geography of desperation and flight and fear? The images of people who transmitted their genes to me? Would any of them, I wonder, have come looking for me?

It is a satisfaction to have traced the missing branches of the family tree. But what I have traced is only an outline. I can never know about the small joys and large sorrows of their lives. Beyond the telling, I do not know if I can ever connect their lives with mine. Our circumstances have been too different. They know what it is like to be white but can never know what it is to be black.

Now I have photographs of most of the missing relatives. They were a striking group. I am fascinated by and attracted to the beauty of my great-uncle Edward as a young man. I keep coming back to his untroubled gaze. Cosmetically at least, I have restored the missing faces to the family scrapbook. But I have given up their ghosts. I think I have lost at least some of the anger and resentment toward my family that was not my family. Not all. As Professor Adrian Piper once admitted, "Trying to forgive and understand those of my relatives who have chosen to pass for white has been one of the most difficult ethical challenges of my life." And I am not sure I have consistently overcome the challenge.

I framed the pictures and put them in a separate group on the wall in what I call my "white corner." Melissa asked why I did not intermingle them with the rest of the family. "Why separate them, after what you have learned and the efforts you made to bring them back together?" A legitimate and thoughtful question. But from my point of view, there was no honesty in integrating them after the fact. Still, I look at them often, and I think and I wonder.

I began the search for my mother's family believing that I was looking for black people "passing for white." And they did indeed pass. But what I ultimately found, I realized, were black people who had become white. After all, if you look white, act white, live white, vacation white, go to school white, marry white and die white, are you not "white"? Can race be simply a matter of context, whether in Buffalo, Cleveland, the Eastern Shore, Anaheim, Idaho, Sutton Place, Vermont, East Hampton or Palm Beach? A case in point: When he was a freshman at Amherst College, my husband joined a group of his white classmates for dinner at a Chinese restaurant not far from the campus. As my husband went to sit down, the maitre d' said to him, "So sorry, we do not serve colored people here." "Who told you I was colored?" my husband asked grandly. "Oh, so sorry," the flustered maitre d' repeated as he showed Harold to his seat. It is a mystery to me what he had become in the waiter's eye or in his mind.

My white relatives have missed the tangled richness of being black in America, the different joys, the different triumphs, the different strengths. But they have also escaped the special pain and anger that most black Americans feel. I suppose I should congratulate them for that. But in their metamorphosis, what personal demons did they create? What levels of hell, what rage, what stunted psyches?

It has occurred to me that my mother was the scapegoat for the Morris family. As the youngest survivor, she was the logical choice. The family divested all its blackness into her. She was their Other, and she fulfilled the role, by marrying the darkest man and living the blackest life. She literally became her family's heart of darkness.

But my mother was never a tragic mulatto. Her absent and rejecting family made her an orphan doomed to search on for that perfect love, that perfect family. But she also became a voluntary Negro, graced by fortunate circumstances. Her marriage brought her new family, and for the most part we have been successful and content.

I often look at my "white corner" and wonder whether I am a racist because black people are at the center of my comfort zone. Or are my feelings the result of a wound that is slow to heal? Am I a racist when I think about all the evil and violent things "they" have done to "us"? Am I not "them" as well as "us"? Or am I carrying the flag from one generation of color to the next to warn of the hatreds that separate the light-skinned from the dark? Will my semaphore be understood?

All in all, I have grown a great deal less certain about the vagaries of race and know that I am ambivalent about its implications. But I am comfortable with that ambivalence, for it keeps my doors and windows open. It allows me to keep learning. I do not know how I could for so long have failed to understand fully the manipulative nature of the designation "black" for anyone who had even the fabled "one drop." If asked, I would probably now describe myself as a person of mixed race rather than as black, although I know I will never lose my black feelings. My journey has made me more cautious in labeling or pigeonholing others as well. And I have more sympathy for those who made the choices to leave the black part of their lives behind. In my eagerness to condemn, I had never looked too closely at the circumstances that provoked such decisions.

It is a consoling idea that everyone on this earth is a shade of the protein called melanin; that black and white alike, we are all a gradation of a color called brown. I know that in the blueprint for every human being, there are some three billion units of DNA, arranged over twenty-three pairs of chromosomes. Spread through-out that mix are about a hundred thousand genes. No one has counted the human couplings that resulted in genetic mixings and crossovers. And Lucy, that ancient group of fossil bones found in Africa, is the mother of us all.

Selected Bibliography

The Afro American (newspaper), various issues, 1920–1935.

Alexander, Adele Logan. *Ambiguous Lives*. Fayetteville: The University of Arkansas Press, 1992.

Aptheker, Herbert. *American Negro Slave Revolts*. New York: International Publishers, 1963.

Ayers, Edward L. *The Promise of the New South*. New York: Oxford University Press, 1992.

Baldwin, James. *The Price of the Ticket*. New York: St. Martin's, 1985.

Bancroft, Frederic. *Slave Trading in the Old South*. New York: Frederic Ungar, 1969.

Bell, Derrick. *Faces at the Bottom of the Well*. New York: Basic Books, 1992.

Bennett, Lerone. *The Shaping of Black America*. Chicago: Johnson Publishing Company, 1975.

Branch, Taylor. *Parting the Waters*. New York: Simon & Schuster, 1988.

Brewer, James H. *The Confederate Negro: Virginia's Craftsmen and Military Laborers, 1861–1865*. Durham, N.C.: Duke University Press, 1969.

Campbell, D. C., Jr., ed., with Kym S. Rice. *Before Freedom Came*. Charlottesville: University Press of Virginia, 1991.

Cox, LaWanda, and John H. *Reconstruction, the Negro and the New South*. Columbia: University of South Carolina Press, 1973.

Cruden, Robert. *The Negro in Reconstruction*. Englewood Cliffs, N.J.: Prentice Hall, 1969.

Davis, Charles T., and Henry Louis Gates, Jr., eds. *The Slave's Narrative*. New York: Oxford University Press, 1985.

Desmond, Alice Curtis. *Martha Washington*. New York: Dodd, Mead, 1967.

Early, Gerald, ed. *Lure and Loathing: Essays on Race, Identity and the Ambivalence of Assimilation*. New York: Allen Lane/The Penguin Press, 1993.

Fields, Barbara Jeanne. *Slavery and Freedom on the Middle Ground: Maryland During the Nineteenth Century*. New Haven: Yale University Press, 1985.

Fitzpatrick, Sandra, and Maria R. Goodwin. *The Guide to Black Washington*. New York: Hippocrene Books, 1990.

Franklin, John Hope. *Race and History: Selected Essays*. Baton Rouge: Louisiana State University Press, 1989.

Franklin, John Hope, and Alfred A. Moss, Jr. *From Slavery to Freedom: A History of Negro Americans*, 6th ed. New York: Knopf, 1988.

Frederickson, George M. *The Black Image in the White Mind*. Middletown: Wesleyan University Press, 1971.

———. *White Supremacy: A Comparative Study in American and South African History.* Oxford: Oxford University Press, 1978.

Gatewood, Willard B. *Aristocrats of Color: The Black Elite, 1880–1920.* Bloomington: Indiana University Press, 1990.

Gibbs, Jewelle Taylor, and Larke Nahme Huang. *Children of Color.* San Francisco: Jossey-Bass, 1989.

Giddings, Paula. *When and Where I Enter.* New York: William Morrow, 1984.

Gutman, Herbert G. *The Black Family in Slavery and Freedom, 1750–1925.* New York: Pantheon, 1976.

Hacker, Andrew. *Two Nations.* New York: Charles Scribner's Sons, 1992.

Higginbotham, A. Leon. *In the Matter of Color: Race and the American Legal Process, The Colonial Period.* New York and Oxford: Oxford University Press, 1978.

Higginbotham, Evelyn Brooks. *Righteous Discontent: The Women's Movement in the Black Baptist Church, 1880–1920.* Cambridge, Mass.: Harvard University Press, 1993.

Hooks, Bell. *Black Looks.* Boston: South End Press, 1992.

Ione, Carole. *Pride of Family.* New York: Summit, 1991.

Jernegan, Marcus. *Laboring and Dependent Classes in Colonial America, 1607–1783.* Westport, Conn.: Greenwood Press, 1931.

Johnston, James Hugo. *Race Relations in Virginia and Miscegenation in the South, 1776–1860.* Amherst: University of Massachusetts Press, 1970.

Kaplan, Sidney. *The Black Presence in the American Revolution.* Washington, D.C.: Smithsonian Institution Press, 1973.

Katz, William Loren. *Black Indians.* New York: Atheneum, 1986.

———. *The Black West.* Seattle: Open Hand Publishing, 1987.

Kennedy, Adrienne. *People Who Led to My Plays.* New York: Theatre Communications Group, 1987.

Kulikoff, Allan. *Tobacco and Slaves: The Development of Southern Cultures in the Chesapeake, 1680–1800.* Chapel Hill: University of North Carolina Press, 1986.

Lane, Roger. *William Dorsey's Philadelphia and Ours.* New York: Oxford University Press, 1991.

Larsen, Nella. *Passing.* New York: Knopf, 1929.

———. *Quicksand.* New York: Knopf, 1928.

Lesko, Kathleen M., Valeri Babb, and Carroll R. Gibbs. *Black Georgetown Remembered.* Washington, D.C.: Georgetown University Press, 1992.

Lewis, Ronald L. *Coal, Iron and Slaves: Industrial Slavery in Maryland and Virginia, 1715–1865.* Westport, Conn.: Greenwood Press, 1979.

McElroy, Guy C. *Facing History: The Black Image in American Art, 1710–1940.* San Francisco and Washington, D.C.: Bedford Arts in association with the Corcoran Gallery of Art, 1990.

McLaurin, Melton A. *Celia, a Slave.* Athens: University of Georgia Press, 1991.

Morgan, Edmund S. *American Slavery, American Freedom: The Ordeal of Colonial Virginia.* New York: W. W. Norton, 1975.

Morgan, Philip D. *"Don't Grieve After Me": The Black Experience in Virginia, 1619–1986.* Hampton, Va.: Hampton University Press, 1986.

Mullin, Gerald W. *Flight and Rebellion: Slave Resistance in Eighteenth-Century Virginia.* New York: Oxford University Press, 1972.

Newton, James E., and Ronald L. Lewis, eds. *The Other Slaves: Mechanics, Artisans and Craftsmen.* Boston: G. K. Hall, 1978.

Pendleton, Leila Amos. *A Narrative of the Negro.* Washington, D.C.: R. L. Pendleton, 1912.

Perdue, Charles L., Jr., Thomas E. Barden, and Robert K. Phillips, eds. *Weevils in the Wheat: Interviews with Virginia Ex-Slaves.* Charlottesville: University Press of Virginia, 1976. Reprint. Bloomington: Indiana University Press, 1980.

Piper, Adrian. "Passing for White, Passing for Black." *Transition* 58 (1993): 4–32.

The Pittsburgh Courier, various issues, 1920–1935.

Redding, Saunders. *They Came in Chains.* Philadelphia: J. B. Lippincott, 1950.

Root, Marla P. P., ed. *Racially Mixed People in America.* Newbury Park, Calif.: Sage Publications, 1992.

Rose, James, and Alice Eichholz. *Black Genesis.* Detroit: Gale Research, 1978.

Russell, Kathy; Midge Wilson; and Ronald Hall. *The Color Complex.* New York: Harcourt Brace Jovanovich, 1992.

Saxon, Lyle. *Children of Strangers.* Boston: Houghton Mifflin, 1937.

Smith, A. E. *Colonists in Bondage.* Chapel Hill: University of North Carolina Press, 1947.

Smith, Kathryn Schneider, ed. *Washington at Home.* Northridge, Calif.: Windsor Publications, 1988.

Smith, Lillian. *Killers of the Dream.* New York: W. W. Norton, 1949.

Sobel, Mechal. *Travelin' On: The Slave Journey to an Afro-Baptist Faith.* Westport, Conn.: Greenwood Press, 1979.

South, Stanley A. *Indians in North Carolina.* Raleigh, N.C.: State Department of Archives and History, 1959.

Spickard, Paul. *Mixed Blood: Intermarriage and Ethnic Identity in Twentieth-Century America.* Madison: University of Wisconsin Press, 1989.

Takaki, Ronald T. *Iron Cages: Race and Culture in 19th Century America.* Seattle: University of Washington Press, 1979.

Troupe, Quincy, ed. *James Baldwin: The Legacy.* New York: Simon & Schuster, 1989.

Tyler-McGraw, Marie, and Gregg D. Kimball. *In Bondage and Freedom: Antebellum Black Life in Richmond, Virginia.* Richmond, Va.: Valentine Museum, 1988.

West, Cornel. *Race Matters.* Boston: Beacon Press, 1993.

Wetmore, Ruth Y. *First on the Land: The North Carolina Indians.* Winston-Salem, N.C.: John F. Blair, 1975.

Wharton, Anne Hollingsworth. *Martha Washington.* New York: Charles Scribner's Sons, 1897.

Williamson, Joel. *New People: Miscegenation and Mulattoes in the United States.* New York: Free Press, 1980. Reprint. New York: New York University Press, 1984.

Wood, Peter H. *Black Majority: Negroes in Colonial South Carolina from 1670 Through the Stono Rebellion.* New York: Knopf, 1974.